ESSAYS IN TEACHING

Essays in
TEACHING

Edited by

HAROLD TAYLOR

President,
SARAH LAWRENCE COLLEGE

HARPER & BROTHERS PUBLISHERS
New York

Contents

Preface

We wrote the essays in this book to set down some of the things which we believe it is important to teach to young people, and to show how we go about teaching them. What brings us together in one book is the fact that we have all been working in the same college, we have developed a set of ideas about how we think teaching should be carried on, and have put them into practice. We believe that knowledge is for the use and enjoyment of life. We teach because we like to, because we enjoy the company of young people and are interested in ideas, liberal values, a free society, and education. Our aim in teaching is to develop persons who will use and enjoy the knowledge we can give them, both in their personal lives and in the service of other people. This has led us to discard the traditional theories of education, to invent new ways of teaching, and to accept newer theories of learning. In actual practice, each teacher, whether he is a scientist, a poet, or a psychologist, is responsible for his own students and is free to work out his own best way of developing within them the ideas, facts, and values which are the content of a liberal education. This means that there is the most freedom and the most individual responsibility which it is possible for us to arrange, both for the students and the faculty members.

We agree on one fundamental principle—that each student is different from every other, and that education, in order to have meaning for the person who is receiving it, must be carried on in a way which can bring out the most that is in each person, and which puts the duties and rewards of learning squarely in the hands of the students. In other words, we agree that the education of young people in the liberal arts and sciences must be built upon the existing needs, interests, and talents of each student who is being educated, and must not be constructed as if all students were the same, had the same role in life, and needed the same academic equipment to carry it out. Although such a principle seems, on the face of it, only to be sensible and obvious, when it is applied fully to the task of making a college of liberal arts and sciences, it produces a program which is radically different from that of the conventional college.

It means that the things which matter most are the students and the faculty. It means that the College budget is spent principally on having enough teachers in the College to deal with the students, and to keep the classes small enough to do close work with individuals. It means that a radical form of democracy must exist for the students and the faculty, in which the administration of student affairs is in the hands of the students, the faculty makes no hierarchy of rank, has no formal departmental organization, and makes College policy in cooperation with the President and the Board of Trustees.

The College itself is intended as a center of intellectual and social freedom, in which the function of the Board of Trustees and the administration is to provide a situation in which each student and member of the faculty can make his greatest contribution to the life of the College and gain the deepest personal satisfaction from his experience in it. It means that all the usual ways of teaching are questioned, and, if found inadequate, are discarded in favor of new ways, which in turn are tested by experience. It means that we lecture to students only when this seems to be the best and shortest way of conveying a set of ideas, interpretations, or facts. There is, accordingly, little lecturing, more independent reading, original research, discussion, seminar work, field work, and a great many conferences between students and faculty. It means also that there are no required courses which all students must take. There are courses planned by the faculty and students together. It means that there are no formal examinations, grades, or other academic obstacles put in the way of the learning process. Education is conceived to be a process in which the student moves toward deeper levels of insight and wider areas of knowledge, in ways most suited to his or her particular talents.

When we first decided to do this book, we began by writing what each of us thought about the things we are teaching. Each essay was then read by all the other authors and discussed at meetings devoted to the separate chapters. As a result of the meetings, a great deal was rewritten, and the present essays are the product of the joint criticism and the rewriting. The series of discussions took place over a period of a year and a half. There were many other faculty members, whose names do not appear in the present list of authors, who had a share in shaping the book, and many others whose work at Sarah Lawrence in the early days makes our present work possible.

We are especially indebted for our educational ideas to John Dewey, Alfred North Whitehead, William James, Sigmund Freud, Jean-Jacques Rousseau, Ralph Waldo Emerson, Montaigne, Walt Whitman, and Thomas Jefferson. In the College we represent, our effort is to carry on the great tradition of those who have believed in the open future and the possibilities of mankind, and who have taught that it is more important to make use of knowledge to release the latent powers of creative thought than to repeat the ideas of their predecessors.

My gratitude for help in editing the book goes to the group of authors, particularly to Esther Raushenbush, Helen Lynd, and Horace Gregory. Mr. H. F. Willkie, of Louisville, Kentucky, first suggested the idea that we write a book of this kind, and we are grateful to him for his encouragement. We hope that these essays may give some notion to other teachers, and to people interested in education, of the way in which a group of scholars, artists, and scientists at Sarah Lawrence College are helping young people to learn and to use the liberal arts.

HAROLD TAYLOR

Sarah Lawrence College
Bronxville, New York
March, 1950

ESSAYS IN TEACHING

The Idea of a College

HAROLD TAYLOR

I

What should be taught to the young?

Every age and every culture has a different answer. At various times in Western society it has been Latin, Greek, theology, rhetoric, history, French, German, philosophy, science, technology, literature, militarism, obedience, nationalism, monarchy, fascism. In other societies it has been religion, ritual, communism, pacifism, czarism, socialism, clericalism, agrarianism, emperor-worship, totemism. The variety is endless. But each answer gives away many secrets. It tells the truth about the hopes, customs, and ideals of any society, and reveals a conception of human life. In the centuries before our own there were dominant patterns of religious, social, and moral philosophy which went unquestioned in Western society, and a conception of human life which was generally agreed upon. Human life at its best was represented by the aristocrat, the gentleman, the monarch, the statesman, the cleric—those who occupied positions of rank in the social system. Young people were taught the system of ideas, practical skills, and moral values which underlay the structure of this society. Those specially privileged were given the higher forms of education to fit them for their higher status. Those who were born into families without money or position were taught the vocational skills appropriate to their station. Everyone knew what should be taught, since there was general agreement as to what was true and what was right.

But now everything is up for questioning. In the world of contemporary thought, moral values have been investigated and analyzed, probed and dissected, explained and dismissed until, for the philosopher, ideals are grunts of approval; for the psychologist, they are evidence of temperamental preferences; for the economist, they are patterned responses to social conditioning; for the anthropologist, they are local customs. The absolute certainty with which

1

the values of Western civilization were formerly regarded, and the belief that ideals existed as intrinsic parts of a universe constructed on a rational pattern—both these certainties have been chipped away, along with the certainty that reason can be trusted either to give us universal truth or to give us a solution to social conflicts.

We now exist in a complex of relativisms, of half-truths invented by governments and political parties, of partial goods vouched for by famous men, advertising agencies, and national publications. We have to look for truth in a welter of lies. The twentieth century is the first in which reason itself is continually suspect by the intellectuals. Reason, in fact, seems powerless, the will toward good seems paralyzed by the politics of power, and the individual seems unable to effect any change of the direction in which he is swept along by the flow of contemporary history.

What should we teach in such circumstances? We cannot behave as if the world in which we live is the same as it was. It is radically changed, and it would do a great disservice to the young to lull them into adjustment to a world which has gone. Nor can we recapture the dogmatism of the older philosophies in the face of the skeptical intelligence of modern youth—unless, of course, we wish to restrict the scope of the critical faculty, or unless we wish to construct a society in which only one set of truths is allowed. The most we can do is to teach modern youth to find a way of judging truth and ideals for themselves. This is the primary need, both for the education of the young and for the future of the democratic form of society.

From every side there are pressures upon the individual to think and act in a standard way. The world's present method of solving social problems is by force, terror, and coercion, and everywhere in the world the individual human being has shrivelled in importance. Yet everywhere, in every country, there are individual human beings, each with his own aims, desires, interests, and needs, each trying as best he can to achieve a special destiny. "Our situation is due to the interaction of myriads of wills, each pursuing its own limited purposes, but for their accomplishment combining in larger and larger units, and finally producing a total state of things which no one foresaw and no one wanted. . . ."* In modern world society, larger and larger groups of men and women have united in trade unions, cities, political parties, nations, coalitions among nations, and have finally united in two massive centers of collective power, the United States and the Soviet Union, two centers of power which transcend all individuals, and, in one way or another, affect their lives for good or evil. The world has increased the size of its own organization to such a degree that it has become literally too big to handle. We now seem to be at the mercy of our own social creations. We have made a collective industrial world society, and now seem about to be swallowed by it.

Everywhere there are indications that the social context of violent change coincides with a disintegration of moral, religious, social, and philosophical ideas. I do not mean to say that one has caused the other, or that the contemporary social crisis is simply the result of a moral and intellectual failure. It is much more complicated than that. But for the purposes of education, our constant concern must be with the moral and intellectual life of the individual, and it is in the world of ideas and values that the teacher makes whatever contribution he can. His greatest contribution is made when he teaches young people the ways in which the modern world can be understood, through art, science, literature, history, philosophy, or any other form of knowledge.

In American education since the second World War, the tendency has been to deal with the most urgent aspects of the contemporary crisis by moving away from them. One dominant trend is that towards the revival of the classical curriculum, which suggests that the cure to cultural and social disintegration lies in teaching the young to value the Western European heritage through a study of its most important documents. Another, and more widely dominant trend, has been towards unifying the content of the student's knowledge by a survey of material drawn from the arts, the humanities, and the natural and social sciences. Neither of these proposals comes to grips with the central issue which education must face, which is the issue of how the individual student can gain a level of intel-

* Moberly, Sir Walter, *The Crisis in the University*. London, SCM Press, Ltd., 1949, p. 15.

lectual and emotional maturity sufficient to answer the questions and make the choices which contemporary life thrusts upon him. The conservative educational programs approach that issue obliquely, advancing a system of general studies by means of which the student may equip himself to draw appropriate conclusions. What is missing is a lively awareness of the nature of the contemporary world, a concern for the kind of knowledge necessary to understand it.

This is not merely knowledge of international affairs, contemporary literature, or of politics. It does not consist in being merely up to date. There are certain demands which contemporary society makes upon the educator and the student. Education must deal with the personal, moral, and social questions raised by our present state of society. Some of these are the eternal questions of human destiny, freedom, and the nature of life. They are eternal because they have appeared at each stage of the recurring present during the past centuries of Western and Eastern civilization. They have been answered in a variety of ways by religious thinkers, poets, scientists, philosophers, novelists, and workers. The answers have formed the germ cells around which our social institutions have grown and by which our personal values have been established. We thus have a variety of religions, governments, schools, moralities, industries, and universes. Since no one of the answers is absolute and complete, it is the responsibility of the teacher to raise continually the great questions in the urgency of their contemporary social and personal setting. By the study and valuation of ideals and realities, by the careful and attentive consideration of the answers given in the past and present, we must make up the content of contemporary knowledge as best we can.

We must do so because the present world is new, and its problems have never appeared before in their present form. The social and intellectual history of preceding periods is of first importance in understanding the present, but only if it is studied in order to gain that understanding. The origins of modern disintegration lie in the intellectual history of the nineteenth century, when the sharpest questions came with the increase in the prestige and use of scientific ways of answering both the immediate and the ultimate enquiries.

The century was marked by a growing belief in the ultimate validity of the scientific answer and a strong belief in the idea of progress. It was assumed that a faith in rational modes of thought would take us forward to a freer and better society, and that the destruction of all dogma, whether religious or secular, would free the human mind and, with it, human society. This was nineteenth-century liberalism.

It is difficult to overestimate the impact which this double philosophy had upon traditional values and beliefs. The philosophers made devastating applications of the new discoveries of their scientific colleagues, and revised the universe in a way which simply deprived it of former meanings. Man became an incident in an obscure cosmic development. Those philosophers who found in the discoveries of science no reason for despair or regret, constructed a meaningful world by absorbing both science and philosophy in a new pattern of ideas. We then had the work of Bergson, James, Santayana, Whitehead, Dewey, Russell, each restating the knowledge gained from science in a fresh and different way. What these men held in common was the view that in matters of knowledge concerning the universe and man's place in it, science provided the basis for belief. Dewey, Santayana, and Russell form the transitional group between the nineteenth century and our own. They extend, by their present lives, the old into the new century. They illustrate by their personal intellectual history the shift in philosophic opinion from the prescientific to the scientific era.

The nineteenth century produced more than a new universe. It developed a new mind in a new society. It did so by investigating the social and personal origins of beliefs about man and society. It started a radically new line of enquiry, which has been taken up with great vigor in the twentieth century, into the nature of belief, thought, reason, knowledge, and custom. We now have conclusions which have cut the ground from under older conceptions of human nature and society and have refuted absolutes of all kinds. A rejection of the absolute has marked the arts of the twentieth century. The classical forms have been broken, and the objects of art have become mutual constructions of the person who creates them and the person who observes them. A new and more personal assertion has entered, and art is conceived as the means by which an experience is communicated from artist to audience. It is not the objective presentation of a principle of beauty recognized by all.

In the immediate past, society has demonstrated its own rejection of absolutes by overturning the moral values upon which a stable world was thought to rest. Consider the contemporary European writer, who reflects that change. He suffered at first hand the impact of European moral, political, and physical disintegration. He saw the approach of German fascism, knew what was going to happen, said so, found himself crushed by what did happen, and saw the open cynicism of those European political leaders who betrayed Western society. The killing of the Jews in Germany and Poland, the occupation of European countries by the Germans, represented to him the final destruction of all hope and moral principle. In the meantime, unless he wished to shut his eyes to reality, he found that the advertised idealism of international communism was drained of moral content by the actions of its Soviet leaders.

Not only is the social awareness and personal frustration of the European writer a phenomenon typical of the twentieth century, but his intellectual and moral character belong in the center of contemporary history. Having observed societies without moral ideals destroy themselves, he rejects all ideals as meaningless, and accepts his own personal life as the only certainty. He has only those ideals which he chooses to have. He has no freedom except the freedom he makes, no obligations except those he imposes upon himself. He expects nothing, even of himself. He returns the questions of philosophy and moral choice to the individual human conscience, and says there are no standard guides in which to trust. In one hundred years we have come to the opposite end of the scale. The European writers and thinkers attack the idea of progress, suspect the value of reason.

In America we are more optimistic. Our economic and social system was not destroyed, nor did we feel the immediate impact of the European events. But what is under attack in Europe, in America, is the entire philosophy of liberalism, and with it the pattern of liberal education. The nature of the present world is such that it is now an act of faith and not a demonstrable principle to believe that human nature is potentially good and that creative intelligence can plan a society for the enrichment of human life. We face the realities of power in the hands of the illiberal.

The idea of a college must therefore be that of a place where liberal values can survive and can be put to the use of society. The task of the college is to teach liberalism—not the philosophy of an ethnocentric, middle-class, nationalist, Western, white man's ethic, but liberalism conceived as a classless philosophy which draws individual human beings closer together, teaches a concern for the welfare of all social groups and all countries, and judges the value of acts and societies by the effect they have upon the enrichment of individual human lives. This is not done by teaching science, the humanities, the arts. It is done by teaching young people the content and meaning of these forms of knowledge with the intention of developing in them a liberal attitude toward life and toward society. It involves taking part in the contemporary conflict of values, philosophies, and power, and giving to the life of the student a meaning and a direction which will help to push his society into more creative forms of human experience and social change. The age demands a commitment from its intellectuals and its teachers. We can no longer assume that the liberal and humanist spirit will survive by its own intrinsic merit. It is our responsibility as scientists, scholars, artists, and teachers to furnish to the new generations an immediate sense of what it means to apply the philosophy of liberalism to human affairs.

II

From the moment we are born we are taught the things people wish us to know. We become accustomed to the ideas of others, and learn to accept them before we realize they are not our own. We get used to the world gradually and accept a reality which other people have prepared for us. This has to do with what is good or bad, true or false, pleasant or unpleasant, desirable or undesirable, interesting or uninteresting, beautiful or ugly. Whether or not these truths and goods are actually valid, for us or for anyone else, they become the means by which we approach all future reality. There are many who go through an entire life without knowing that there are any other ideas than the ones prepared in this way.

Reality accumulates around the growing self, layer upon layer, until sometimes at an early age the self has disappeared and there is nothing left but a set of automatic responses to conventional stimuli. The spontaneity of the 'original impulse of the child, the freshness of the uninhibited and questioning mind, and the vitality of its response to life become slowly dulled by the usual, the proper, and the expected. This is what Christopher Fry has called the "domestication of the enormous miracle." The aim of the teacher is to peel away the layers of customary reality and to restore vitality and nourishment to the individual consciousness beneath.

Society has its own ways of creating stability, and one of its ways is by education. Most education is designed to present to the young those ideas from its history and its present situation which a society accepts without question. It is designed to classify life and knowledge in such a way that it can be taught conveniently to students. Its purpose is to increase the ease with which one generation of young people may slide into the intellectual habits and social customs of the one preceding it.

Yet the world which actually exists is not the standard model of the schools. It is a world which must be created and recreated by each person as he comes to know it in experience and as it becomes real to him through his own efforts to understand it. The task of education at its highest is to help the student to break through the patterns of language and thought to the inner core of meaning which makes it significant for him. In this sense, books, formulas, art objects, laws, concepts are all records and symbols which stand between the human being and his knowledge of the world. They are guides to where knowledge may be found, or they are clues to action which may be taken, to experiences which may be felt. When all of these records, books, and other devices are assembled into an institution of education, the primary reason for their existence there is to make possible a variety of intellectual experiences for the individual student. The college must be organized around the collection of individual students who compose its student body in such a way that the quality of the individual's experience is both the aim and the test of the whole organization. There is no substitute for the direct experience of the human being with the actual object of his thought. The content of a poem or of an equation lies in the experience of the individual in getting from it the meaning concealed within.

Education, or knowledge-getting, is a process in which the student involves himself. Otherwise it is simply a name for organized information. Until the process of learning begins within the life of the student there is no content in education, there is only a set of materials waiting to be transformed into knowledge. Knowledge exists as something known by someone. When enough people know together, and are believed by others, what they know becomes an accepted part of the truth of their time, only waiting its own transformation into the next truth by those who transform it. Contemporary knowledge, in one important sense, contains everything else, and knowledge from any age is contemporary if it contains the insights and information necessary to understand present issues and questions.

With one or two rare exceptions, the entire stream of education in the history of Western culture has clung tightly to the rationalist's illusion that knowledge is independently real, and that once it can be stated in sentences and talked about or read, it has achieved an independent existence. This has led to the further illusion that, since knowledge has independent existence, is contained in abstractions, and can be communicated in sentences, education must consist in training the mind to understand the right set of abstractions in the proper order. On the contrary, knowledge is created freshly every time an individual human being takes hold of an idea and makes it part of his own understanding. Those who have preceded each one of us in the history of knowing have gone through a similar process—sometimes at a higher level—but nevertheless similar. ". . . all the while," says William James,* "the world *we* feel and live in will be that which our ancestors and we, by slow cumulative strokes of choice, have extricated out of this, like sculptors, by simply rejecting certain portions of the given stuff. Other sculptors, other statues from the same stone. Other minds, other worlds from the same monotonous and inexpressive chaos."

The philosophies of organism, those of Bergson, James, Whitehead, and Dewey, whose roots lie in the biological sciences, in

* *Principles of Psychology,* I. New York, Henry Holt & Co., 1890, p. 289.

psychology, in the conception of the universe as a state of process, have influenced thinking about contemporary art and science. The results appear in new attitudes to music, sculpture, painting, poetry, the dance, theater, anthropology, the social sciences, and, of course, the whole of the natural sciences. But little effect may be seen in the contemporary forms of higher education. The philosophy of process has shown itself chiefly in the work of the nursery school and the elementary school. In other kinds of education the mind of the child, the adolescent, and the adult is treated by the educator as if it were a rational entity complete in itself, constant throughout the whole of human nature, and unrelated to the social, psychological, and personal conditions of its origin. Accordingly, curricula are arranged to present to all students that cluster of ideas and facts which academic custom has associated with higher education. The assumption is made that the relevance, value, and use of the ideas are perceived by the student. The function of the college is said to be that of making rational minds more rational.

Yet we have evidence that the mind is but one aspect of a total character in each individual, and that it works by a process which can only be understood by investigating the particular facts connected with the process. People think, learn, and understand in their own ways and are capable of many different kinds of insight. To lump them all together under the word *rational*, or to assume that there is a standard kind of reason possessed by each, in more or less degree, is to misconstrue the nature of human intelligence. The ability to think logically and productively, even in the most exact sciences, is a process much more like that of the individual artist than of the logician. The art of learning can be acquired only by an effort of a creative kind on the part of the student. The rest is sheer memory-work.

As far as the education of the student is concerned, knowledge is not a matter of subjects to be studied, but an activity to be undertaken. Truth itself is a matter of ordering and relating the facts and values one finds in experience. The philosopher, for example, is one who has developed an oversensitivity to the ordering process, one who is not content with reality as it is commonly expressed. His pathology is that he cannot rest content with the things, thoughts, and feelings which appear natural to others. He sees relations among things normally felt to be disparate and sees differences between things normally felt to be the same. The poet works in a similar way. The psychologist approaches the field of knowledge with certain interests and attitudes. He investigates one segment of material which is related to other materials, and he temporarily isolates it for the sake of his investigation. The chemist, the painter, the economist order the forms of knowledge into patterns satisfactory to them as individuals, and satisfactory to the general demands made by the empirical rules of scholarship. There are no gaps between fields of ideas unless they are artificially invented for the sake of academic administration. Knowledge, when conceived as subject-matter, or as something which is only conceptually real, is defined by Auden when he speaks of a character in *The Age of Anxiety*, whose knowledge had "lain oddly around in a corner of his mind like luggage left long ago in an emergency by some acquaintance, and never reclaimed."

The reason for the existence of the college is to aid the individual student to develop the most that is in him. Scholarship, research, teaching, community life, administration are all means by which the student may be developed into the full growth of his emotional and intellectual life. This means that the usual programs of the college curriculum must simply be reversed. They must be planned from the inside out, from a knowledge of the students and of what they are capable of learning. I am prepared to face the fact that throughout the United States there are areas of the American student body where there is insufficient interest in intellectual affairs and where students have not been prepared for a high level of intellectual effort. The interest, because of the American culture pattern and the animal energies of youth, is more in sports, ballroom dancing, clubs, and meeting people who may be useful later on.

The way to deal with this problem, however, is not to take a poor view of students, abolish what is called the extracurricular, and set about training the mind as if it were a muscle. A better way consists in drawing together the various parts of the student's life into a meaningful pattern, so that his energies, both in the classroom and out of it, are devoted to the total aim of learning to know himself and his world. As far as the college is concerned, the task is to find the means by which the student as an existing reality, complete with the faults and virtues of his society and of his own individual character, can be drawn from an absorption in some aspects of life which we consider of lesser value into other aspects of greater value. The lesser values will not negate the greater, but will provide a foundation upon which the new values may be built.

This way of learning proceeds by a kind of infection of the individual with the interests and values of his teachers. The qualities of character shown by the teacher at his best, the love of wisdom, the sensitivity to ideas and people, the respect for fact, the generosity of outlook, the ultimate liberalism of the honest mind—these are the qualities which we wish the young to develop, no matter what the field of studies they undertake to investigate. The process of learning represents in a different way the process of creating a work of art or a new idea. It moves by an inner drive towards the knowledge of something which the individual wishes to know. A desire to know must precede the knowing, as hunger is a condition of eating. The student moves towards fuller knowledge when he realizes he needs it, or when he is drawn towards it by the attitude of his teacher. When a positive attitude to learning has been developed, the education goes forward under its own momentum.

For many students the desire to learn is already present, more or less subdued. In many colleges it is not fashionable or even respectable to admit the presence of such a desire. If it is not present, we can only hope that the atmosphere for learning which we, as teachers, can make will bring it on. Often the college and its teachers assume that more can be done than is actually possible. We can prepare students for the act of learning, we can show how their senses may be used, we can give them clues to information and its sources, but at the crucial point we can only withdraw and wait for the act of learning to occur.

The depth of interest in learning varies from student to student and from college to college. The motivation differs in each case. For most of those enrolled in the large institutions where mass education methods are used, the motivation lies in a firmly held set of material aims, and a compelling ambition for economic advantage in the world after college. To know, in this sense, is to provide one-self with the materials of knowledge, whether literature or engi-neering, in order to meet the requirements for a college degree, and thus to become commercially valuable and a more expensive piece of social property. In the competitive system of examinations and grades, additional motivation is provided by rivalry and the social and economic approval of the straight A record. To know in this sense is to defeat the aim of education for the sake of vulgar success.

On the other hand, when we speak of the interests and needs of students, it is best to remember that most students do not know what they are interested in, because they have only become inter-ested in those things which people expect of them. If it is expected that they will develop the collegiate habits and the philistinism of the late adolescent in college, they will do so. If it is expected that they will talk about the ideas of Proust, Aristotle, Marx, Planck, Faulkner, Adam Smith, Picasso, Kierkegaard, or T. S. Eliot, the young people will begin to do so by the sheer contingency of their minds with those already working in these areas. They want to do what is expected, and if what is expected proves to be interesting and fruitful in its consequences, they will become the kind of think-ing person whose role in life we are teaching them to play. Similarly, the student learns quickly the genial cynicism towards higher learn-ing and intellectuals which is the mark of the astute and informed collegian when he finds himself in the presence of teaching un-related to his capacities, interests, or needs. He learns quickly to disguise his ignorance, to ignore his responsibilities, and to repro-duce the emotional and intellectual insincerity of the mechanical academic system.

The majority of students now in college are there because their employment opportunities are being improved, because the life is pleasant and has its own tradition, and because their families want them to be. The desire to become intellectually independent, socially useful, informed, mature, and sensitive to aesthetic values is seldom an aim which the student consciously holds. It is the function of the educator to help the student to develop these qualities, whether or not he first comes to college to achieve them. Otherwise we have the constant reflection in our colleges of the value patterns of the society in which they are located. These value patterns in America revolve around a hard core of materialistic aims which the young American finds he can achieve, in part, by going to college. One central aim, consciously held by many students, is for the development of the individual self into a socially approved and attractive person who can be assured of money and power in later life. Hence the elaborate rituals of the fraternity-sorority system, the anxiety to join the fraternal élite, the constant need for popularity, the effort to build a good college record of high grades, many friends, many activities, and a long paragraph in the college yearbook.

Where there is opportunity and encouragement for intellectual interest and growth, the students educate each other by their mutual concern for meaningful ideas. Before anything serious or important can be accomplished in a college, it is first of all necessary to establish, by the efforts of the people who teach, an intellectual vitality within the community of students. This can become a community where, as Newman says, "the conversation of all is a series of lectures to each, and they gain for themselves new ideas and views." The community "will give birth to a living teaching, which in the course of time will take the shape of a self-perpetuating tradition, or *genius loci*, as it is sometimes called, which haunts the home where it has been born, and which imbues and forms, more or less, and one by one, every individual who is successively brought under its shadow."

III

In the beginning, in medieval Europe, the universities were the centers of learning which formed themselves around hand-written manuscripts and the scholars who read them. The manuscripts contained all that could be recorded of what was known. The rest was carried in the social experience and habits of the race, and in the heads of those who had learned from conversation, discussion, and meditation. The scholars were, in fact, a special group of individuals interested in a special set of problems related to religion and history. They met to study what was known, to discuss it, to comment on it, to teach it, and to share a look at the manuscripts with younger men who were interested.

From time to time new ideas developed in the midst of the scholars. When this happened, a period of twenty-five to one hundred years of controversy and bitter resistance set in before the new was admitted to the known. In the meantime, the advocate of the new had either been burned at the stake, condemned, excommunicated, or exiled. Whatever knowledge had been accepted by the authorities was collected in written form and was asserted to be true, since it had the approval of the Church, and thus, the State. The Church and the State found the universities a good place for scholars to comment on those things which it wished the people to know. The purpose of the university was not so much the advancement of learning, as is usually held, but the assertion of a set of intellectual and moral principles, and the spread of an established truth.

Persons who were interested in speculation, thought, and scholarship, and who lived outside the universities, went ahead with their own lives and made most of the significant discoveries in philosophy and science, as well as most of the great works of art, music, poetry, and literature. The universities chose to remain "the sanctuaries in which exploded systems and obsolete prejudices found shelter and protection." In this curious way, higher education built up what is now referred to as a body of knowledge, a set of revered book lists of works written by nonuniversity people—in short, the Western tradition. There are many educators who propose that the function of the liberal arts in the college or university should be simply to pass on that tradition. The reason for doing so is substantially that expressed by Thomas Hobbes, when he says:

> For seeing the Universities are the Fountains of Civil and Morall Doctrine, from whence the Preachers, and the Gentry, drawing such water as they find, use to sprinkle the same (both from the pulpit, and their Conversation) upon the People, there ought certainly to be great care taken, to have it pure, both from the Venime of Heathen Politicians, and from the Incantation of Deceiving Spirits.

There have been revolutionary shifts in the social order since that earlier time when the Preachers and the Gentry sprinkled the rest of mankind with purified doctrine. We have managed to free the University for the most part from control by the Preachers and the

Gentry. We have managed to ward off the incantations of deceiving spirits. We are now at work daily on the problem of resisting the Venime of Heathen Politicians. But in general the idea of the University has remained static since Hobbes and the seventeenth century and, as a result, exerts less than its share of moral and cultural leadership. It is conceived to be a place where approved civil and moral doctrine are contained, safe from the agitations and excitement of the rest of the world, and from which knowledge suitable to various professions and industries can be obtained at a certain fee and under certain conditions.

The scholars and scientists, busy with their own private researches, arrange themselves in hierarchies of rank, so that those with the highest rank and the greatest number of books or pamphlets printed can give the least number of hours to the students. A body of knowledge, approved by committees, is then transmitted as a direct transaction from teachers to pupils. As in the thirteenth century, a text, or printed manuscript, is presented. A person trained in academic custom, whose blood has been drained away by the ordeal of the Ph.D., either gives comments upon the text or repeats the text as a lecture. The students record the salient points under numbered headings, and report the information back when asked.

The difference between the older university and the modern American institution is that our natural talent for organizing is such that we have expanded the whole enterprise to the proportions of a big business, and we can now handle the matter much more efficiently than earlier scholars ever dreamed possible. With the invention of television as a medium for mass distribution of knowledge, and the invention of mechanical tests and IBM machines to check on the reception of the distributed knowledge, we are rapidly approaching that happy time when we can simply take the body of knowledge and one professor or former radio announcer and cover the entire American student body without the need for anything else except a staff of engineers, a list of books, and a commercial sponsor. Under these circumstances it is likely that the great works of music, art, theater, literature, philosophy, and science will continue to be created among those who are outside the colleges and universities, and that the cultural vitality of the country will depend, not upon the centers of learning, but upon the individuals who rebel against the academic tradition.

The college of liberal arts is not a shelter for a body of knowledge. That is a library. Nor is a college a place where truth is dispensed so that thought and action may be orderly and quiescent. A college is a place where the creative aspects of life have a chance to grow freely, and where human energies and talents are devoted to the discovery and invention of fresh knowledge about man and nature. The college in its true state consists of people, some of them teachers, others students, who are working in the arts and sciences because they enjoy it. They compose music, write books, or investigate phenomena because it is natural for them to be doing it, and it is equally natural for them to want to teach what they know to younger people. They enjoy the satisfactions which can only come from the free use of the intellect. They are also interested in testing out ideas and beliefs by the active processes of thought, and in raising questions about those matters which affect the political and social future of man. Accordingly, they become an agency through which ideas may be transformed and related to action, and learning may be used for the better guidance of society.

In this sense, education and the college are instruments of social transition. Their role is to infuse the social order with ideas concerning the changes which are taking place within it, and continually to make judgments about the direction and quality of those changes. Without the college, there is no agency through which the ideas and values of contemporary society can be continually tested by men and women who can give most of their time to it and who care most deeply about it. Without a continual concern by the college for the growth of intellectual and emotional maturity in the American student body, there is no way of developing the social leadership essential to this country's future.

Thus the function of a college is to act as the creative agent of cultural and social progress. It follows that in order, to carry out its function, the ideal college must be the model for a democracy, since the effort to reach the variety of forms in which truth presents itself demands that each person be encouraged to say freely what he thinks, to respect the ultimate political and social freedom of his colleagues, and to give honor to everyone who contributes to the total good sense of the society of the intellect. A further consequence is that the college must remain closely in touch with the social issues which make up the content of contemporary history. It should not withdraw from its surrounding society in order to protect the purity of its doctrine, but must, in fact, enrich the store of its own ideas by continuous reference to the ideas of the world within which it exists. It has the obligations of intellectual leadership when questions are raised in the urgency of present controversy. It must give help and direction to the student mind in answering political, social, and cultural questions. If it refuses to do so, on the usual academic grounds that scholarly objectivity cannot be preserved in the confusion of present controversy, it has betrayed its chief duty in the education of the young. That duty is to help the student to understand his world and to take an active part in the conduct of its affairs. Otherwise the conduct of its affairs rests entirely in the hands of those who have the power and the ambition to remain in control, whether or not the power is wisely used in the interests of the total community.

When the college is considered to be an instrument of social and cultural transition, when it takes the stand that its purpose is to create the conditions of freedom as a model for the whole of society, its aims conflict with the rest of society. Society as it works from day to day is suspicious of the intellect, of new forms of art, and is often resentful of free thinking, since radical thought is a threat to social stability. Any institution which fosters the free use of creative energies, whether in aesthetic, moral, political, scientific, philosophical, or social matters, is bound to be dangerous to established precedent, since its function is not to sustain all existing values with equal enthusiasm but to create new precedents, new forms of knowledge, new ideas for the use of society.

Dangers to the integrity of the college come both from outside and inside the college community. Inside, they come from the more discreet human weaknesses—a craving for the security which full professorships can bring, pedantry, the acceptance of standard academic authorities, interest in increasing departmental powers, the development of a bureaucracy of the intellect, pride of intellectual status and prestige; in short, a muffling of the imagination. The common form of the danger shows itself in an academic attitude which consists in speaking always in long sentences full of *perhapses, and buts, on the other hands, frames of reference,* sentences composed to ward off the necessity of committing oneself to any particular point of view. Those who take care never to commit themselves to anything specific can achieve high academic recognition for being sound and capable of objective judgment.

Another way of putting this would be to say that when the members of the college community cease to bring the total and individual experience of humanity to bear upon the problems common to all humanity, they fail to refresh and recreate the store of knowledge which others have accumulated. They begin to rest content with what is known, to the exclusion of knowing what is new. The concern for ordering human experience into categories of thought then strikes at the root of experience itself, and the intellectual becomes alienated from the stream of contemporary life which gives his work its ultimate meaning.

The dangers from outside the college are those connected with the pressures society puts upon it for conformity to its own pattern of ideas and values. Sometimes this takes the form of legislation against political, religious, or social heresies; at other times it takes the form of investigative committees for detecting heretics, usually described as communists; at other times, threats of withdrawal of financial support by college graduates or by the state legislature; at other times by a pervasive threat of condemnation and suppression, carried through the Board of Trustees or Regents to the President, and thus to the working areas of daily teaching by faculty members. In the history of higher education the continual threat of suppression of ideas has had the effect of discouraging faculty members from taking part in controversial issues and from expressing their own views about such issues in the presence of students and colleagues. This has been true since the time of religious orthodoxies, and has now been transposed into the area of political and economic orthodoxy. At the same time, the continual struggle by intellectuals against the pressures of conformity has made a tradition of intellectual freedom, with its own heroes, and has served to remind the intellectual who teaches that his relation to society is quite direct, even though his position in society is usually one which detaches him from some of the more immediate impacts. We have the example of the German universities before us to demonstrate what can happen to the intellectual life of a country if it takes no interest in the social, economic, and political changes which are occurring outside the university, and if it submits to control by groups in the state who are allowed to set the pattern of social thought. The relationship between the college and its wider community is one which benefits both. The benefits to each can only be maintained when the college stands firm upon its right to seek its own truth, to sustain its own values, and when it refuses to be bullied by those who wish to control its thought. This sets the task of the college as that of teaching liberalism.

There are two major criticisms made against this idea of a college. The first is that to relate education to the needs of the students and to contemporary life is to give the young a shallow, pragmatic, and inadequate knowledge of society and its history, since it is impossible for the student to understand the nature of the issues themselves without a background of their historical antecedents and principles. The second is that this kind of education, in stressing the need for making judgments about contemporary events, and in advocating a point of view, deserts the standards of objectivity essential to the scholar and the teacher. The further argument is made that it is only by study of the past as a separate area of knowledge that the student can learn to observe the rules of objectivity, since it is only in the settled past that we can see events in their actual perspective.

There is substance to the criticism, and those who propose a philosophy of liberalism and a philosophy of the present must meet it. If students learn to treat each contemporary issue, whether it be one concerning race relations, foreign policy, the meaning of modern art, or the nature of the universe, as if it had no antecedents and as if one could settle it by sheer enthusiasm in the absence of knowledge, the criticism is justified. But this is not the proposal of a philosophy of the present. The proposal is that the student and teacher together deal with the issues of contemporary society, in order to involve the education of the student in a study whose relevance and significance may be clearly understood. Once the student becomes involved in the effort to understand the nature of the issue, the knowledge which can aid him to understand becomes an essential, and is sought, not as a separate enterprise connected with an academic program, but as an integral part of his effort.

To think of objectivity as suspension of judgment is to confuse a logic of rationalism with the total process of thought, and to separate the knowledge of fact from the valuing of fact. Any object of knowledge is valued at the same time that it is known, and by the same process of intellectual and emotional effort. Every teacher has a set of working assumptions upon which his judgment rests, both regarding the selection of knowledge which he believes his students should possess and regarding its meaning for the lives of his students. What produces academic sterility is the fact that the teacher so often assumes that there is something intrinsically valuable in sheer knowledge, provided it has been approved by the proper intellectual authorities. This achieves objectivity at the expense of relevance.

On the other hand, the kind of partisanship which simplifies the richness of the field of ideas and makes of Plato "merely" a fascist, or socialism "merely" a police state, betrays objectivity in order to advocate a point of view. Objectivity consists in weighing evidence according to certain tests for truth which generation after generation of scholars, scientists, and thinkers have been able to devise. The final authority is not an appeal to precedent, but an appeal to the empirical fact. The need of the student is for experience in making objective judgments himself, and for trying his own judgment against the judgment of others, with the aid of those who have had the advantage of more mature experience in making judgments under the disciplines of evidence. To teach the student only the truths of a settled past is to inhibit his power to interpret events independently and to refuse him the experience he needs in reaching his own conclusions. It is for this reason that the spurious objectivity of textbooks has such a paralyzing effect upon the process of education, since it presents under the guise of established fact a series of conventional conclusions based upon what has come to be accepted as true by common consent. That is not to say that what is accepted by common consent is therefore false, or by its nature suspect, but only that to present knowledge in this way deprives the student of his right to discover what objectivity means and of the right to build up his own pattern of belief and knowledge from the original sources.

Those of us who have joined forces in making an educational institution at Sarah Lawrence College hold a variety of points of view about politics, poetry, art, philosophy, science. When we talk with each other and with our students we say, as honestly as we can, what it is we think and what are our grounds for thinking it. This has some influence upon ourselves and upon our students. Our views become modified and changed by the arguments which our students make against them. We also believe in taking sides when there are social issues to be considered, both inside and outside the College, or when there are educational issues to be considered in planning the future of Sarah Lawrence College or of American education.

We teach that racial discrimination is immoral, and that social segregation of any group of human beings is wrong. We teach that each human being must be valued in his own individuality, and that his social or financial status are matters of no importance to his worth as a person. We teach that the use of force, violence, and war as a means of settling social conflict is immoral when it destroys innocent human lives. We teach that it is wrong to oppress nations, and that international cooperation in which the rights of each nation are respected is the only alternative to war. We teach the necessity of social equality, the value of freedom. We advocate these values with objectivity, knowing on the basis of historical experience that without them life becomes narrow, selfish, and, eventually, self-defeating. Unless each college and its faculty teach these aspects of liberalism, there are few places in the modern world where they will be taught, and few influences upon the young American men and women to lead them towards a respect for the liberal spirit. We believe that these are responsibilities shared by all teachers, and that a liberal education is one which aims to develop people whose feelings and ideas are liberal.

The trouble with most education is that it is boring. What makes education boring is that it puts people into institutions for the improvement of their minds and organizes the enjoyment out of learning. An educational apparatus, a syllabus, a curriculum, a well-used body of knowledge become the means for shaping behavior into conventional form. We wish to avoid this error and to keep the college program flexible enough to allow every new idea a chance to try itself in an open and free situation, yet firm enough to take full advantage of the body of experience which has been built up during the past years. We see no point in starting the College all over again every year.

It is therefore essential that the College be administered by teachers, since others would have difficulty in applying the continuous flow of knowledge about education which comes from the teaching and learning of the whole community. It is also essential that there be a radical degree of equality and democracy for the students and faculty in the administration and planning. Otherwise, good ideas might be lost simply because they were thought to come from an inappropriate quarter.

The philosophy we teach is not weakened by this diversity nor confused by its content. The central aim of liberalism, and of our effort, is to increase the scope of the creative intelligence. In order to make this possible it is necessary to form a society of human beings whose condition of freedom lies in the fact that cooperative effort is essential to the government of themselves. If this can be accomplished, in whatever small way, within a college or within a larger society, it can serve to demonstrate a kind of life freed from ignorance, fear, prejudice, and oppression, and open to a wealth of new possibilities for further experience. The idea that this is a better kind of life than other kinds has been taught by humanists and sustained by civilizations. Liberalism measures human values by the quality of the individual experience available to those who are free and furnishes an ideal towards which we can help the younger generation to move.

The Teacher and the Student

ESTHER RAUSHENBUSH

*If our faces were not like, we could not discerne a
man from a beast: If they were not unlike, we could
not distinguish one man from another.*
—MONTAIGNE

A great many people who do not teach in colleges talk about the
education of college students, and what they say often profoundly
affects the people who do teach. This talk is important, and we
need all the light which observers and theorists can throw on the
process of education. But the most important thinking about this
subject has always been done by teachers because they are able to
consider not only the aims of education, but also the ways in which
their knowledge, scholarship, and understanding may fulfill these
aims.

In spite of all the wide-ranging discussion about education there
are in fact only two ways of thinking about how to teach. One or
the other of these shapes every educational program.

One way is to consider the sum of the world's knowledge and
decide how much of it we can transmit to our students. This is the
way the people who taught most of us proceeded. The task of
education, then, is to train the minds of students to receive this
knowledge. This task gives a teacher a sense of high calling, imparts
to him a feeling of responsibility, of being dedicated to the task of
conserving, selecting, and keeping alive in our descendants the
world's learning.

The other way of thinking about education is to consider what
education can do for one's life; what teachers can do to help
students who are growing from adolescents to adults; and how
knowledge may best be used as an instrument for this growth and
for the experience of living. Then learning is no longer an accumulation of facts, or even an analysis of ideas; it is the process of

24

finding and using knowledge that will help in this growth. The curriculum, if this is the aim of education, is not the list of courses in the catalogue. It is, rather, the total educational experience which the college provides for its students. The curriculum is made by the faculty on the basis of their understanding of the needs of their particular students in this stage of their development, in this society and period of history, and by the way their own knowledge, values, attitudes, and intentions help to meet these needs. Central to the educational planning and to the decisions about what to teach and how to teach are the students, with their potentialities for learning, and the teachers, with the uses they make of their knowledge.

This idea of education has prompted the building of Sarah Lawrence College, and it is implicit in the work of the men and women who teach in the College and who have written here of their experience as teachers. There are many differences of opinion among them, but they agree about the most important matter— the meaning of education. This common understanding of what education means is responsible for the decisions they make about their own teaching, and the decisions made jointly in the College about how our students are to be educated.

Students living through their late adolescent years have accumulated a sum of experience that is intensely important to them, and they are acutely sensitive to the impact of the events of life. They have begun to see the complexity of human life and of the world they live in. For them the range of possible experience has steadily widened since childhood, and they have still to learn the limitations which they will discover as adults. If schools have not succeeded in drying up their natural curiosity they will bring to college a great capacity for learning about the world. They have many intellectual concerns and many emotional needs. Some of these are articulate and form the expectations with which students come to college and which lie at the root of their judgments about what they would like to study. Many of their needs exert on them severe demands which they do not remotely understand, but which it is surely the business of education to consider.

The complicated and in many ways ill-defined roles women must play in our society are responsible for some of the most serious concerns of young women students, and these concerns make relentless demands on their energies and emotions. Students cannot check them at the campus gate, and we must recognize their importance in the educational process or we will blind ourselves and fail to see our students as they are. These girls, both the more and the less intellectual, will marry and have children, and they are well aware of this future whether their teachers are or not.

As we all know, the early history of higher education for women was marked by strong competitive feelings. Women felt they must prove that their intelligence equaled men's and educators believed the only way to do that was to make women's colleges as nearly like men's as possible. Some recent alternatives to this have been attempts to introduce into women's colleges courses in cooking and managing domestic budgets, and making the most of one's looks. But this is not a legitimate alternative—there are other more appropriate places to learn these crafts.

In thinking about the education of our students, however, we must take into account the fact that for most of them the principal occupation of their adult lives will be the creation of a family and a home, and this occupation will demand as much understanding of human relations, of growth and development, as much social understanding and community responsibility, and as much wisdom in ways of enriching the life of the family as they can learn to have. Students are implicitly or consciously aware of these demands, and it is reasonable for the college to recognize them too in thinking about their education.

The character and the needs of students cannot be of primary concern if we plan a curriculum by selecting as essential a particular fraction of the world's knowledge, by assuming that our function as teachers is to transmit this knowledge to students, and by defining the education of students as the acquisition of this knowledge. The acquisition of knowledge is important, but it is important only for the uses it can serve in developing the life experience of the person who seeks and acquires it. Educators have always taken a kind of false aristocratic pleasure in talking about the importance of "knowledge for its own sake," an idea which has little meaning and which has led to endless sterile learning. Knowledge is significant only as it can be used for all life purposes. There is no discipline, intellectual or any other kind, which cannot be better developed by knowledge which has meaning for the one who is learning than by knowledge which has none.

In planning the education of our students the faculty at Sarah Lawrence College tries to be mindful of the questions, the areas of concern, and the expressed and implied needs of their students; and their efforts to meet them are reflected in the teaching throughout the College. The psychologists on this faculty hold various views about the structure of personality, and they have by no means the same ways of explaining behavior. But they agree in recognizing that the desire of most students to study psychology is rooted in the need to seek some explanation of human behavior; that young people are deeply involved in reflections and feelings about the relations of parents and children, about the role of the individual in society; that they are concerned about the relation of the life of reason to the emotional life. Such concerns are a strong incentive for learning. For this reason teachers begin to teach psychology by discussing with their students the questions about human behavior which appear important to them, by giving them books to read which will bear on these questions and will raise others, and by helping to interpret what they read and observe. The teaching of psychology does not confine itself to the students' questions, nor end there. But that is a good place to begin.

This attention to the questions that stir the imagination and reflect the anxieties of students and stimulate them to inquiry is found in all the teaching—in biology, literature, social philosophy, or art. The function of the teacher is to sharpen and direct the experience of students, to deepen their understanding, to use knowledge as a means to their intellectual and emotional growth. If this is their purpose they have to be interested in matters other than "covering the subject."

The literature teacher who undertakes to help students examine their social, aesthetic, or moral concerns or prejudices and uses his knowledge of literature for this purpose may never manage to survey English literature from Beowulf to Thomas Hardy. The teacher of philosophy who knows that students have philosophical questions to ask before they have ever looked into a philosophy textbook will be unlikely to engage in a comprehensive study of all the systems in Western philosophy, if he undertakes to consider the students' questions as a way of teaching and studying philosophy. Students do not study philosophy in order to learn the history of philosophy, or to be able to describe a dozen philosophical systems. They do come with the expectation of discovering that the questions bothering them have been answered by the philosophers, and they would like to know the answers. It is an important educational experience for them to learn that the questions they ask are questions the philosophers ask too; and when they study philosophy or art, literature or science, they discover that the process of inquiring and learning about important issues is a permanent quest; and finally, they learn that the purpose of education is not so much to find answers as to discover which questions are important, and which ones, therefore, they should spend their time examining.

The biologist and the psychologist both need to deal with the physical manifestations of emotion, and a biologist's discussion of this problem with a group of psychology students invariably makes some of them see the need of studying the biological sciences— even students who had rejected altogether the idea of such study. It is not difficult to kindle the enthusiasm of students to learn something which they know to be important for things they want to discover.

As we plan the curriculum, we think about ways to use knowledge and ways to use the energies and abilities of the students as means to educate them.

We must therefore scrutinize all the academic conventions. The study of painting or sculpture, for instance, is often excluded from the curriculum of a college on the grounds that art is not an appropriate academic subject; or students are permitted to study painting or music seriously if they are particularly talented and plan to become painters or musicians; or they are occasionally permitted to study art (with a small amount of academic credit attached to the art course) as a means of "self-expression" and a proper pastime for an idle hour in the midst of more serious studies. But the study of art as part of a liberal education is neither primarily for the particularly gifted nor for the dabblers. It is not to create painters or to provide emotional release. It is to help students discover what the world looks like, to help them to see and to understand what they see. Its discipline, as rigorous as the discipline of logic or mathematics, is the means by which many students learn new ways of thinking about experience, and the study of art should be part of the education of many students. For instance, I recall an intelligent student who "learned" quickly, who generalized easily about experience, who tended to oversimplify, to make quick verbal organization of ideas and events; and we advised her to study painting. The first report of the teacher remarks that "she has always done the assigned work with great care and thought. If these thoughts have occasionally turned out to be literary thoughts rather than visual ones, I might point out that this is the reason why she is in this course. She has learned very well to distinguish between these different ways of thinking, and it becomes more apparent in her work. She must see more exhibitions. Her visual imagination and capacity to observe are still rather limited—not 'by birth' but because she has not exposed herself enough to the work of people who have it."

The painting studios will not, therefore, turn out the number of skilled painters that might develop if other criteria were used in selecting students and other objectives set for them. But the learning that goes on in the studio, when painting is an experience of ways of seeing and understanding the world, becomes part of the total life of the student who may never become an artist.

The classroom experience of teachers sensitive to such educational problems, the conversation of a group of teachers about a particular student, the consideration of these issues in the committee which plans the curriculum, lead to new thinking about how to teach and how to use the substance of one's knowledge in the interest of students. A composer on the staff undertakes to write an opera for student production, and as soon as it is under way the faculty and students in the field of theatre, music, dance, and design find new sources to draw on for their common work, and individual students find new opportunity for using particular gifts.

The kind of teaching described here, and this way of making a curriculum, escape the common error of treating students as though they had intelligence of one sort or another but no history or emotional life or personality. We cannot look on them simply as fresh minds to be instructed and made wise—a view that has made planning education relatively simple for many college administrators and faculties. If we are to understand students at all we must discover as much as we can about their intellectual and emotional concerns, the kind of energy they bring to their education, the curiosities, prejudices, and resistances which are, whether they know it or not, such positive forces for us to use in educating them. Before a teacher can begin to educate his students in the terms described here he must know something about the qualities the students bring to their education, and he must find ways of understanding them early in his association with the students.

The information colleges usually ask students to give them at entrance is not enough to enable the college to know what is educationally significant for the students. College Board records, school grades, and a list of the subjects studied in high school all tell something about a student, but not some of the most important things we need to know. At Sarah Lawrence College, therefore, we ask for other information. Each student who applies fills out a questionnaire which is one of our most important guides, not only in deciding whether or not the student should come to the College, but in helping us to know what kind of person she is and how we can best work with her when she is here. What does she expect the College to give her? Which studies up to now have meant most to her, and which have been least important? What teachers has she worked with best? And which ones have been most difficult for her to work with? Is she interested in any political or economic questions? In any of the arts? What books has she liked, and why? What in her school life has been most important to her so far, and what experiences outside of school? The student is asked to write a brief autobiography as part of this admissions material.

The teachers who have this kind of knowledge about students see not only the common concerns determined by their age, the pressure of their times and their common cultural life; they also see students at once as a variety of individuals, each at a different level and kind of maturity, of interest, of energy, and of ability. It is then impossible to assume that all these freshmen can be educated by any single plan of studies if we as their teachers are to think of their intellectual growth and not simply of our own knowledge. Therefore, immediately upon arrival at Sarah Lawrence College, each student begins to work with a member of the faculty in putting together her own curriculum of courses. Registration does not mean listing on a form the courses freshmen are told to take. It means talking about expectations and hopes, abilities and difficulties, about the student's idea of what her experience might be, the adviser's judgment about what she might do. It means, for us, discovering all we can to begin with about what areas of knowledge, what ways of working, what kinds of thinking might have the meaning for a student that will make her use her abilities as fully as possible.

All the members of the faculty, as they come to know the College and their colleagues, serve to advise new students. This is part of their function as teachers, and during this registration time, as at other times, the teaching, counseling, and administrative parts of the educational program are merged and carried on together. None of the teachers advising freshmen has more than seven or eight to work with, and the teacher is able to spend enough time with each student during the registration week to arrive at some basis for planning with each one the way in which she may best begin her college career. During this week students consult many faculty members for whose courses they are eligible. They attend meetings conducted by faculty members in different fields to learn more about the courses offered in the College. They meet with returning students and learn about the College as the students know it.

During the past five years criticism of the elective system has become more vocal and more severe than it has ever been. Under this system, as it developed in our universities, students could select whatever subjects they chose and piece together a course of study. There is a body of opinion that holds that the only alternative to this chaotic situation is a highly organized program of study in which all or most courses are prescribed. The aims of education and the ways of teaching described in this book would be impossible to achieve under either system. Planning in terms of the interests, needs, and goals of students, on the other hand, does make it possible to create the flexibility which an all-required program destroys, and to make the constructive plans which an unguided elective program does not permit.

The student entering Sarah Lawrence works out a program of studies for her first year with the help of a registration adviser and by means of her interviews with other members of the faculty. One of her teachers becomes her don, or adviser, for the rest of the year. This teacher keeps in touch with her progress in all courses, talks with her about her work and life in the College, and gives the counsel that will help her make the most of her college experience. Working in this way makes both teachers and students sensitive to the possibilities in teaching and learning, and greatly enriches the life of the College.

In reading the record of a student entering the College who had lived in a small community in the South, we saw that to her most of the important social issues of our time seemed to be settled. She was not interested in studying "politics or economics or anything of that sort," wanted to study literature and the arts, and was obviously out for "Culture." In her mind the College was to serve this purpose. This is a student who had a good high school record, passed the College Board examinations well, but seemed to the faculty members who talked to her upon her arrival at College to be insulated against the possibility of education. She was allowed to take a literature course, but we saw to it that it was one that would clearly require her to think about some of the issues she assumed had already been decided; a course in history that did not threaten her by a direct approach to contemporary issues, but which was certain to deal with them obliquely; and a course in art. Her life in the College was the process of emancipation from the stereotypes with which she had come, and no time was lost in attempting to deal with her obvious needs and to remove the hindrances to her education.

The experience this student had in working with teachers who were able to begin to free her from these intellectual difficulties is one which many students have in many colleges. A student may happen on an interested and perceptive teacher in any situation. The effort at Sarah Lawrence College has been to bring this kind of self-discovery as soon as possible wherever it is needed, and not to trust to luck that it will develop by itself or that some teacher will happen to see the need.

Such association between teachers and students lies at the center of the educational program and determines the character of the curriculum. Not the academic disciplines but the students are the subject of education, and knowledge is the instrument. It is, therefore, important for students and their teachers to have time for consultation, for students to have time for study and the opportunity to spend long periods working without interruption. This cannot be achieved if students study five or six different subjects and sit in classes many hours daily. To allow time for intensive work, most students here take only three courses, although if it seems appropriate they take four. Classes meet only once or twice a week, and students have conferences not only with their advisers but with all their teachers each week, or every two weeks. All teachers have access to the cumulative records on each student and these records, the small classes, and the frequent conferences give teachers the opportunity they need to discover how students are responding to their studies, and how to carry forward their education.

Instead of giving freshmen the most formalized kind of studying to do, advisers plan with students in such a way that they will be able to begin by studying something which they have an initial desire to learn. And since this exploratory freshman year may in some ways be the most important period in the college life of students, instead of assigning them to the least experienced teachers, graduate assistants, or new instructors, we try to have them taught by the most experienced and wisest teachers, who will know how to deepen and extend the questions which the students bring, and to help their search for answers.

A faculty adviser remarked in his first report about a certain student that she had grown up in "a restricted and authoritarian environment," and that she was rebellious against the degree to which she had been subjected to the demands of this environment, although her rebellion was covered by a veneer of conviction that this "has been good for my character." Her comments on books were constricted; she spoke of liking and disliking but with no analysis or explanation. She was status-conscious and made many comments indicating that she needed the approval of people in authority. Her work from the beginning was formally good. She met all assignments, she listened attentively to the teachers, and made clear that she heard and believed what they said. She said little in class discussions, and when she spoke it was to corroborate what had already been said and had apparently been approved. She would have made excellent grades on an objective examination planned to test how thoroughly she had read and studied her lessons. If they had had no concern for the further aims of education, her faculty could have been lulled into comfortable acceptance of this girl as "a good B student," and she might easily have grown into an informed pedant. Her teachers' initial knowledge of her attitudes and ways of working made it obvious that for this girl, who had intelligence considerably above the average college student, education meant more than anything else freeing her from these compulsions and finding ways of making her work and life at College something more than a routine experience. She studied, perhaps, the same "subjects" she would have studied under any circumstances—a freshman course in literature, a science course, and economics. But everybody saw to it that she was given work to do that would stretch her imagination, that would make it difficult to give routine answers, that would give some opportunity to understand and evaluate her relation to ideas and people. Her adviser, who was also her literature teacher, was able to help her in the process, not only in terms of his work with her in this course, but in terms of his knowledge of the problems she met in the rest of her work. A record of his experience in teaching and advising her, and the experience of the rest of her teachers, is made accessible through reports, made three times in the course of the year by her faculty and three times by her adviser, which are part of the permanent record. The faculty members in the following year thus have something much more than a series of grades to help them understand this student and to plan her work with them.

At the end of the year each student works out with her adviser the plans for the courses of the following year, and it is the sum of her work to that time, her ways of working, her intellectual and general educational needs as these have emerged through the year, that determine what she should do the following year. One sequence of courses may be necessary for the goals of one student but not for others; no one sequence can, therefore, be the determining factor in planning our courses of study for all students. The advisers of students have the responsibility of discussing their education with them, of helping them to discover their needs, of examining the seriousness of their interests and aims, and of planning with them in terms of these goals. The premedical student must meet the demands of the medical schools, but, while doing so, it is no less important that she become educated in other phases of her life.

Naturally, when education is planned in relation to the student, the progress of the student from course to course, and from lecture to lecture, does not occur with the same regularity and order as in the prearranged curriculum. Particular demands made upon some students are not made upon others, since to make the same demand in all cases would be unrealistic, both for the teacher and for the student. In planning a course, the teacher assigns some work that all students must do as the basis for discussing the subject at hand; but beyond this he may range widely in planning individual aspects of the study for different students.

When troubles develop, or when a student is unable to deal successfully with her educational problems, a teacher usually calls a meeting of the faculty members who are working with the student to discuss her difficulties. I remember a bright, imaginative, but disorganized student who early attracted the attention of her teachers by her interest in large, philosophical issues, and her ability to ask questions which seemed penetrating. She sought the most complex and profound subjects for study and wrote long papers on important problems. But it became apparent that her thinking about these problems was not developing; her intellectual experiences were exciting, but she was disinclined either to learn anything more about them or to write about them in an orderly and intelligent manner. When the faculty members teaching her met to talk, they found that the same difficulties existed in her work in psychology, in international relations, and in literature. By agreeing on certain changes in the reading and writing demands made on her they were able to save her months of floundering and to prevent a failure.

Teaching in this way means that teachers must treat their students seriously. If, in the beginning, teachers set themselves the task of transmitting as much of their information as possible to their students, it would not matter much whether the students experienced anything in the process or not—the information could be transmitted whether or not it made any difference to the student. But almost everything the teachers who have written this book, and the others who teach with them, say about their work involves the effort to help students find ways to use their studies in thinking about their lives, in determining their attitudes and ideas, in guiding them toward ways of acting. Unless teachers are convinced that these ends can be achieved, it must be impossible for them to work with the students at all. There would be no appropriate "subject matter" for them to teach with, and no reason for teaching.

The students must take themselves seriously too. It would be destructive to work in the ways we do with students who were indifferent or frivolous in their own attitude toward their education. They must take an active part in their education; they must work at the planning, too, because this cannot be done by the College without them. A passive attention to the events of the classroom, or the passive reading of books, will not help in finding significant use for what is being taught or learned. One of the most heartening things about education is that most students, if given half a chance, show serious concern with important matters. When this does not happen, it is likely to be because either teachers or institutions have failed to give students an opportunity to read and talk about such matters.

There is repeated evidence in this book of teachers' concern with helping students discover a way of proceeding from one point to another, from one set of ideas to another, of creating an end rather than reaching one already known, or of discovering an end that exists by virtue of all the steps along the road. These teachers all say that students must learn to find their way to a goal which the teacher might not even see in the beginning, although he has much more to see with than his students have. Their road may be one which he too has traveled, and so he may be able to predict their discoveries. But sometimes, and this is the reward of original teaching, the discoveries students make, created as they are by a new combination of the teacher's knowledge and their own thought, experience, and feeling, are new to the teachers as well as to themselves.

Finally, if we accept the use rather than the acquisition of knowledge as a goal of education, teachers have to decide what they want to use knowledge for. This means that they have to make value judgments—they have to examine and understand their own attitudes toward experience and toward their lives as individuals and as members of families and of society. This is a necessity not only for faculty but for students as well. We cannot subscribe to the current fiction among academics that only "facts" are the business of the teacher, not opinions or attitudes. We know too much about the elusive nature of a fact to believe this fully in any context. In teaching and studying it is obviously impossible in many situations to separate fact from judgment, and if we try to do so we again try to reduce education to a simple acquisitive act. For this reason teachers must take responsibility for making judgments, and they must not hide behind a fiction of objectivity where it cannot exist. For the purposes of education, what writers, experimenters, teachers, and students think about what they know is as important as what they know.

As faculty and students work together, as the educational purposes and the life purposes of those who make up any college become more articulate, the style or character of the institution emerges. Where faculty, administration, and students are most conscious of their values and attitudes, the character of the college is most sharply defined.

It is interesting to observe, in reading the chapters of this book, the recurrence of certain ideas and certain problems of value. This is not the result of deliberate planning; it has happened because the climate and character of this College are congenial to interest in problems such as these. The men and women whose "subjects" are literature, psychology, history, philosophy, or art, use what they know about their special fields to deal with issues they think important. For instance, there are a number of discussions in the following chapters about the relative significance to our lives of the concepts of competition and cooperation. This shows up sometimes in political terms, sometimes in dealing with psychological issues, as a problem in education, in a field work project, or in almost any aspect of the conduct of life. Another recurring question is one which has to do with how we can order life to achieve a maximum degree of freedom and a maximum degree of security. This question is discussed whether teachers are talking about a novel, about parent-child relations, or about the structure of a state. The relation of the individual to society, of his obligations to society and the responsibilities of society to him, is also a frequent subject of concern, and one which teachers and students consider whether they are talking about Plato, or *Hamlet*, or the behavior of the children in the nursery school.

The quality of all the life in the College is shaped by our educational purposes and methods which are shared by faculty and students. In the dormitories, students live under the sole supervision of their fellow students. The Student Council is a self-governing body which has many activities important to the functioning of the College—for instance, a Civil Rights Committee, and an Arts Exchange which brings students from other colleges to discuss painting, music, or literature. A Student Curriculum Committee works closely with the Faculty Curriculum Committee and takes a serious part in evaluating our course of study every year and suggesting changes.

What kind of teachers are needed for a program such as the one I have outlined here? For one thing, the question of how much of a specialist the college teacher should be is one which is troubling many people seriously concerned with the problems of teaching college students, and is even beginning to trouble the graduate schools. Obviously a chemistry teacher must be a good scientist or he cannot be a good chemistry teacher; and a teacher of literature must be widely read and have imagination and insight into the meaning of literature or he is a poor teacher of literature. But there has been so much pressure for graduate students who are to become college teachers to embrace a corner of the knowledge of their fields and possess it completely that we sometimes forget that the college teacher should be an educated man.

For the kind of teaching described here the possession of a little plot of detailed knowledge will not serve. The lines between anthropology and psychology, between history and philosophy, are of our own making and have hindered the education of students as much as they have helped scholars. Few of the students coming through our schools read other languages than their own as well as they might. But the rigor with which literature departments have excluded the reading of any literature not written in the English language has greatly impoverished the study and the reading students do in college. We have not drawn these lines. A teacher of literature, himself widely read in literature in many languages, uses the whole range of his knowledge to bring to his students any book, from any literature, if in an English version it can enlarge their vision and their thought.

There is indeed only one way for the teacher to thrive in this situation—he must continue to study and read, to learn from his colleagues, and to discover, along with his students, those things he needs to know in order to be able to teach in the most imaginative way he can.

In selecting teachers, as in planning for the work of our students, we cannot be satisfied with routine information about them, with evidence of a good graduate school record and ability to do research. These are desirable, but they are not enough. Teachers must like their students and be able to work with students in the ways described in this book; they must have the quality and depth of knowledge that has been indicated here. They are not easy to find, and the President of the College and a committee of the faculty with him spend many hours seeking the kind of men and women we need.

The best evidence of what they are like as teachers and as men and women can be found in the class and conference rooms in the College. The fraction of this evidence which we have been able to put between covers will be found in the subsequent chapters of this book.

On Teaching Literature

HORACE GREGORY

I

In America the teacher of literature in a liberal college has behind him at the back of his mind's eye the double images of Emerson and Coleridge. The Emerson he sees and whose voice he hears is the Emerson who composed, quite as if it were a symphony and not a lecture, *The American Scholar.* Today that voice is overheard as though it were the voice of a ghost, given overmuch to the sounding of rhetorical platitudes; yet if one listens closely, what a lively and disturbing ghost it is! And when it speaks well its truths are as true today as they always were:

> Thought and knowledge are natures in which apparatus and pretension avail nothing. Gowns and pecuniary foundations, though of towns of gold, can never countervail the least sentence or syllable of wit. Forget this, and our American colleges will recede in their public importance, whilst they grow richer every year. . . .

Emerson's warning holds an essential meaning that is not to be forgotten, for "the least sentence or syllable of wit" is still the necessary ingredient in the teaching of literature. And what of that other ghost, Samuel Taylor Coleridge, who is equally troublesome and haunting, but has the good fortune at this moment of being in better repute than Emerson? What of him, who having failed in the spring of 1796 at publishing and editing his periodical called *The Watchman,* turned his distracted mind to education and to the prospect of opening "a school for eight young men" which had, still formulating in Coleridge's mind, the following course of studies:

> 1. Man as an Animal,—including the complete knowledge of anatomy, chemistry, mechanics, and optics; 2. Man as an intellectual being,—including the ancient metaphysics, the system of Locke and Hartley—of the Scotch philosophers and the new Kantean system; 3. Man as Religious Being,—including an historic summary of all religions. . . . Then pro-

ceeding from the individual to the aggregate of individuals, and disregarding all chronology, except that of mind, I should perfect them: 1.—in the history of savage tribes; 2.—of semi-barbarous nations; 3.—of nations emerging from semi-barbarism; 4.—of civilized states; 5.—of luxurious states; 6.—of revolutionary states; 7.—of colonies. During these studies I should intermix the knowledges of languages, and instruct my scholars in *belles lettres* and the principles of composition. . . .

During his lifetime Coleridge's school never came into physical being, and though he was obviously unfitted for the offices of headmaster and college president, he contributed brilliantly to the education of his friends, including William Wordsworth—and, of course, the world. How clearly he held before him the important principle of the integration of studies and, held at its center, the figure of man! Man as always is the disturbing, troublesome element in the making of plans for his education; his external appearance is always changing; he yields to the pressure of his fellows, and at spectacular moments finds the power to resist it. His apathy is often overwhelming, and it would seem that out of his very weaknesses he discovers (like Coleridge) a source of strength. The condition of man is such that in an age of mechanical science like our own, and in the United States, the study of humanities (and this is where literature plays its part) becomes an increasing problem in his education. As for Coleridge's school, the ideas behind it gave it life and persisted and grew. One can find its list of studies in many liberal institutions of learning today: the literal titles have undergone a few temporal changes; the names of Nietzsche, Marx, Freud, Goddeck, Kierkegaard, and Hegel have been substituted for those of Locke and Hartley. The "history of savage tribes" has found a new title under the word "anthropology," and today after the psychic shock of two world wars, "Man as Religious Being" emerges in a new disguise. It is of some moment, I think (since Coleridge was a poet), that he placed the instruction of *belles lettres* and the principles of composition at the bottom of his list.

It is easy to admit that Coleridge's prospectus of a school has in it much that we now define as "liberal education," but it is not so easy to keep the word "liberal," with its various political and educational meanings, free of misuse and misapplication. I bring this troublesome question up because Coleridge and lip service to his ideas have been appropriated by institutions that are anything but liberal, and within them the principles on which Coleridge founded his idea of a school have been completely lost or unwholesomely distorted. His idea of a school still stands as one of the few brilliant illustrations of what a liberal education can do and is; few descriptions of what a liberal education means are as clearly presented as his idea, and his stress upon man at the very center of his scheme is of a kind that brings the study of the humanities to its rightful position in the curriculum.

But to return to the last item on Coleridge's list, *belles lettres* and the principles of composition. I suspect that it was not modesty that made Coleridge place it last. The part played by literature within the study of man can be taken for granted and placed last because of the nature of literary art whose primary and final intentions are to reveal the sources of man's being. All other esthetic values are secondary to these intentions, and the intention to be artful is not enough to endow a work of fiction, a play, or a poem with its necessary resemblance to life. Coleridge himself had very little need to worry visibly about instructing his students in the values of *belles lettres*. Although he was often capable of vast self-deceptions, he knew himself well enough to know his disposition to talk fully and pointedly on such occasions when the names of Shakespeare or Donne, Thomas Gray, Milton, or Wordsworth flowed into the stream of conversation. Coleridge, for one, could well afford to let the principles of composition come as they may; and in his later years his study of man included a profound revelation of the psychology of poetic composition. In his plan for a school he had already advanced the notion of disregarding all chronology, except that of mind, a procedure which closely resembles the approach of those who have rediscovered the continuous and active participation of myth in literature. This idea can be discerned in those interpretations of literature which allow a discussion of nonliteral reality to take its rightful place, and within it literature of the past is not merely a view into a distant vista of time and space but is an enriched perception of being alive, of being aware of the forces which shape human existence. It is by this path of understanding that one begins to unfold the meanings of a work of art, whether the work happens to be Joyce's *Ulysses* or a cycle of Sophocles' tragedies or the poems of William Butler Yeats.

No theory of teaching literature is likely to find itself in dispute over the latest mutation of Coleridge's dismissal of chronology in education; the point of argument rises over methods of advancing it, of presenting it to students, and then relating literature to life itself. That is where schools clash and educational ideologies are at war. Although in America it is generally agreed that studies in the mechanical aspects of the sciences are to be placed first in order because they are easy to acquire and, in a literal sense, eminently practical, few institutions have the courage to drop literature from the curriculum entirely. Great lip service is paid to the teaching of humanities of which literature is the core; and the American genius for mass distribution of goods finds an application in the teaching of literature by the means of "great books" courses, which are nothing more or less than extended survey courses for which textbook anthologies are provided. The British Victorians were justly noted for their hypocrisy in dealing with human emotions that were all too obviously related to sex; and in matters of educating young people in the humanities, the Americans of the mid-twentieth century are no less hypocritical. In conservative institutions mass methods of teaching literature are in high favor: the same extracts from the same books are read by thousands at the same hour every week, and as the hour closes, the homage to literature is paid and the whole matter dismissed. Under these circumstances, a necessary ingredient of Emerson's *American Scholar*, "the least sentence or syllable of wit," has extremely infrequent chances of being overheard; the mechanical process of lecturing, teaching, reading has found its groove within that part of the educational system reserved for the humanities. The very few who, so it seems by accident, have caught fire from the pages of an anthology, are selected from the larger mass and taught the process of analyzing literature and are again handed textbooks on "how to read" or "understanding poetry"—and these mid-twentieth-century American scholars, if they are industrious enough, will enter graduate schools and emerge as teachers of the same process to thousands of other scholars.

I think I have sufficiently indicated the point at which educational ideologies are at war. In a liberal college the youthful Coleridge's idea of a school, however impractical that idea was for him, still retains, in respect to a study of the humanities, a positive release from the general "curse of bigness" which afflicts the majority of educational institutions in America today. In Coleridge's school the progress of learning moves from the individual to "the aggregate of individuals," a concept that can be put into practice, literally enough, among small groups of students; the concept in itself showed the way Coleridge's idea could be put to work. The liberal college is in a fair way of making a mid-twentieth-century contribution to the more radical facets of Coleridge's idea, of taking it back to the liberal sources where it belongs, refreshing it with Emerson's demand for wit, and giving it renewed life by paying proper respect for the needs and abilities of individual young men and women.

II

The progress of an education in literature which I have begun to describe demands an enthusiasm that can be applied to the values of individual thinking and feeling as well as to the values of teaching imaginative literature. It presupposes that anthologies and textbooks should be set aside in favor of readings at their source. It becomes the responsibility of the instructor not to clutter the intelligence of his students with opinions gathered at second or third hand, and no "shortcuts" to learning are advised. In this environment the question that the teacher frequently asks a student is why a certain book is to be read at all. Why read *Moby Dick* or *Look Homeward, Angel,* or *Bleak House* or *Crime and Punishment* or *Don Quixote* or Malory's *Morte d'Arthur*? Why, why? It is from the student's answer that actual motives for the study of literature are brought to light—and the question of how to read arrives after the question of why to read at all is answered. The question has a kinship to the title of Dr. Robert Lynd's book *Knowledge For What?*, a pertinent question which places a share of responsibility for education on the shoulders of the student—and the question "why?" leads toward the mature consideration of what the results of a study of literature may mean. With these questions in mind, the instructor has no authority but his own learning to consult; he must then refer to his own ability to read, his own imagination, his own ingenuity—and, most important of all, his interpretation of why his students elect a course in literature. When the motives for the reading of literature are clarified, it is often found that the student's primary concern refers to man's place in the universe and where the individual stands in relationship to human experience. The student may elect a course in literature for the more immediate desires of learning how to teach or how to write, but even underlying these "practical" desires the subjective question, "What is my place in the world?" awaits an answer.

It has long been one of the properties of literature, either ancient or modern, to extend the ranges of individual experience and to provide a vantage point from which the intelligent reader may view the world. One example that readily comes to mind may be drawn from the pages of Henry James's story *What Masie Knew*, and the intelligent reader can, after some interval of reflective thinking, find in that story of the unhappily situated child several distinctly interwoven threads of human experience. To some of us the story may well be a part of the universal, and so often painful, experience of "growing up," of the child learning to see her unworthy and self-centered parents, not as they seemed to be or as they wished to appear but as they are. Others may read the story as a parable of the division between the adult world and that of childhood and, in Masie's case, of innocence, precociously assuming a worldly air, emerging deformed and somewhat soiled from the encounter with what are so often called the "facts of life." Still others will read it as a comment on the frequent consequences of divorce, a situation in which the child becomes the unwilling instrument of torture, mutually inflicted upon the other, of two people engaged in the art of destroying one another. I think it can be agreed that James's story is far more enlightening and has within it more facets of human experience than the latest report of a sensational divorce case in the morning paper, for the story, timely as it may be, has already acquired a timeless air, and with the story before them, both the social moralist and the philosopher would find something appropriate to say. The story's excursion into the nature of education is by no means pedantic or usual, and those who read it are often impressed by the wide ranges of its application. Certainly the experiences that the very action of the story involve are not entirely irrelevant to situations that the college undergraduate may have faced or should be prepared to face today; in any case, the story can be shown to have its bearing upon even the most subjective interpretation of the question, "What is my place in the world?" and "Where can I go from there?"

I hope I have not implied that James's little narrative *What Masie Knew* is so singular, so rare an illustration of what I mean, that it excludes other kinds of insights and other types of fiction; Thomas Mann's *Death in Venice* and his *Felix Krull* could be advanced to chart other areas of human experience, and so could Turgenev's *A Lear of the Steppes*, or Sherwood Anderson's *Death in the Woods*. Yet, all the stories I have mentioned have this in common: each extends the range and reaches further into the depth of what is frequently regarded as everyday experience; none of the stories could be interpreted as mere fantasy and therefore outside or irrelevant to human motives and fears, human hopes and desires; each story holds within it possibilities of more than a single interpretation of its action and its theme; and each, not unlike life itself, is worthy of more than a single rapid glance at the motives which underlie human action and emotion.

If something like an answer is found to the student's larger questions, then the student begins to know what being a "well-educated" person means, and the discovery leads to what the Greeks meant by the phrase "self-knowledge." Literature in itself cannot pretend to give a direct and final answer to this kind of question, but it does furnish a number of illustrations of how an answer can be found, and some of the best-known examples are those which are derived from courses in comparative literature, the tragedies of Shakespeare and Sophocles, and in the pages of the Old Testament in the Bible. It is here that the understanding of the teacher plays its dual role: an understanding of what the student is looking for and an appropriate understanding of the literature which brings into view the answer to the student's question.

This kind of teaching cannot depend upon the textbook for solution of student questions, nor can the single text of translations from classical literatures be regarded as the only version of a play or poem. The reading of a prose translation of Homer's *Iliad* is followed by readings in Chapman and Pope, which also include some understanding of Renaissance and neo-Classical interpretations of Homer's masterpiece. In the reading of classical literature in translation it is natural enough for the student to ask what "divine envy" means and to question whether or not a relationship exists between the trials of Oedipus and those of Job. One way of answering these questions involves Coleridge's "historic summary of all religions," and the student turns to rediscoveries of ancient problems in twentieth-century anthropology. Or another student, guided by Lessing's *Laocoon*, turns to esthetics rather than ethics and religion, rereads Aristotle's Poetics and Arnold's essay on translating Homer, and from there moves onward into a rediscovery of neo-Classicism in contemporary criticism. This kind of learning is scarcely aided by selected presentations of "great thoughts," for it demands the student's ability to follow out the consequences of making a well-deliberated choice. One of my students, charmed by a reading of Aesop's fables, found them an appropriate example for writing fables of contemporary life, while another student related them to the neo-Classical wit of La Fontaine. Within this kind of educational environment it becomes natural for the teacher to suggest a revaluation of Aeschylus in terms of Nietzsche's essay, *The Birth of Tragedy*, and to contrast it with classical esthetics as well as the contemporary neo-Classical position of T. S. Eliot.

The progress of this kind of education, in relationship to literature, rests on the premise that young men and women have a valid interest in the world in which they live, that a book is not read merely because it has the reputation of being "a great book" but because it has survived the moment it was written since it had, and still has, something to say. It is in this area that the liberal college must continue a process of unlearning students who arrive from schools that encourage tabloid learning in strictly regimented departments, departments in which surveys of literature are offered in preparation for further rapid surveys of anthologies of literature. No general surveys of literature *per se* exist in the kind of education I am describing, no courses that pretend to review readings in English literature from Chaucer to the latest volume of verses by W. H. Auden, for the fallacies of this kind of teaching have been in evidence so long that even the most conservative colleges in America are troubled by the problems they create.

III

In the teaching of literature there are two main approaches to the general subject: one is to name an area of reading of which the student has heard vaguely but knows nothing, the other is to find out what the student has read and to proceed from there onto unfamiliar ground. The first approach is an appeal to the student's curiosity: What is Russian literature? the student may ask. What are its values, and why is Russian fiction of the nineteenth century something that has "universal" meaning? Or another student may ask, What is the relationship of a course in mythology to "the myth" in literature as it is referred to in current critical reviews? Or why is *Paradise Lost* considered a great poem? What is Realism in fiction and what is Symbolism in poetry? All these are questions which arise out of overhearing conversation about literature and, naturally enough, adolescent curiosity is aroused. The flaw in this otherwise commendable desire to know things and to expect large answers is that this kind of curiosity about literature tends to disassociate it from living experience and often raises the false hope that, after certain literary terms have been explained, a sudden transition will take place and the learner will be elevated from a state of general ignorance to one of all-embracing worldly wisdom.

At the opposite extreme from students who select courses in literature to satisfy their curiosity are those who have read little and do not wish to imperil the safe ground on which they stand. One illustration of this kind may be found in the student who has no wish to extend a range of reading beyond "science fiction," because it was the kind of reading that had been enjoyed, if not completely understood. It was then the instructor's duty to release the student from a haze of contented bewilderment and guide her, with the help of H. G. Well's *The Time Machine*, into other phases of contemporary writing where imagination took the place of fancy and social criticism took the place of desires to solve the problems of the world by floating through stratospheric space.

The successful use of both approaches to studies in literature implies a knowledge of the way a student's intelligence works, what its potentials are, and what emotional factors have steered the course of the student's life. With these considerations in mind, the arts of persuasion in teaching are of more enduring value than those of dogmatic utterance. I am well aware that from a raised dais behind a lectern or in that reserved position at the end of a room behind a teacher's desk, the arts of persuasion are at times less spectacular than those of dogmatic force, that the lecturer who is deaf to all other sounds but those of his own voice can, on occasion, provide lively entertainment for his students. I am also aware that some few students in the group before him may, in the excitement of the moment, become noisy champions of whatever convictions the lecturer reveals to a fascinated audience. But in the process of the further education between student and student where ideas and concepts are recited and reviewed, something that resembles reason comes to light. And in America where students not only may but do talk freely among themselves, extreme faculty opinions are tested and undergo transformations that are often cheerfully reassuring and refreshing.

The teaching of literature has its happiest aspect whenever it reveals its kinship to the art which it endeavours to interpret and describe. E. M. Forster once remarked that contemporary criticism should hold spiritual parity with the works of art that it surveyed, and what is true of criticism in its best sense is also true of teaching. Nor does this mean that teaching becomes (through exercise of taste and discernment) a flaccid, unscholarly art, an irresponsible, though liberal step-brother of the professions. The twentieth century has few examples of critical scholarship to equal John Livingston Lowes's well-known study of *The Road to Xanadu*, an example, by the way, that is completely unhampered by rhetorical invective.

So as not to seem to wander too widely from one of the central figures whose appearances have already been mentioned in this paper, I speak of Dr. Lowes's *The Road to Xanadu* advisedly. It could be said that Coleridge is the hero of that book and that the search inward, following the traces left behind Coleridge through his reading, is the adventurous action of Dr. Lowes's narration, so artfully disguised as literary analysis and criticism. Yet Dr. Lowes did not sacrifice seriousness to the pleasures of art; and critics of literature in universities, as well as out of them, have yet to improve upon the strictness of his scholarship in a book which first saw the light of publication in 1927.

As Dr. Lowes's study of Coleridge so ably proved, a student of literature should know something of the origins that gave it being in order to find a path through which human sources of inspiration are rediscovered; and when education attempts to find fresh motivations for the understanding of literature, the creative aspects of research enter the classroom. I remember one student who translated passages of the *Aeneid* from the Latin into English, then tested her literal version (which was in prose) with Dryden's version in heroic verse, and the results of this exercise were compared with Vergilian imagery in *The Waste Land*. The immediate end in view was to discover whether or not Eliot's sources were in Vergil or in Dryden, but the larger prospect which came before her was the psychology of poetic composition—which is, of course, one of the means of understanding poetry. This kind of research is avowedly experimental, and is best pursued in an environment that encourages a liberal attitude toward learning, where stress is placed upon the doing of things rather than hastily gliding over half-realized experiences in reading. The object of her research was not to "pass" an examination in comparative literatures but to know something of the way poetic imagination brings one aspect of classical literature to life.

IV

One of the major problems in education today is to rediscover the place of studies in literature in the college curriculum. If the effort of a literature department is solely to keep what is so often called a "dying culture" alive, the effort is a wasted one and is probably doomed to fail. What is more, those who teach what they believe to be a "dying culture" develop a strident and sometimes fearful inferiority complex in respect to what they teach. What follows this condition of mind and feeling is the complaint that students have lost an interest in literature. And the conclusion is that literature must be forced down the throats of unwilling thousands before its values can be accepted and understood. What should be remembered is that the arts of communication are always with us and that the written word is not likely to cease publication. Every generation from Queen Elizabeth's day to this has expressed its fear that language as literature is facing an untimely death, and even that fear has been expressed in excellent verse. Meanwhile the written word has remained at its best a precise and revealing expression of human emotion and ideas, and each generation as it creates its own way of viewing itself and the world before its eyes transforms the means of its expression. In the kind of teaching I have described the student is frequently inspired to feel and think creatively, to discover the relationships that exist between the arts of the drama, painting, sculpture, and literature; and in more than a few cases literature assumes the position of providing a center where all branches of learning are open for discussion.

The underlying reason why this kind of teaching has the character of renewed freshness at the beginning of each college year is that the entire curriculum, including the studies in literature, are modified to the needs of the students rather than those of the institution. This reason is at the root of all experiments in education, and it also recalls what Emerson meant when he spoke of "inquiry" in his essay on Self-Reliance, for such adjustments in methods of teaching awaken independent thinking; teaching of this order does not stir intellect alone, but it also brings light to other resources of human understanding:

> The inquiry leads us to that source, at once the essence of genius, of virtue, and of life, which we call Spontaneity or Instinct. We denote this primary wisdom as Intuition, whilst all later teachings are tuitions. In that deep force, the last fact behind which analysis cannot go, all things find their common origin.

The teaching of literature should awaken the beginnings of the primary wisdom which Emerson discerned, and the instructor should be able to guide the student in the early expression of them. This means that a study of literature should be profound enough to uncover more than one aspect of its value; if it happens to delight the intellect, it may also be worthy of deeper inquiry.

To give an example of what I mean, no understanding of Thomas Campion's airs can be made complete without some knowledge of the music he composed; in other words the lyrics must be heard as well as read; and in all works of art, if viewed in their completeness, a proper balance is struck and usually concealed within the primary gifts of intuition and intellect. It is not until the student knows the completed work and its associations that a fruitful inquiry into its sources can be made: it is at this level that the work begins to take on meaning for the student; the student's merely personal emotions, if not forgotten, are directed to the origins of instinct and intellect, and it is at this point that a first step toward self-knowledge may begin. Emerson's American scholar was, however—and significantly enough—an active creature, and by making him so, Emerson penetrated deeply into the recesses of the American psyche. It is little wonder that Emerson's idealism was so quickly followed by the cheerfully active philosophy of William James; but what is in danger of being forgotten today is that Emerson took it for granted that the American scholar was also a man of thought, that he enjoyed thinking, and that to him thinking was a partial act. Emerson went to some trouble to say as boldly as he could that adult thinking was reflective, and with this conclusion in mind it is well to remember in the teaching of literature that the ability to reflect is an end in view of which four years spent in a college should provide the means of attaining eight years later. Though it may seem less attractive to outward view— for to look at someone in a reflective mood may inspire neither love nor affection—that exercise is not to be ignored, and deceptive as outward appearances may be, the exercise is by no means static. It is the gathering together of forces which in college leads one to read or act with discrimination. It is to be hoped that a reading of literature continually broadens a knowledge of the world and intensifies self-knowledge. Under circumstances which provide understanding of what one reads, a modest search for truth may be conducted. One then learns not to believe everything one hears by way of radio or sees among the flickering shadows of a television screen. There may be times in the future when even a modest search will be difficult, but those moments have also been a part of human experience in the past. Meanwhile, the arts of teaching literature in a college that permits its students to translate the spirit of Emersonian inquiry into terms of mid-twentieth-century thinking need not fear either the future or the past.

Experience of Philosophy

HELEN MERRELL LYND

Philosophy springs from sources deep in human nature—wonder and need for refuge. Wonder arises when the strangeness of the world invites exploration. When strangeness becomes too threatening, men shrink before it and seek refuge in authority.

But in formal education, philosophy tends to become a system of revered answers rather than a way of making fresh discoveries. Teachers find it easy to believe, with Plato, that speculative thought can be an outcome only of maturity and training. And since every younger generation is untrained, exposing the young to the classic answers is accounted the only wise education.

Children constantly refute the view that philosophic inquiry comes only in later years. Anyone who has watched and listened to young children cannot miss the intense concentration, the total use of self, which appears in their exploring—of a hole in the ground, of the inside of a cupboard, of the wings of a fly; their delight in discovery—of the moon in a daytime sky, of water filling a trench in the sand; their curiosity about death—of a grandfather or of a mouse; their attempts to separate animate and inanimate, idea and metaphor, necessary causation and chance sequence; their endless why's in the insistent search for meaning. Records of children's questions and soliloquies are sufficient refutation of the belief that wonder expressed in speculation comes only relatively late in development and after formal cultivation.

The three-year-old who asked the meaning of the overheard phrase "traffic congestion," and in response to his mother's casual reply, "A great many cars," insisted "You mean a great many cars in the same place at the same time, don't you?" had begun to be aware of the meaning of space and time.

A five-year-old on the same playground wondered aloud:

A voice is a fast thing, isn't it? It's a sound! Are other sounds voices of things? Is your voice *in* your mouth? Are all the words stored up some place in your mouth? How can you get food in if all those words are there? How much space does a word take? Words are thin little things. But some of them make a big noise. You couldn't take hold of a word. What if the words were made of something? I mean if they were real, if you could touch them, if they were *things*. Then there would not be room for anything else in the world, would there? Who decides about the words? Who made them up first? Why do you use the words that somebody else decided? Why couldn't we make up some for us?

(As he was digging in the playground.) What is a hole? It is a thing, but it is nothing. There is really not anything there—just an emptiness. It is not a thing, but it is so *much* nothing that it *is* a thing. It is funny to have a name for something that is not.

If I have my tooth pulled, will I still be me? I can't be the same me, because some of me will be gone. It will be a different me. But if it's different, then it's not really me.

Another five-year-old, with somewhat embarrassed laughter, expressed honest perplexity at the limits of imagination: "Of course, I really know the world began a long time before I was born, but it's hard for me to believe it."

For children with some basis of security the unknown world about them is interesting and appealing rather than frightening. The unsolved problem of education is how children growing up can acquire the greater possibilities of maturity, and the knowledge necessary for adult life, with their happy curiosity unimpaired. Too often the process of education, in home and neighborhood as well as in school, is what Kafka has described as the "parrying of . . . children's impetuous assault on the truth." Ernest Schachtel comments: "The capacity to see and feel what is there gives way to the tendency to see and feel what one expects to see and feel, which, in turn, is what one is expected to see and feel because everyone else does." So in each new generation various conventional versions of the Emperor's New Clothes are perpetuated. It is by no means impossible to acquire specific knowledge and skills in maturity if a person has learned how to learn. It may be impossible to recapture curiosity blunted by learning out of context or encased in alien standards. Inquiry is natural in children, but once dulled is not easily regained.

With the beginning of college both wonder and fear once more become strong. College offers to education a second chance. College freshmen are late adolescents, overflowing with fresh expectancy of the world. Coming to college means a break with what have been their familiar boundaries; they are beginning to be aware of themselves as independent adults with their own way to find. The very sense of wide possibilities brings bewilderment to many, particularly today when everywhere they turn they are confronted with other men's broken hopes.

Why have hopes for lasting peace always failed? they ask. Can a person have a happy life in the world now? Is selfishness always wrong? How can I be sure that what I think is right to do is really right? If it is true that people always do things because of their early experience, how can you ever choose what you want to do? How are choices different for men and for women? How do you know when a thing is really true and when it is a matter of feeling or opinion? Can idealism be practical in any political party? Can I believe in science and in God? When everything is changing so much, what can I trust?

With such questions as these, they try—now in love and friendship, now in religion, now in science, in politics, in socialism or world government, or in art—to find basis for belief and a sense of direction.

It is no good to meet such urgency with statements that the questions they want to work on are "too big" and that they will have to get more "foundation" or "background" before they can attack them. Some young people bring to college a latent store of such questions from which "preparation" for college has diverted them. If they can't begin to work on them directly when they come to college, when can they begin? If stopped once more, the inquiring imagination may again be compressed to conformity. It is sometimes better to let a student start on a problem absurdly big from a more sophisticated point of view, and then to help him to discover how he can limit and restate it and build up methods to work on it, than to short-circuit the whole process by insisting in advance that he work on something more manageable but with less meaning for him. This involves risk of confusion; and there is undoubtedly danger in feeding a young person's appetite for big ideas. But avoidance of this kind of danger invites sterility. One of the shortcomings of the American college is its tendency to plane down big ideas to chips of knowledge. Our culture conspires to make thinking discrete and safe. There can be no quick exorcising of perplexity. Some wandering in the wilderness is inevitable. Those young people for whom entrance into adulthood brings concern about the profound problems of existence demand that education help them to find a way into these problems, not safe ways around them.

Today these questions of what men can believe and what they should do have special urgency for two reasons. The great social drama being enacted all over the world forces itself on our attention. We may call it the struggle for power between rival social systems, or we may see it as a social upheaval bringing about a new epoch in human freedom; but, however we describe it, we cannot avoid trying to understand it. And also, the liberal tradition of the unique importance of each individual, combined with the work of Freud and his followers, has made us aware that a no less complex drama occurs within each person. Whether we stress the impact of world struggle on personal conflicts or that of individual frustration on war and industrial strife, in some way we must deal with this central problem of our time: how can we re-discover the meaning of individual freedom in twentieth-century society? How can students, as young men and women, realize their potentialities in the contemporary world?

Some may find in natural science, in social science, in literature or in art, a way of approaching these problems. Others turn to philosophy. Not that being labeled "philosophy" alters the nature of this inquiry. An idea is neither better, nor worse, nor in any way different, for being called a "philosophical" idea. But any curriculum should and does include many courses carefully circumscribed in areas covered and techniques mastered. It is precisely the function of philosophy not to take limits for granted, to investigate starting points, to question axioms about the nature of truth and beauty, of moral value, the relation between body and mind, subject and object, the individual and the world. Nothing is by definition too big or too remote to be a valid problem of study. Here there are no stop signs of "Thus far and no farther"; or

"There you leave our legitimate subject of study and get into speculative questions which are not our concern." Every immediate experience, every common-sense expression, every conventional version of life has significance in itself; but it is the role of philosophy both to discover this meaning and to say: "This is not all. There is something beyond what this seems to be which may be discovered. Even with deepening recognition of the tragedy in human existence, the world may yet become more various, more beautiful, more new, than we had imagined."

Every culture, and particularly our own, tends to strip, compress, and distort complex experiences and concepts to brisk, rule-of-thumb shorthand. Questioning of meanings behind accepted labels invokes impatience and scorn. At this point philosophy enters. Philosophy embodies the persistent thrust of life against custom. Through philosophical exploration a given experience is recurrently placed in a different context to invite fresh insights; we are able, in Rilke's words, "from what is closest, from things that are at hand under all circumstances, to take the leap into the most spacious."

This effort at understanding requires all the resources young people can bring to it. Nothing they have ever felt or known, nothing they have read, feared, or dreamed is irrelevant or is enough, for all can be directed toward further discovery of what is involved in their questions. The very attempt to use all their own resources brings the realization that these are not adequate, and the young inquirer turns to others who have known the delight and struggle of such exploration and who have made such problems the central concern of their lives.

However immediate and personal are the questions which have led students to turn to philosophy, they early come to see that their insistent concerns are not wholly their own. The alerted sensitivity with which a particular individual faces the universe may have become focussed in a specific situation—a sudden revelation of beauty, decision as to life work, conflict between a religious background and developing scientific interest or the reverse, the loss of a fiancé in the war. But each such problem bears within it at least three aspects: some form of a recurring human question, the meaning of which men have sought for centuries; a particular form as it arises at this time when one period of history is coming to an end and the outlines of its successor are not clear; and an immediate personal importance. Sense of shared experience with others in the past, and in the present, allays fear and helps more forthright facing of problems. If others have been similarly puzzled one need not ask "Is something wrong with me that this worries me so?" Seeing one's present perplexity from a broader perspective does not "solve" the problem involved, but it decreases isolation and gives a firmer stance for making the next move.

The young person begins to enter into an active working relationship with these others who, like himself, have been attracted and bewildered by the strangeness of the world. He discovers that the work of these "great philosophers" whose names appear in the history of Western thought was in many ways more like the limitless searching of children, or like his own quest for significance, than like the solidified categories of the Schools. The philosophers did not initially separate reason and emotion, theory and practice, fact and value, but brought all their varied resources to focus on the relentless exploring of particular problems. Kant, too, pondered: What can I know? What may I hope? What should I do? He observed no formal boundaries of "philosophy," but found study of the movement of tides, comparative anthropology, literary style, organic evolution, human motivation all relevant to his demanding questions. With complete intensity not unlike that of a child he combined the manifold resources he could discover in his time in his search for truth.

Plato wanted to find truth, restore Athens, realize human justice, educate the young; his philosopher-kings embodied his belief that contemplation and direction of the affairs of the state were interdependent; he not only discussed aesthetics but wrote as a poet. William James, like Aristotle, came to philosophy by way of medicine and the science of human behavior. Like both Plato and Aristotle, Bertrand Russell and Whitehead found it impossible to separate mathematics and physics from philosophy. These men did not regard themselves as custodians of truth. Rather, starting with their immediate grasp of reality, they moved out to embrace wider areas of meaning. Philosophy for them was not a thing apart, but a probing and transcending of familiar experiences to gain heightened awareness; not an area mapped out, but an uncharted voyage.

This way of understanding—this going beyond the obvious to acute awareness of the nature of a particular experience, and at the same time of its relation to wider perspectives, this combination of focus and connections and of thought and feeling—is, of course, not confined to men whose names appear in histories of philosophy.

T. S. Eliot has described this experience as it appears to a poet: "When a poet's mind is perfectly equipped for its work, it is constantly amalgamating disparate experience; the ordinary man's experience is chaotic, irregular, fragmentary. The latter falls in love, or reads Spinoza, and these two experiences have nothing to do with each other, or with the noise of the typewriter or the smell of cooking; in the mind of the poet these experiences are always forming new wholes." He stresses the awareness of each separate "object as it is," the "direct, sensuous apprehension of thought," the "recreation of thought into feeling" which constantly reshapes the world into more significant wholes.

Henry James regards this ability to focus and enlarge experience as the greatest "source of strength" to the novelist: ". . . the faculty which when you give it an inch takes an ell. The power to guess the unseen from the seen, to trace the implication of things, to judge the whole piece by the pattern, the condition of feeling life, in general, so completely that you are well on your way to knowing any particular corner of it. . . ."

In Gardner Murphy's view, a similar transforming of the familiar into the new takes place for the inventive psychologist as he substitutes for earlier specializations new centers of study; for example, in making the young child an area of specialization, thus substituting richer concepts for those that had become abstract. Such reshaping of areas of research occurs for every scientist.

It is, indeed, partly a matter of accident and tradition that determines which people turn up as "philosophers" in histories of philosophy. Why does Kant appear in the histories while Rousseau who had great influence on Kant frequently does not? Why is

Machiavelli included but not Dante or Petrarch? Why has Hobbes and not Nietzsche a place in a textbook on ethics?

There is point in becoming acquainted with the people who do compose the official "history of Western philosophy"; they have to a large extent set the forms of thought by which we think, ground the lenses through which we perceive and interpret the world. It is important to become aware what these forms are, their possibilities and their limitations, and how they have arisen. But there is point, also, in obtaining fresh light on philosophical questions from people whose speculations do not fall within the usual "philosophical" patterns. Paul Schilder's *Goals and Desires of Man*, Freud's *Beyond the Pleasure Principle*, Dostoevski's tale of the Grand Inquisitor, or Dorothy Lee's study of value systems in primitive societies suggest highly significant ways of approaching values not to be found in technical discussions of the theory of values. Such books as Planck's *Philosophy of Modern Physics* or Philipp Frank's *Modern Science and Its Philosophy* make clear in simple and penetrating terms conceptions basic to understanding of the theory of knowledge. Studies of the relation between the perceiving person and the world outside him in Kahnweiler's account of Juan Gris and the eras of painting which preceded him, or Wertheimer's *Productive Thinking*, or Köhler's *Place of Value in a World of Facts* give kinds of understanding of subject-object relationships hard to find in technical "philosophic" discussion of these problems.

Capacity to find new ways of interpreting experience may come slowly to a student; but once the timidity bred of conventional categories begins to yield, the ability to see things freshly grows at an accelerating pace. The excitement of discovery returns as the student feels that each new formulation is his own. In dealing with the kinds of materials demanded by such a wide approach to the problems of philosophy, any teacher finds his own competence inadequate. He is fortunate if he teaches in a college where he can call freely on his colleagues for suggestion, correction, for taking over a class, or for the supervision of a particular investigation by a student.

To approach philosophy in this way is not to glorify diffuseness or any sort of free-and-easy amateurism. Just as a person who will never be a great artist can understand more of what is involved in painting or in music by trying to paint or to compose than by confining his study to the work of the masters, so, by trying to find his way through problems of importance to him, a student may learn more of what it is to engage in philosophical thinking and share more of the method, as well as the content of thought, of great philosophers than by confining himself to the results of their work. To begin with students' questions does not mean that we are working with them in a vacuum, nor that we are neglecting the impersonal study of philosophies and philosophers. It means that we undertake such study in order to provide the indispensable material for something the student wants to find out, in the context where it will have most meaning for him.

To start with his own problems is to confront him with the difficulties of working on such problems—the fallacies in his unconscious assumptions, the things he needs to know, the necessity of narrowing focus without losing what is, to him, the heart of the matter. The problem is to learn rigorous method while preserving imagination and sense of importance. "Discipline" is more often an outcome of education if it is gained in pursuit of what the student wants to find out than if it is made a separate end in itself. Nor does this apply only to the more verbally adept. One of the revelations of teaching is how much can be done, even with a student who seems at the outset to have little capacity for generalization, if we can begin with things he genuinely wants to know and gradually deepen his sense of their meaning and his capacity for working with them.

Once the student has begun to have the sense that his problems are some version of recurrent human experience he moves on with eager curiosity to the questions: Who has written about this problem? How did he go to work on it? At this point he reaches for the fat books with formidable titles on the library shelves. The first contact may repel. Many students have to learn how to read: What is the writer trying to say? And how does one get the sense of his imagination and curiosity through the opaque wall created by forbidding terminology?

Here two contradictory attitudes, sometimes alternating in rapid succession, may block the young philosopher: "But what right have

I to have a judgment on that problem which has puzzled leaders of religion and philosophy for centuries?" And, on the other hand, "Why must that man split hairs so over plain questions! If he has anything to say he could say it more simply."

In answer to the first question, the student may be reminded that Amos hesitated to follow his individual road to truth, demurring that "I was no prophet, neither was I a prophet's son; but I was a herdsman, and a gatherer of sycamore fruit"; and that Hobbes averred "Fear and I were born twins." The philosophical education of one student at Wellesley began when she wanted to take a course in Greek Philosophy but thought she was debarred because she had not had the required introductory course, Philosophy 9. A great teacher replied: "So far as I know, Plato had not had Philosophy 9 either. Be prepared to put everything you have into it and take the course."

As to the second barrier, the student who is impatient with Aristotle's classifications or with the geometrical form of Spinoza's thought may become aware of the difficulties they faced by making his own attempt to construct a basis for ethics or the nature of reality. The antimonies of Kant, the manifold meanings of each Hegelian term were not devices especially contrived to weary or delude the unwary, but their efforts to approach truth. Through the austere discipline necessary to enter into their form of expression, to follow the course of their thinking, it is possible to learn far more than by beginning with critical appraisal and placing each of them in the appropriate historical niche.

If the student is to have the experience of working intensively on philosophical problems and coming into active working relationship with philosophers, the teacher may have to resist the temptation to "cover" in a brief course, or in a series of courses, the fruits of Western thought, to have a class move, even though hastily, across the grand panorama of the conclusions of the "great" philosophers. To work with a philosopher the student must stay with him long enough to know him. Not only more insight into particular problems but actually more awareness of the dynamics of historical development may sometimes be gained by focusing in a year on three or four individuals and using them as centers of study. The persons selected for study may range from Plato to John Dewey, but each should be someone who has worked on questions important to a particular group of students, who is influential directly or indirectly in contemporary thought, and who represents a markedly different stream of thought from the others studied.

Study of each person selected involves the twofold experience of putting ourselves into his time and place, and seeing him in the whole sequence of historical development before and since his time. Jacob Loewenberg has described this double process, as Hegel employs it, as a combination of dramatic impersonation and comic absurdity. In the first mood one seeks to understand a philosophic view from within, taking it in its full concreteness, regarding it for the time being as if it were all there is. Comic absurdity, on the other hand, brings realization of the folly of *any* philosophy which assumes that it is the sole key to reality. This Loewenberg calls the irony of "the partial masquerading as the complete." It is nothing less than this difficult combination of seeing every philosopher and philosophy both from within and from without, which a student must attempt in order to experience philosophy.

To see a particular philosophy from within, to see the world through the eyes of the person holding it, involves asking such questions as these: What was he trying to do and how was he trying to do it? What was the common sense and what were the characteristic metaphors of his time? What resources in economic development, in scientific knowledge, in understanding of history and of human personality did his time give him; what limitations did these same techniques and ideas impose? What to him constituted proof? Where does he place the "natural" limit and where the "institutional" limit on human desires? Was his interest to preserve existing ways of life or to question and supersede them? What was he fighting for and what against?

Trying to see any philosopher from without leads us to extend dimensions in space and time, to carry the understanding derived from him backward and forward in history. From what sources came the ideas that found focus in him? How have his ideas radiated out since his time and how have they been altered in the process? Does his method give us the means of criticizing and going beyond his conclusions? How far are the common problems which led us to select him for study the same for him as for us? Where are they different? To what interpretation of particular contemporary situations does his philosophy lead us?

Whitehead has written eloquently of the importance of variety and rhythm in learning. This applies notably to ways of getting into the study of a new person or problem. Sometimes students are asked to write a paper about a philosopher—Plato or Jeremiah or St. Paul or Marx—before reading him. Usually such a request is met by a horrified response: "But I know nothing about him. I am not quali- fied." If the student can be persuaded, "Of course, you are not qualified. But his name means something other than X to you. Make clear to yourself what that something is, and then test that impression by what he actually says," the result may be a sharpened edge of attention in reading and some insight into the changes which any system of thought undergoes as it becomes incorporated into popular opinion. Or, before beginning the study of Renaissance and Reformation philosophers, students may be asked to write a paper on some of the questions a thoughtful person would raise during the waning of the middle ages, selecting a particular hypo- thetical person. This will bring out such questions as: Can men reach goodness through legal reform or through progress of science rather than through faith? What other aim in life can be substituted for preparing for life after death? How far should heresy be tolerated? Some students will introduce the idea of conflict between genera- tions, between a secularly-minded son and a religiously-minded father, or between a trade-oriented son and a guild-oriented father. Or again students may turn directly to the text to be studied with no previous consideration of the period; they may then try to dis- cover what problems Locke or Hume were concerned with, or the different preoccupations of fifth-century Athenians and of the writers of *Job*, by reading what each wrote and thus building up the background of his time.

The attempt to translate from one philosopher to another, from one vocabulary to another, and from the chief concerns of one philosopher to those of another may further understanding. Could Plato have written Bacon's passage on the idols of the cave? How would Aristotle have criticized Hume's theory of causation? What would Kant have thought of the assumptions about human nature in Brock Chisholm's *Psychology of Enduring Peace*?

Variety in the modes of study also promotes awareness of the different kinds of thinking required by philosophic exploration. It is relatively easy to help students to realize the fallacy of drawing conclusions without an adequate basis of factual knowledge. It is no less important and considerably more difficult for students to recognize that insistence on more and more "facts" may in itself become an evasion of responsible thought. Clear analysis and any effective action demand the ability to do "as if" thinking. To the student who protests, "How do you expect me to have any judgment on that! I don't know enough" it may be useful to say "Of course, you don't. But assuming that such and such is established as factually true, then what is your judgment? What evidence would cause you to change that judgment?" Students may be asked to alternate analysis of some situation with which they are thoroughly familiar, such as a disputed issue in campus politics, with analysis of one in which they cannot possibly be in command of all the data, such as the Civil War in China. A thoroughgoing attempt at both sorts of analysis is bound to increase their capacity to use logical tools needed in different kinds of situations.

Gregory Bateson has said that all thought demands some such alternation: between loose and strict thinking; between "wild 'hunches' and . . . more formal thinking about those hunches"; between "looseness of thought and rigid concreteness." He urges examination of concepts so that the terms describing them will stand "not as fences hiding the unknown from future investigators, but rather as sign posts which read: 'UNEXPLORED BEYOND THIS POINT.' "

This alternation of method can be embodied, also, in the tempo of work. At times, a week or a month may be spent on a few pages —discovering precisely what it is that a writer is saying, the roots of his particular way of saying it, and various interpretations of its import. This kind of experience may come as such a revelation to a person, giving such a startling awareness of all he has missed in everything he has ever read, that he may feel that reading is useless unless it can be done in this fashion. But not every person and every paragraph need be studied in this way. One cannot know everything so intimately, but one need not be helpless before an inescapable ignorance of many things. It is necessary to establish some kind of working relationship with what one cannot know intimately, to realize that wherever one finds oneself, with whatever tools of knowledge, language, skills, one can find some place to take hold and begin to learn. It is possible to make some kind of contact with a period of two centuries or with an unknown civilization in a month. At times it may be as educationally important to do exactly this as, at others, to spend a fortnight on a page. Otherwise, it is too easy to have a view of the universe as distorted as the New Yorker's misshapen map of the United States. Buddhism and all Eastern philosophy may appear as an incidental fringe on the philosophy of the West; or the history of Europe may be a blank in the centuries between the "fall of Rome" and 1066; or "Greek history" may appear to have occurred in one detached area of the globe, Hebrew history in another, the history of India in a third. Certainly there are risks in attempting to develop any sense of the relation between Greek and Hebrew thought in a month. Awareness of these risks and of the extent of the unknown is part of the learning involved. The risks are not met either by ignoring the existence of areas of ignorance or by systematic cramming to give the illusion that all gaps have been filled.

Whether the treatment of any given piece of work is brief or intensive, students should not rest on the kind of cavalier distinction they sometimes make between "facts" and "theory." It may not have disturbed Lady Beaconsfield not to know "which came first, the Greeks or the Romans," but however much a student may focus on a few philosophers, he cannot, if he is going to understand them, dispense with periods, dates, facts, historical sequences. He must gain some sense of the relation between Plotinus and Jesus, between Locke and Mill, of what Descartes or Bentham had lost that St. Augustine had. Concentrating on a few people in a particular course is not a way of dispensing with understanding of historical development. It is an attempt to get a more living sense of it.

At any stage of their work young people can realize, also, that raising the basic questions of philosophy is no turning away from action in this demanding society, but a way of more effective participation. They may analyze a proposed bill in Congress, a political platform or a State Department document and, again, taking a comparable proposal later in the year, discover what greater resources they have to bring to understand it. I commented to one student, a veteran who submitted at the end of the year a searching analysis of the bill on Universal Military Training, "You couldn't have done that kind of thinking in September, could you?" He answered, "I couldn't have done it even a month ago. I would still have been trying to find arguments to defend what I wanted to believe." Reason is purposive activity, whether it is speculation about an abstract scientific construct or search for the grounds for an immediate decision. Even these polar aspects of thought are interdependent. Kant was as insistent as Marx that "good in theory but not in practice" is meaningless. "A logically consistent mathematical formalism," as Nils Bohr has said, can be adequately tested only by observation and experience. Action, on the other hand, reaches anticipated, rather than unanticipated, consequences to the degree that it is grounded in understanding of its ends and of the means of attaining them.

This relation between theory and fact, understanding and life, carries over into what a student demands of himself. Forming a working relationship is a two-way process. All the questions we put to the philosopher we must also put to ourselves, constantly reexamining the assumptions and questions with which we started. Everything we see in the world is the combined result of what is there and what we bring to it. The more aware we are of what we bring to it, the more we can be sure of what is there. We must realize the way in which the things we are looking for influence the things we find in any philosophy. Students can gain insight by formulating early in the year what they regard as fixed points of belief, which they use as criteria by which they judge good and bad, true and false, and then by keeping a record of how these change in the course of the year. Emphasis falls less on the particular conclusions the students reach than on the kinds of assumptions and methods of thinking they use in reaching them.

The teacher is not a cipher in this situation. His wider experience and his sense of the implications of initial student questions are the reason that he is a teacher. In exercising this role his own sense of what is significant forms a part of group discussion. The purposes of "objectivity" in teaching are better served if, in addition to presenting as fully and fairly as he can various points of view on a particular problem, the teacher declares, rather than attempts to conceal, his own conclusions. If they are openly stated, students have more effective means of appraising and of differing from them in the process of forming their own philosophies.

An important element in the growing awareness of the young philosopher is his changing relation to words. The kind of relation, largely unconscious, that students have to language may in the beginning block their full use of what has to be their medium of study. They may accept without active thought familiar usage of words which has dulled the sharp edge of meaning, or they may use fine sounding words without close inquiry, as a kind of intellectual snobbery, or with vague euphoric enjoyment. Their very facility in use of words sometimes blocks understanding.

Very early, however, they can learn to restate questions in more accessible form. A simple thing like always using a complete sentence rather than a phrase, such as "the meaning of human existence" or "freedom versus determinism," can help to push a vague query toward a precise, productive question. But asking "Am I free to choose?" or "Is the world rational?" may lead to nothing but more arid definition. Probing further, the student may begin to glimpse how many different and sometimes contradictory meanings may be masked by such words as "freedom" or "reason." Groping, or even false, formulations may be the beginning of wisdom, if they are recognized as beginnings.

Often people who have come to conclusions which they particularly value fall into the way of using the words in which they first encountered those insights as substitutes for further thought. Such use of words as final argument or arbiter occurs in every after-dinner conversation, in every professional meeting, certainly in every classroom. Different students develop certain words which they use as all-answering. For one it may be "logical," for another "objective," or "practical" (or its more academic version "operational"), or "scientific," or "dialectical," or "moral," or "liberal," or "productive," or "correct." The reverse of these are usually condemnatory; and certain words are almost always devil words: "authoritarian," "evasive," "escapist," "indecisive." "Rational," "metaphysical," "relativistic," "subjective," "complex" may be honorific or derogatory according to one's philosophical position. In any case, if a person finds himself habitually using the same words as standards of judgment, it is time to reexamine them to see whether they are being used as tools of analysis or as substitutes for analysis. A student's understanding of philosophy as something in the making rather than as something completed may increase if he is told: "If there is genuine meaning in what you say, you can find some other way of saying it; not that what you say is untrue or unimportant, but you don't have to put all your weight on that one phrase."

This fresh examination of habitual usage includes questioning of labels which have become conventions in philosophy. A label or a definition which would be a useful tentative formulation for the beginning of exploration is often used as if it marked the end— as if using the label answered the question, disposed of the matter. Saying that Kant and Hegel have been called "idealists," or that Hobbes and Marx have been called "materialists," or that John Dewey is a "naturalist" can be an excellent beginning of investigation. But if any of these terms is used as if it were a complete description or classification, it serves to nullify thought. Such falsifying use of definition, labels, or categories reduces the meaning of philosophy. Stating the "six major points" of Aristotle or Kant or Hume may be a convenient way of classifying, but restatement in the philosopher's own words, or in any easy summary, is dwarfed learning.

This tendency toward reduction of meaning continues for many who have come beyond passive acceptance into a more vigorous relation with language. They may attempt to force words into a kind of exact representation of life which limits and distorts the nature of language.

It is possible both to catch the delight of discovery as a new word clothes and illumines a concept and at the same time to realize that no words ever precisely correspond to "reality." Today the temptation is to *reduce* the meaning of language for the sake of a limited precision and the illusion of understanding—rather than to give ourselves to the process of Schopenhauer's or Santayana's thinking in an effort to apprehend what they were trying to reach with the words they were able to lay hold of. Part of our difficulty with Hegel's vocabulary is that we want words to mean less than they can mean. We do not want the labor of entering into the experience which led to his use of *Aufheben* or *Begriff*. The attempt of the logical positivists to assimilate language to mathematics and the records of empirical science has strengthened this tendency toward reduction of meaning. A. T. Ayer's *Language, Truth, and Logic* condemns all other uses of language as "nonsense." Graham Hough in reviewing it comments:

> . . . if this view is correct, the analysis of nonsense assumes a hitherto unsuspected importance. For though many of the propositions which Ayer classes as nonsense have indeed no bearing on anything, many of them have a powerful effect on the way people actually behave. Nobody goes to prison because he believes that the snark is a boojum, but some people have done so because they believe that killing is wrong. If these statements are both nonsense, at least they are nonsense of very different kinds.

Language has possibilities which differ from those of mathematics. Both the fluid myth-making possibilities of language which Cassirer describes and the precise verbal symbols associated with scientific thought have possibilities and limitations. Neither should be judged solely in terms of the other. Emery Neff points out that in France the eighteenth-century effort to be scientific, combined with limited aristocratic usage, had succeeded by the end of the century in reducing by almost two-thirds the rich vocabulary of the sixteenth century.

The problem is to inquire with the utmost care how a particular word or phrase is being used by a student of philosophy without assuming that there is an inevitability about that particular usage, and that there is a single "correct" usage. As R. G. Collingwood has said, "You cannot tell whether a proposition is 'true' or 'false' until you know what question it was intended to answer."

Learning genuine communication with other members of the

class may be an important means of gaining further insight into
one's own problems. Although one student may start from questions
about how to reach a specific personal decision, another from the
meaning of human freedom, a third from need of religion, a fourth
from the adequacy of science as an answer to all things, it is impossible to go very far in the exploration of any one of these questions without encountering others. Common reading and certain
assigned papers for the whole group help to establish the meaning
of a common vocabulary and give texture for group discussion,
while diverse meanings and questions are explored further in individual papers and conferences.

Accuracy as well as enhanced meaning results from asking what
a particular philosopher was attempting to do, and what he was attempting to avoid, by the words he chose, and then putting the
same questions to ourselves. I remember the indignation of one
ultra-intellectual, ultra-logical student when, in the midst of a violent classroom battle over definition, she was insisting on the single,
logical possibility of the meaning of a particular word, and I asked,
"Why is that so important to you? What do you want it to mean?
What are you afraid it will mean?" She had gifts of scorn and of
eloquence and she employed both in denouncing the irrelevance of
introducing "emotional" factors into a purely intellectual discussion. Her astonishment was great, when she and all of us in the
group had finally submitted to the answering of these questions, to
discover that in the process greater *intellectual* clarity had emerged.
To paraphrase Chesterton, it is well to know when you are going to
march to Trafalgar Square whether you are doing so "to rid yourself of your temper; not to rid yourself of your tyrant."

The history of particular words gives insight into the concepts
with which they are associated. Why has the meaning of subject and
object reversed itself from Aristotle to the present? What attitudes
toward the world and toward the self are implicit in that shift? Why
do we retain the earlier meaning in "subject of study"? We have
begun to enter into some understanding of the processes of thinking
of different philosophers and different periods if we glimpse why
"opposites" to Plato meant something different in source, in aim,
and in import from "opposites" to Hegel or to Marx, and that both
were very different from "opposites" to the seventeenth-century

metaphysical poets, or to Paul Schilder and the Gestalt psychologists. Similarly we may try to discern the different meanings of abstraction to Plato, to Aristotle, to Hegel, and to modern Gestalt psychology. How much of what Groddeck included in the word *id* did Freud retain when he took over the term? Were Freud's id, ego, and super-ego intended as the precise mapping of areas of personality or the effort of a great scientific imagination to enter into the unexplored?

Words are sometimes sensitive instruments of precision with which delicate operations may be performed and swift, elusive truths may be touched; often they are clumsy tools with which we grope in the dark toward truths more inaccessible but no less significant.

If study of philosophy has been experience of philosophy, this experience continues throughout life. As it is true that "our lives are governed by the emotional tone of events which we have forgotten," so, in similar fashion, the power to focus emotional and intellectual energies in new discovery, cultivated through study of philosophy, continues long after technical details have disappeared from conscious memory. Often students say that they really begin to realize what they have learned from philosophy five or ten years after they graduate. Or that in the midst of some puzzling new situation they realize in a flash, "Oh, *that* was the meaning of that class discussion; and that is the way I should work through this problem."

Whether students have come to philosophy early in college, eager to explore an unknown world or to find sureness in a world which baffles them, or in their last years want to discover through philosophy a way of drawing together separate areas of study and experience, they often cherish the hope that somewhere truth lies ready-made if they can only find the way to it. Perhaps, they think, no one person or no one philosophy has all the answers, but surely if they can only lay hold of the right way of thinking or the right way of viewing the world, they can find a means of distinguishing good from bad, true from false, of knowing what one may hope and what one should do. It may be a new kind of philosopher's stone which they seek, but is should work something of the traditional magic. They want in some way to pin down the universe and are disappointed when it refuses to be so pinned down.

But when we ask the ultimate questions, whether about the direction of our own lives or about the meaning of human existence, the outcome of thinking is not an "answer" but a transformed way of thinking, not propositions to assent to, but heightened power to think with.

Realization that what they have sought comes to them in this form is sometimes disturbing to impetuous young philosophers. They are more familiar in our present society with rigid, cautious, denying methods, the attempt to find a limited truth in clear-cut categories, by process of elimination. They want to "dispose" of problems, to find "reality" empty of contradiction; and find conflict an essential part of the process of reality. They want to create a social utopia, and they are disturbed to find that it is not a new order of creatures but the human beings of this planet who will engage in the making of any better world and live in it afterward. They search for "truth" as something already there and find it difficult to recognize it as also an unending task ahead. They want to rest on certainty which is like granite and discover that they may have to rest on certainty which is like the sea.

Truth is larger than our grasp and will not be bound. What philosophy can do is to help the student to live with and use seemingly conflicting phases of living rather than to become frightened at the discovery that things do not automatically fit together or lend themselves to any final arrangements. A working hypothesis is not weak or unimportant because it is an hypothesis rather than a finally demonstrated conclusion. The student can learn that when he says "Rousseau is inconsistent; he contradicts himself," he has not disposed of Rousseau nor finally classified him; that it is more rewarding to understand Rousseau then to label him. Or, when the student says, "But I can't be two persons at once!" he has not disposed of the responsibility of realizing the conflicting potentialities within him. Emotion and reason, conscious and unconscious, particular and general, self and others, thought and action, fact and value, proximate and ultimate—these different emphases have been descriptively separated out as ways of coming closer to reality. But we err when we harden metaphors into what we treat as separate entities, or when we ascribe to qualitative differences hierarchical values. These so-called opposites are continuing parts of the flow of experience.

To discover a sense of direction in the midst of such fluidity, to be able to find oneself and continuing values in whatever time and place and orientation one may be churned into, is particularly important in a time which offers no assurance of stability in the world. The last few years have shown many examples of adherents to inflexible philosophies who under the pressure of events proved to be no more than weather vanes in the wind. There is nothing more difficult than putting everything one has into a specific course of action while still recognizing the possibility that one's present beliefs may not encompass the whole world, and that there may be more light to come. But such ability to move imaginatively and freely in space and time, multi-rooted, with a variety of methods of discovery, always with a developing core of self in relation to the world, offers more promise of genuine consistency than absolute adherence to an all-or-none creed.

Here some student throws up his hands in despair with the cry, "Then everything is only relative! We are condemned to relativism." Relativism is a word. If we mean by it that in order to talk of anything at all we have to say what it is we are talking about, and that this can only be done by defining it in relation to, relative to, other things, then it is true we can not "escape" some form of relativism, or, more precisely, of relativity.

"But," asks the student, "what about Kant's absolute ethical standard—treating every human being as an end in himself?"

"Is this expected of a six-months-old child in relation to his mother?"

"No, of course not. I didn't mean that."

Then already we have begun to define what it is we *do* mean, with what limitations, under what conditions. In approaching a creed, a philosophical system, a code of ethics, a program for social reform, we may ask not "Is this true or false?" but "Under what conditions, in what relationships is it true?"; but not "Is this of any use?" but

"What kind of use has this?"; not "Has this any meaning?" but "What is its meaning?"

The fear in the student's mind when he talks of being "condemned" to relativism is that, if any statement of principle is "qualified" at all, the implication is: Then there are no standards of anything; nothing makes any difference. This does not in the least follow. By qualifying something we give it quality, content, meaning. We say what it is that we are talking about. The fact that Kant's ethical imperative does not apply to an infant does not mean that it does not apply to an adult in deciding whether he shall protest suppression of civil liberties. On the contrary, it gives surer grounds for saying why and how it does apply in such a case.

Being clear about the context within which a particular principle applies does not weaken its truth there because it is not true outside of that context. Newton's principles of physics are as true as they were before Einstein within the particular framework he was describing. The farmer who says the sun rises in the East and sets in the West is not simply a fool who never heard of Columbus; within the limits of his acres he describes correctly the behavior of the sun. Recognition of the existence of different frames of relationships enables us to raise more pertinent questions and draw clearer implications within each of them. It also gives a basis for reexamining which aspects of the world are unalterable and which may be changed closer to men's needs and desires. History may be viewed as a process of pushing back walls of inevitability, of turning what have been thought to be inescapable limitations into human possibilities.

We live in the midst of an inner and outer drama of which our time has made us peculiarly aware. Each individual thus has a twofold problem. He seeks to know within himself when his "idealism" is productive thinking and when it is "escape" from what are actually inevitable limitations. And in his view of the world the individual attempts to distinguish between limits to men's hopes which are set by the nature of man and the world, and those institutional limitations which are man-made and therefore can be changed by men. In both endeavors he can find through philosophy some guides for productive understanding.

Second Thoughts of a Psychologist

RUDOLF ARNHEIM

A psychology teacher who walks into his classroom for the first meeting with his students can count upon an attitude of trustful anticipation. The students have many weighty questions, and they expect to have them answered. The reasons they give for their interest in psychology are apt to sound pragmatic: I want to understand myself, learn how to tackle other people, how to get out of trouble. Undoubtedly, the usefulness of what the students expect to be a handy kit of tools plays a role in forming their attitude; but I have the impression that often, and perhaps always, these alleged motives are also a rationalization of a less practical and even more enjoyably human impulse. The students may not be aware that there survives in them some of the old curiosity about the nature of the enigmatic powers that run our lives. They approach our science with a productive shudder, comparable to the experience of tourists who, behind the guiding monk, descend the steps to the Roman catacombs and explore the darkness of the subterranean passages with the weak light of the tapers that have been put in their hands.

Interest in psychology may have as many reasons as there are fields of psychological subject matter and approaches to them. It is true, however, that every decade will create its own preferences. At a time when the early experimentalists proudly confessed that they were practising a "psychology without a soul," measurements of sensory observations were almost identical with psychology. Later, mental processes were banned entirely, in favor of bodily behavior, which, in turn, was reduced to highly specific and mechanical reactions. Today, students are surprised to learn that psychology deals with anything else besides "personality"; i.e., the central pattern of forces which determines attitudes to the environment and the self. Not long ago, a student asked me: "Why should I study visual perception? There is nothing wrong with my eyes, but there is plenty wrong with my personality."

Such a reaction is understandable as long as the more peripheral mental functions are thought of as independent mechanisms, no more connected with the vital center of human striving than a microscope or a calculating machine. By now, however, the teacher can take advantage of the many attempts to show the dependence of these specific functions on central processes. This is true, for instance, of the studies concerned with motivational factors in perception and with the effect of personality on learning. In addition, basic structural principles are emerging, which underlie the marginal as well as the central functions. They can often be demonstrated more concretely in the relatively simpler performances and readily rediscovered later in the more complex ones; as, for example, when the perception of visual figures is shown to involve the same kind of creative organization which distinguishes productive thinking.

Should, then, the teaching and learning of psychology be limited to those aspects which can be related to the vital core of mental functioning? Except for strictly preprofessional training, this would seem to be a reasonable working principle for the teacher. We are bound to lose some material which is scientifically valuable and would profit some students; but the loss is more than compensated by what is gained through cutting out dead wood. This holds true particularly for the first course in general psychology, which is looked upon by many instructors as a second-rate job and is approached with little enthusiasm. Actually, it is the key course in the psychology curriculum. It often depends on this course whether a gifted student will decide to take advanced work or to keep clear of psychology for life. It is also the only systematic contact with the field which many educated people will ever have. If such a course offers knowledge for knowledge's sake and is cluttered up with technicalities whose bearing on the business of living is not evident, it will scare people away from the truly useful achievements of psychology and leave them with "How to make friends" and "Be glad you are neurotic."

Among the questions which concern modern psychology and ways of making it profitable to the young I will single out two. The first deals with the relationships between the raw material of experience and the formative concepts by which such material is digested. The second refers to a topical problem of subject-matter, namely the functions of the normal and the abnormal in psychological thinking.

I

Psychology is as old as humanity, if by psychology is meant the ability of sensitive individuals to infer thoughts and feelings from how people look and behave and talk; to understand why people do what they do; to extract rules that allow prediction. Astonishing feats of psychological insight come from children, judicious mothers, experienced businessmen, and, of course, from the poets. And while many people are distressingly wrong in their judgments of others, it is nevertheless true that, through the centuries, innumerable observations have been transmitted, tested, and generalized. An imposing coral-reef of psychological wisdom has been piled up, which belongs to all.

Enjoyable and indispensable as these insights are, they lack precision and proof. Though some polishing of concepts was done by the philosophers, who were the professional psychologists of the past, even they felt no need of, and had no tools for, factual proof. Since then, one more rib has been removed from the body of philosophy, and psychology has been established as a natural science.

Two factors seem to underlie psychology as it is practised today in laboratories, offices, and classrooms: the backlog of popular assumptions and the sudden aspiration for scientific exactness.

The young students share the advantages and disadvantages of both. They have used psychology practically from birth. The infant who finds out that one has only to cry to make mother's face bend over the crib has discovered a psychological law. During the years of childhood and adolescence many more discoveries are made, and not all are sound or justify generalization. Before becoming students, they have talked psychology with parents and friends, have gathered popular notions from many sources and not necessarily clarified them in their own minds. A mathematics teacher can be more certain than he would like to be that he will start his course with a *tabula rasa*; whereas every psychology class begins as a gathering of vaguely preexposed minds.

The teacher, too, has had this kind of informal training and has combined it with what he has learned as an academic psychologist. Since he is expected to know many more answers than are provided in the scientific literature, he is constantly tempted to satisfy trustful believers with advices that would be received with due caution if they came from the housekeeper. However, even a conscientious psychologist may feel that this trust is not entirely undeserved. He may well be convinced that the few times he succeeded in finding words that struck home and lit a corner of the young mind, perhaps for life, he was not applying carefully tested experimental findings but was relying on experiences which he had more keenly perceived, more objectively weighed, more tidily analyzed by virtue of the discipline of thought his training had given him.

Some measure of self-reliance is needed in any case, since the psychologist as teacher cannot rely on a solidly founded body of professional knowledge with the same assurance as most of his colleagues in other fields. The most faithful retailer is not necessarily the most dependable teacher. It is probably in the nature of a young science, born in our time, that there should be so much no-man's-land between the writing desk of the theorist and the apparatus of the experimenter. Looking around for suitable class material, the teacher finds on the one side the pioneers of psychological speculation. Some of them are admirably clear-minded. Others are inspired by the vapors of myth and madness to produce fascinating but distressingly intangible revelations. The teacher then turns to the other side. Here he finds hundreds of earnest scholars pressing stopwatches, offering word lists to children and electric shocks to rats, processing populations by formidable machines, and publishing one paper a year. A patient consultation of the journals leads now and then to the discovery of a piece of research which has succeeded in translating a crucial question into an impeccable experimental setup, thus bridging the gap between ideas and statistical tables. But in order to find it the teacher has to wade through dozens of articles in which the obvious and the inconsequential are copiously verified. For the sake of quantification, the life of man and beast is traded in for census data and test scores, and human speech is reduced to yes, no, and can't tell. The results are all significant statistically, but it is less certain that the questions answered in the Summary and Conclusions are the same which aroused curiosity in the Introduction.

Yes, some self-reliance is needed. The psychology teacher cannot depend on the authority of the few or the consensus of the many. He must be prepared to find that a colleague condemns as dull and flimsy what he himself had recommended to his students as a cogent and sound piece of thinking. The inevitable standardization of psychological knowledge freezes artificially what is actually in a state of flux. Thus, to many a good teacher all textbooks seem inappropriate, except the one he intends to write during his sabbatical year. The teacher has to make his own selection, apply his own accents. I was not surprised when recently an alert veteran student who attended my course in general psychology told me: "Before I went into the army I took a course in general psych at the University of ——; but nothing of what you are talking about reminds me of anything I have ever heard before!"

An integration of most of the available material is possible only in more advanced sciences. In psychology some findings and ideas can be organized in a systematic survey. Others neither agree nor disagree, but bypass each other obliquely so that a synthesis would presuppose a thorough reshaping of the approaches themselves. For instance, what is the relationship between gestalt psychology and psychoanalysis at the present time? Both are meant to apply to the same human mind. Yet only with regard to a few problems have they met thus far on a common basis for comparison and decision. Any science grows unsystematically, sometimes filling one of two correlated gaps but not the other, forging ahead in one area and neglecting another. Since the striving for integration is one of the more arduous tasks of science and, to some extent, identical with scientific progress itself, textbook-writers or teachers cannot be expected to do the job. For this reason any attempt at an all-embracing eclecticism is hard on the student; because in a presentation of this type, things that do not fit each other are either distorted or wrapped in a protective cloud, but still render each other incomprehensible.

The best partial integration the teacher can expect to offer is the one that derives frankly from his own point of view. He will not

cover everything valuable in the field, but in tracing from a center
some guiding radii in different directions, he may hope to build
with his students a fairly unified network of theory and counter-
theory, evidence and counter-evidence. As to the omissions, he will
find comfort in reminding himself that over-all structure, rather
than piecemeal completeness, constitutes a whole. The aim for the
student is not to learn everything, but to grasp the essentials. Most
important, the teacher will try to keep alive the feeling in his students that they are not touring a well-established settlement but
pioneering in a wilderness where they must conquer if they wish
to profit, and suspect if they wish to be safe. It is this spirit of the
self-reliant and bold, but cautious, adventurer that psychology can
convey more naturally than many older fields of study.

Concepts serve to make the raw material of experience accessible
to the searching intellect. Through concepts we grasp the constant
in the fleeting and sift the essential from the accidental. We cannot
perceive what we have not fitted to an appropriate form. However,
concepts have a way of opening and closing the shutters at the same
time. While providing an enlightening order, they tend to petrify
insight at the attained level. Concepts not only give form to substance; they also take the place of substance and block our view of
reality if we are not careful. Useful terms such as "aggressiveness,"
"stereotype," "neurosis" tempt even the experienced psychologist,
let alone the young student, to seal the living matter with labels,
which stop fresh observation. Since thinking starts with global
generalities, the concepts of a young science are particularly broad
and sweeping. They are bound to require much modification, suggested by further experience. Loosely anchored to the facts, they
are easily swayed by prejudice and preference.

In modern psychology, such conceptual detachment is reenforced
by the increasing specialization which has tended to shut the scientist
off from humanistic wisdom. In the past, philosophy, science, literature, and the arts were so intimately connected that they could not
help checking each other's insights. Today psychology suffers from
inbreeding. Moving within the enclosure of his well-defined terms,
the psychologist may not be aware that his affirmations, consistent
though they may be, often bear little resemblance to anything real;

so that, for instance, an author may talk quite logically about love for two whole volumes without noticing that, in comparison, Stendhal's capricious aperçus on the same subject are miracles of truthful exactness.

In no way does a petty conception of man follow by necessity from the reduction of experience to scientific concepts. It would seem to be among the teacher's duties not only to scrutinize the internal logic of psychological investigations and to check on whether the conclusions follow from the presented evidence, but to make his students ask themselves the scientifically decisive question: Do these theories and the kind of observations from which they are drawn measure up to the wisdom we find reflected in the writings of the philosophers and poets? Do they fit real life?

Take the example of a psychologist who sets out to study human learning experimentally. There are ways of eliciting some genuine student interest even by a contraption of buttons, wooden blocks, and light bulbs. Often, however, the subjects of such experiments feel little of the incentive which makes genuine learning meaningful. An artificial, extraneous motive is supplied by a "reward" or by the willingness of the subject to help the psychologist with his queer work. Innumerable correct conclusions may be drawn from experiments of this type. But since the setup excludes decisive motivational factors in the subject, the results are likely to be misleading when they are taken as information about "human learning." If the teacher presents this kind of material to illustrate the psychology of learning is he not likely to disappoint particularly the best students, who have known the excitement of exploration and the satisfaction derived from true gain?

Another example is provided by mental tests and measurements. Psychology, like the other natural sciences, develops toward quantification. I take it that this happens because quantification is the best way we know to make sure that people who wish to talk about the same thing actually do so. Experimental psychology, after having limited itself for a long time to peripheral areas, such as sensory perception, is becoming increasingly capable of using measurable performances, even for the study of emotion, motivation, and personality—processes which were believed to be accessible to qualitative description only. The widespread aversion to quantitative study of the more central mental processes is due in part to traditional prejudices—such as that the spirit is differently organized from matter and that rational analysis is inappropriate and even dangerous to spontaneous creativity. On the other hand, such aversion is justified by the degradation to which the higher human functions, intelligence, thinking, learning, talent, sociability, have been subjected by current quantitative tests.

Of what use are these tests for the teaching of psychology? Obviously, an acquaintance with testing techniques is needed by some students for professional purposes. It may also be argued that since nowadays everybody can be expected to run into tests here and there, he should have some knowledge of what they examine and how, and with what results. If, however, we ask what contribution the study of our present quantitative tests can make to the upbringing of a mature and educated person, we must point out first of all that they are essentially indicatory, not explanatory. This means, for instance, that intelligence measurements can indicate, at best, to what extent intelligence is present, but do not enlighten us about its nature. If they are valid, they can be used as a research tool, the way thermometers are used in physics, but there is a temptation in psychology to mistake looking at the thermometer for a study of the nature of heat. This mistake is not serious as long as tests are meant to be nothing but a convenient, fool-proof way of measuring an unknown which happens to make for success in school, army, business, etc. In class, these shortcuts to knowledge are risky. They are so unattractive to an imaginative intelligence that they antagonize desirable students. Others may seize on them as an easy way of getting a firm grip on the human mind. It is convenient enough to let numerical data replace the living matter they are supposed to interpret; but this may lead to serious misconceptions about one's own and other people's intelligence and ability. We cannot blame young students for overestimating the value of present-day testing techniques, when there are fully trained psychologists for whom the human personality seems to have been all but chased away by the dehydrated ghost of I.Q., aptitude score, adjustment rating, and so forth.

No objection is intended to the use of tests as such, but only to the replacement of direct observation by conceptual indices at a time when they are unlikely to represent a true equivalent of their object. In class discussion tests may serve to illustrate the fact that while quantification is the final aim, the living thing must not be distorted or impoverished for measurement's sake. Much valuable spade work consisting of hunches, hypotheses, or descriptive demonstration is ruled out by a rigid insistence on measurement as the only admissible scientific procedure. And the student should be made to realize that even where exactness has been attained there is continued need for that good-natured suspicion which leaves eyes and ears open to corrective experience.

It is not a simple matter for the student to preserve a flexible attitude toward the more formalized findings of psychology if at the same time he is supposed to keep out of the opposite pitfall; i.e., to avoid the tea-time talk which leaks into psychology from every-day language, magazine articles, etc. It would be pleasant enough for teacher and students to spend the hours on what a fellow psychologist has termed "systematic gossip": one exchanges human-interest stories, offers and receives "advice," sprinkles a few technical terms on common-sense reasoning . . . and the time flies.

But the first-hand material of experience as gathered from personal observation, field trips, or case studies furthers psychological insight only when the student attempts to interpret it by concepts which are as sharply defined as the stage of the investigation permits. Without insistence on well-structured organization of the data, clean logic, and valid conclusions the contact with reality will not result in the educational gains expected from scientific study, even though it may produce all kinds of humanly desirable effects, such as arousing pity or inspiring poetry.

Precise, penetrating thinking will not merely help the student to become a good scientist. It is also a tool for the organization of his life, since living involves distinguishing essentials from accidentals and knowledge from belief, viewing details in their relations to the whole, and facing issues objectively. Disciplined thinking may help students to spot the kind of ambiguous, cloudy talk which causes so much trouble because it provokes disruptive misunderstandings and camouflages shrewd selfishness, slander, and injury. A well-trained brain is not sufficient to make an ideal mate, parent, or business partner, but it helps to identify asocial forces that thrive in the twilight of muddled minds.

The plea for ordered and substantial thinking is connected with another educational aim. Students are expected to find out that competence is not acquired cheaply. At present, the main concern of commercial writing and publishing is to make reading matter palatable and thrilling at all cost. While this may be inevitable when instruments of culture are used as commodities, the influence on textbook writing and teaching must not be accepted without protest. It is a temptation for an author to imitate the easygoing talk of popular magazines and for the teacher to strain his capacities as an entertainer. The point can be reached where students—and not only students—get used to feeling that if a thing is hard to understand there must be something wrong with it. They conveniently overlook the difference between the stuffy intricacies of the "academic" mind and the concentrated substance of true thought. Do we have to be reminded that the more solid creations of man do not run after us, but stand by until they are patiently explored? *The Divine Comedy* cannot be read on a cross-town bus, and a Beethoven quartet cannot be taken in while one reads the newspaper. Any good piece of work must be as simple as possible, but it has no right to be simple at the expense of its purpose.

It seems to me that no education can be acceptable unless it conveys the notion that thinking and creating, and indeed living, take place at different levels of a pyramid, from the shallow bungling of the many to the high striving of the few. A view of this pyramid of values creates reverence, of which Goethe has said in *Wilhelm Meister* that it is the one thing "which no child brings into the world with him; and yet it is on this one thing that all depends for making man in every point a man." If we whittle down the pyramid to level flatness, there will be easy walking but no reverence and therefore no education.

Psychology courses have an opportunity to acquaint the student with the best of psychological writing in its original form. Modest in stature and number as the classics of our field may be, there is no reason why we should dilute and pamper the young mind with second and third-hand popularizations. It is true that the reading habits of the average student have been effectively spoiled by the time he enters college. He has become accustomed to racing through oversize assignments, so that a rebellious headache may be his first reaction to the kind of reading that deserves the name. But it is also true that once he concentrates all his wit and attention on a few meaty pages, he is likely to enjoy the experience of his own capacity and to feel the impact of the passionate precision in the words of a good thinker.

Naturally, I do not advocate a dogmatic limitation of reading material. I simply wish to point out that in practically all the basic areas of modern psychology the pioneer writings are accessible even to beginning students, if they care to take the trouble. Why should we deprive them of the enjoyable chance to sharpen their own thinking and style by reading James's paper on the theory of emotion, Freud's Introductory Lectures, or Köhler's studies on the mentality of the apes? The same is true even for a number of strictly experimental papers. Once in touch with the sources, the student may need supplementary reading in order to put specific contributions in their systematic and historical context. But he is likely now to apply the standards of the masters to the textbook and to get bewildered and annoyed if he meets shallow evasion in the disguise of popular simplicity. Having become used to the limpidity of the "heavy" writers, he may feel that the "text" is the most difficult book on the shelf—which is all to the good.

The interplay of the raw material of experience on the one hand and conceptual form on the other has been the subject of the foregoing discussion. The same two terms also describe the poles of a personality dimension which has an influence on ways of learning and teaching. There are individuals who are "empiricists," in that their dealings with the world are based essentially on concrete, particular experiences; whereas others strive for knowledge mainly by manipulating abstract generalities. These attitudes, which are related to the total personality structure, will determine how the individual approaches a field of study, what is hard, what easy, and what limitations the teacher must try to meet.

At the one extreme, there are students who like to deal with children, observe animals, attend court trials, or canvass the neighborhood. They are absorbed by what can be watched and touched. They handle people with intuitive wisdom. But they become uneasy when called upon to draw general conclusions, to compare one theory with another, or to evaluate the soundness of a proof. Scientific terms, which they handle gingerly or quite unconcernedly, acquire a strange poetical flavor. When asked to define the conditioned reflex, they may say: "They had a dog on the table, and they made a harmless operation at the jaw, so that they could count the drops of his saliva, and then they rang a bell. . . ."

At the other extreme, there are the clever jugglers. They are in love with terminology and quick in connecting ideas which stem from disparate contexts. But their brilliant short-circuits are often purely formal and therefore unproductive. Detached from the facts to which they refer, concepts drift and combine at random. The careful presentation of evidence makes such students impatient: "Why does he have to go through all these cases since the main idea was clear on the first page?"

Personality differences of this kind will escape the teacher who has to address lectures to rows of anonymous faces. Yet, they obviously have a bearing on how young people study psychology. Both extreme types may be found among interested and intelligent students. Both can succeed in their work. But whereas the "empiricists" do not see the forest for the trees, the concept-jugglers do not care to look at a tree when they see one. What is the teacher to do? The student of the first type may be seized by the story of a struggling human being and, if helped by a key concept which throws light on the problem and shows a way out, may never forget that concept and keep applying it wisely. The other type of student may be baited by a case study which suddenly gives flesh and blood to a glibly used technical term. If the teacher is too "empirical," he will not further the one student and will bore the other. If he is too "abstract," he will bewilder the one and keep the other floundering. But if he is a good enough psychologist to crystallize the floating substance of experience and to fill organized form with colorful content, he may hope to give something to both.

II

In contemporary philosophy and literature there is a widespread tendency to describe man in the most discouraging manner possible. He is made to look as though he were not created by lawful Nature but by Jean-Paul Sartre. So thoroughly has popular thinking been permeated with this conception that students bring it up spontaneously as a most obvious and incontestable thing. Man is selfish, interested only in his own profit, money, and pleasure. He is born lazy and will exert himself only when baited with honor rolls, pieces of candy, or the more durable pleasures of Heaven. He is kept from crime only by the threat of punishment. He does the right things for the wrong reasons, loves himself in loving others, hates his father, is jealous of the baby and almost everybody else, and paints and sings and poetizes because he would like really to rob and rape.* He is aggressive by nature. He can tell what is good from what is bad only by dumbly obeying the promptings of society. He juggles words instead of dealing with issues, he is capable of doing only what he has done very often, he is blinded by his feelings and dried out by his intellect. The masochistic enjoyment of human deficiency has become a matter of pride to the sophisticated. Before a young man learns how to use a razor, a sharp smile has carved a wrinkle around his mouth, and by the time he is fully educated he tends to believe in nothing but his liquor dealer and the semanticists.

What can our objection be to all this? Certainly, there is no denying that many of the unpleasant things which are said about man fit many people we know, such as ourselves, our friends, and our enemies. To judge from the newspapers, most people may be that way. But the psychologically and educationally crucial question is whether or not this dark composite picture is accepted as a description of "human nature." A norm is not established by what the majority of individuals is like. If 90 per cent of the people had rickets because of a deficient diet, one would not conclude that bow-leggedness was part of human nature. Nor would it simply depend on habit and taste whether or not crooked legs were called the norm. In the first place, we recognize that human traits differ in

* The paradigm of man's contemporary repulsive image lies in Auden's *Age of Anxiety*. New York, Random House, 1946.

their positions on what might be called the scale of modifiability; for instance, the sex instinct is relatively hard to modify, whereas the habit of spitting could be corrected easily. Reactionaries have long been fond of charging the laws of nature with what is due to changeable social conditions. In the second place, norms are distinguished from mere preferences or fashions in that they depend on axiomatic values concerning the meaning and aim of life.

Psychiatrists who ridicule the conception of a "normal" man as outmoded could not deal with any patient for even one meeting if they had not an idea of sanity, a norm by which to measure the deviation, a model of adjustment for which to strive. True, everything that exists is stained with abnormity by its very existence. But even though the normal is never perfectly realized, its conception is indispensable for any evaluation of reality.

One can hardly overstate the importance of this point for the teaching of psychology. Growing up in a world which is torn to pieces by the brutalities of selfish nationalism and competition, frightened by newspapers on whose front pages the close-up photographs of murdered bodies crowd out the remnants of peaceful and productive living, entertained daily by the vulgar dialogue of radio-gangsters and the screams of their victims, our young people could not afford the kind of teacher who, thoughtlessly or for some unwholesome satisfaction of his own, would join in the collective attack on their nervous systems.

Radio, the movies, the press, and other media of mass communication are deliberately misused to draw profit from the fascination which evil, violence, and madness hold for the immature mind. Striving for the attention of his students, a teacher may unwittingly exploit the same power of attraction. He may even believe that it is his mission to "shock" them out of a complacency produced by overprotected home life. Or he may simply lack the capacity for presenting the psychology of personality as anything but a museum of deformities. Obviously I am not calling for an expurgated picture of the mind, with virtue and happiness as the only subjects of discussion. On the contrary, it would seem that the average textbook omits much psychiatric and criminological material which is not only admissible but indispensable in the introductory psychology course. What counts is not so much the subject matter in itself as the general framework in which it is presented. An inappropriately framed discussion of maladjustment, crime, and insanity may reenforce the kind of *weltbild* which emerges from many best-sellers produced in our day by acute but shortsighted and basically reactionary novelists and playwrights. In novels of this type, the lack of a frame of reference, which would define the unfortunate characters as victims of distorting conditions, interferes not only with the ethical value but also with the aesthetic validity of a book, in that the narrowness of the view makes for an untruthful image of life.

In teaching, one can observe genuine relief in students who are led to understand that a realistic appraisal of the shortcomings which they find in themselves and others must not blind them to the equally tangible symptoms of basic goodness. The images of the healthy child, the creative thinker, the unselfish leader are powerful protective charms against the entirely unproductive anxiety which the spectacle of human shortcomings arouses when it is presented with the purely hypothetical implication that man is born evil and that human institutions frustrate by necessity. There is no better way for the teacher to activate the precious ambition of youth than by stressing those psychological findings and theories which point to the cultural causes of neurosis, delinquency, or socio-political ruthlessness. We cannot afford a psychology which is not "mental hygiene" in the best sense of the word, and there can be no such hygiene without an ever-present conception of health.

Think of two physicians. One of them, even though thoughtfully concerned with the afflicted, inspires confidence because whatever he says and does is clearly directed toward the goal of recovery. The other doctor, equally competent, has taken to medicine because he is infatuated with disease. He courts the symptoms, and every diagnosis sounds ominous. Under the care of the first, a patient lives through a serious attack of tuberculosis with his mind hopefully set on the future. Watched by the melancholy eyes of the second, a sore throat creates a haunted invalid. Similarly, it will often depend on the attitude of the teacher whether a discussion of psychoneurosis will arouse and strengthen fear or will offer a tool for successful living.

Constant implicit reference to the normal mind is not only good

hygiene but also good science. It was suggested before that in selecting his subject matter and in his way of dealing with it the teacher
keep asking himself whether or not the discussion is likely to add
to the understanding of the basic principles which, in his view,
make up the present scientific conception of the human mind. Isolated facts are likely to be immediately forgotten by the student or
not apprehended at all unless they happen to strike home for some
individual reason. The teacher may hope to rescue the more specific
findings and ideas from oblivion by relating them to a few general
theses. During the last decades psychologists have tended to unify
their science by incorporating outlying areas of research. For instance, at the time when L. Levy-Bruhl wrote his classical treatises
on primitive mentality, the savage was believed to think according
to specific laws which could be deduced from observation and, at
best, understood by empathy, but which were different in kind
from the principles of civilized thought.

Nowadays, we try to show that while human thinking is basically
the same everywhere, it will necessarily produce different reactions
when it operates on a low level of knowledge and at the service of
the particular needs which characterize primitive life. Similarly, in
psychology we owe the most fruitful discoveries to attempts at interpreting pathological behavior as reactions of *the* human mind to
conditions of stress. Thus, Freud was able to show that compulsive
symptoms are not simply irrational madness but reasonable defense
mechanisms of a cornered mind. It is significant that by dealing
with pathology in such terms Freud automatically contributed to
our knowledge of the normal personality.

The teacher can use the same procedure reversed. He can present
pathological phenomena as extreme cases of common behavior patterns which he wishes to illustrate, profiting from the fact that
caricatures tell the truth in a particularly impressive way. And
precisely as caricatures acquire their meaning and lose their night-
marish power by being understood as distortions of a model, psycho-
pathological behavior is humanized by being drawn into the range
of common functioning and is thus deprived of some of its shocking
effect. Reassured and attracted by the insight that mental disturb-
ance does not transform man into a monster but keeps him within

the realm of everybody's concern, the student acquires an enriched, graphic picture of the mind.

Needless to say, present-day psychiatry is far from being able to interpret all known abnormal manifestations by principles of general psychology. For our purpose it suffices to suggest that pathological material has a legitimate place in general education only to the extent to which psychiatric interpretation has been reasonably successful. The course in abnormal psychology which aims at a complete coverage of the field is best limited to the few students who need it for professional training. From the point of view of general education, such a specialized course would promote the unfortunate parcelling-up of the body of knowledge into unrelated members, would cater to the student fascination with the abnormal, and involve no small risk for the unprepared student.

An example may illustrate the role psychiatric material can fulfill in the general psychology course. A discussion of productive thinking leads the teacher to point out that an inadequate perception of a problem situation often results when the self is part of that situation. He suggests that since people find it hard to evaluate their own place and function in a group objectively they are apt to distort the whole picture so that it will fit their egocentric prejudice. Such a warped conception of the situation will hamper them in reacting suitably to it. The teacher illustrates ego-involvement first in particularly concrete and emotionally neutral perceptual experiences. For instance, our eyes see near objects large, far objects small, thus distorting the actual sizes. Near noises monopolize our attention at the expense of more distant ones, which may be more important objectively. In our newspapers, the din of local events often drowns reports about fateful happenings abroad. This egocentric attitude makes it sometimes difficult for people to realize that things going on around us have no intentional bearing upon ourselves. To the primitive, a stroke of lightning is a planned attack on himself. When mother goes out shopping, the young child narrowly conceives of this as: "She is leaving me alone!"

In our own lives, we tend toward such egocentric misinterpretations mostly when we are unduly concerned about ourselves, feel guilty, out of place, ridiculous. Wearing an inappropriate hat, we cannot help thinking that drivers in the street are hooting "at us," that the smile and whisper of the people we are passing by refer to us. It is understandable that such misinterpretations may become habitual and quite strong in people who are driven into an ego-centric position because they feel insecure, inferior, blemished. At this point in the class discussion, the student is ready for an elementary understanding of what psychiatrists call "ideas of reference," which in paranoid states of persecution mania may incite a deranged person to murder.

In this fashion, the description of a clinical phenomenon, which might have disturbed students considerably if presented out of context, becomes an organic part of a survey that cuts across various "separate" fields of psychological study in order to show different manifestations of a basic principle; namely, ego-involvement. The guiding idea gives meaning to every example, connects what seemed unrelated, and, in turn, acquires flesh and blood from the applications.

Not the smallest advantage of such a procedure is that it helps to keep the student from finding all the symptoms of madness in himself. All too easily is he convinced that he is on the threshold of dementia praecox because he often feels coolly detached from his surroundings as, according to the textbook, schizophrenics do. He will be safer from such wrong conclusions if he is prepared to view the clinical symptoms as disruptingly extreme cases of what healthy people experience also.

The present discussion began with a criticism of the tendency to accept aggressiveness, stupidity, laziness, and selfishness as the foundations of human nature. Whether the approach to psychology is based on such an attitude or on the trustful assumption that man is basically constructive, cooperative, kindly, intelligent, and industrious is educationally crucial. It is not a matter of mere personal preference when a teacher strives for the fascination which springs from worry and fear rather than for encouragement and faith.

The "facts" seem to speak in favor of pessimism. But the psychologist is not concerned with external behavior as such. What people do is a symptom of what they are; and symptoms require interpretation. Psychological statements about the underlying mental forces begin to sound encouraging once the initial shock derived from the appalling frankness of the unconscious is overcome. An uncompromising conscience, an almost prophetic insight, and powerful drives toward balanced, courageous, productive living seem to be at the core of the mind, in spite of its unattractive disguise. Evil appears to be a defense mechanism rather than an ingredient of human nature.

These hypotheses of depth-analysis are important also because they establish a connection between the study of personality on the one hand and fundamental principles of experimental psychology and of the biological and physical sciences on the other hand. A view according to which the dynamics of personality are based on discord, disequilibrium, and tendencies to disorder and imperfection is not easily reconciled with the experimental findings of the gestalt psychologists, who have shown, for instance, that processes of visual perception tend consistently toward states of balance and order— tendencies which are also found in physiological and physical fields. Nor does such a view fit Cannon's concept of homeostasis, according to which the household of the human body ingeniously balances supply and demand, thus allowing for a maximum of planned efficiency.

This scientific evidence may encourage the psychologist to accept the working hypothesis that the same tendency toward balance and order will prove to be valid also for the psychology of personality and social relations. It is true that in the course of history we seem hardly to have progressed toward the goal of matching the wisdom of the body with the wisdom of the mind. But the mere conviction that there is such a goal can challenge the teacher to start doing some constructive work. He does not have to wait for the day on which the theories that man is born aggressive, or that cooperation is bolshevism, or that one has to be neurotic in order to be creative, will have been buried quietly next to the remnants of other short-lived fashions.

On Teaching Modern Poetry

STEPHEN SPENDER

A poem has many levels of meaning, and none of them is prose. Are some of these "righter" than others? Is it altogether "wrong" to think that a poem may be paraphrased? Can an appreciation of poetry be acquired? Does poetry have educational value for the student who is incapable of a complete experience of poetry but who can acquire a limited appreciation which may not seem to survive his years at school or college? This last question, which the reader may be inclined to answer with an immediate "No" is, in practice, not so easy to answer. For students who may never completely understand a poem, can often understand other things through the discussion of poetry. Those who prefer discussing poetry to reading poems, look to poetry for an illumination of some of the problems of living. One cannot afford to dismiss this as irrelevant when one is taking into consideration the whole picture of the education of an individual. Many people look to poetry today as an illumination of religious and philosophic problems. Although poetry is not and cannot be a substitute for religion and philosophy, nevertheless it may lead people to think seriously about such things. It may lead them through poetry and out of it into their real interest or vocation.

Probably most modern critics would agree that a poem *means* the sum of everything which it *is*, in language used to suggest not just thought but also imagery and sound. It means a thought which can be paraphrased in prose, plus the sound of the words in which this thought is expressed and which add as much to the thought as color does to drawing in a painting, plus the imagery which becomes a sensory experience to the reader as he reads from line to line, plus the energy of the metre, plus the poet's taste or palate in words, plus even such things as the punctuation and spacing of the poem upon the printed page. All these things become an *experience* which the poem is and means.

96

Most contemporary critics, as I say, would agree about this. On the whole, the tendency today is to judge the poem by the sacred order of the irreplaceable line, and not by the generalized reducible opinions and attitudes of the poet within his poem. This modern appreciation of the concreteness and texture of art is surely one of the characteristics of intellectual life in the twentieth century which we can consider to be an advance over the nineteenth.

Yet, if we do not feel the need to translate poetry into prose, nevertheless the need to explain and annotate it seems to remain. Why else those books explaining the philosophy of T. S. Eliot's *Four Quartets* or of Rilke's *Duino Elegies*? It is all very well for Mr. Robert Graves to declare that his poems are written only for poets, implying that all poems should be that and that only. But evidently, despite the modern purist desire not to lose the poem in the prose translation, poetry expresses complicated ideas and attitudes. This inevitably leads us on from a discussion of the best order of the best words to that of the ideas behind them. Robert Graves may be right in thinking that poetry should be for poets only. But despite his protestations, the overwhelming mass of contemporary criticism of poetry assumes that poetry is written for a reading public who are not just poets: or at least that there is a content of poetry which exists, as it were, apart from the pure esthetic experience which can only be communicated to people who think poetically, as the poet himself thinks.

The teacher of poetry finds that although it is important to stress that poetry *is*, it is also true that poetry is about things. To a certain type of student the "about"ness will always be more important that the "is"ness: and perhaps this student may learn more from having poetry explained to him than the one who understands poetry intuitively and who therefore scarcely requires to be taught.

The teacher is not a poet teaching poets, nor even a literary critic concerned only with readers whose interest in poetry is "pure." He has to accept I think, that the interest of most students in poetry, however serious it may be, will not be for the sake of that which is essentially the poetry in poetry. At the same time, poetry itself is ambiguous, and that which it is about is inseparably bound up with that which it is. If a critic as austere as Mr. T. S. Eliot can argue that a poet as pure as Blake is not a great poet because he has a "homemade philosophy," that means that one approach to Blake is certainly by way of his philosophy. And if many of Blake's readers never get beyond his philosophy to the center of his imagination, that does not mean that they have entirely missed the poetry in Blake: because Blake's thought, which can perhaps be paraphrased, nevertheless remains a part of his poetry. What a poem is about, even if it can be expressed in critics' prose, does take us some way toward understanding that which it is.

Many students undoubtedly try to *use* poetry to help them to develop attitudes towards things other than poetry. Sarah Lawrence College provided me with several examples of such a utilitarian attitude. One student, K., had difficulty with certain modern poems at the beginning of the course, because she disapproved of the views which the poets appeared to her to be expressing in their poems; for example, the pessimism of Thomas Hardy, the mysticism of T. S. Eliot, and the insistence on sexuality of D. H. Lawrence. She thought that poetry should in some way express ideas which contributed to the betterment of human society.

Perhaps I should have argued with K. that poetry had nothing to do with the views of poets and still less to do with improving the lot of humanity. But I only partly did this. I also argued against her views in themselves, quite apart from their relevance to poetry. I tried to point out that the search for a meaning in life, even if it seems to neglect the exigencies of social welfare, is not escapism. The result of allowing her to discuss aspects of poetry, such as the opinions and personalities of poets, which seemed on the face of it to have little to do with their work, was that she did, in the course of a year, develop powers of appreciation which I had not thought possible. A block to her appreciation was removed. She learned tolerance through tolerating poets. Having acquired a certain tolerance she experienced a certain release in her imaginative life which brought her to an appreciation of poetry for its own sake. Her prejudices were not just irrelevant: they were barriers which had to be removed before she could understand poetry at all. Her criticism of every poem—that it said something with which she disagreed—implied a conviction that poetry ought to have a social message with which she did agree. It would have been useless to say that what a poem *said* was irrelevant to the poetry, because to her the saying something was what really mattered, and ultimately her objection was to the expression of any attitudes of mind which she did not consider socially responsible. To say to her that Thomas Hardy's pessimism was irrelevant to his poetry would only be a way of making her think that Hardy not only had the wrong opinions but also attempted to evade responsibility for them. Therefore it seemed best to accept her view that poetry was about opinions which she could not tolerate and to point out that those opinions, within the contexts in which they were expressed, might have a value which she could come to appreciate. When she had learned to tolerate these opinions she was well on the way to understanding the freedom of the imagination of the poet in his poetry. On the other hand, so long as she could not tolerate what she considered antisocial opinions, she would not tolerate the life of the imagination.

K., it transpired, was using poetry as a means of liberating herself from a narrow application of her social conscience to every situation. Her case was not rare. There is a fairly widespread tendency amongst students today to label a great deal of their reading "escapist," for the most superficial reasons. To them, all the poetry of Walter de la Mare is "escapist," Mr. T. S. Eliot is not "escapist" in *The Waste Land* but becomes so in the *Four Quartets*, Mr. W. H. Auden has recently become an "escapist," D. H. Lawrence is escaping from social reality into "personal relationships and mysticism," and so on. Such readers seem to expect that it is the duty of literature to confront them with a social reality, which, in fact, they rarely face themselves in their own lives. They wish poets to stop being what is called escapists and become scapegoats, punished and punishing in their work for all the ills of society. One might reasonably argue that if literature did do this, it might indeed be providing a facile escape in imagination from problems which people ought to be facing in their living. In fact, there is a case to be made for saying that people should be social realists in their lives but not in their literature. For living should certainly be pre-occupied with improving conditions, but literature should be concerned with enlarging our ideas of a significance beyond the paraphernalia of living. Without such a significance, improved conditions themselves become a burden. There must be a goal beyond the goal of social improvement—to give significance to better conditions of living when they have been achieved.

In an ideal world I suppose that living would be involved in problems of living, and that literature would be concerned with values which transcend living. It is these values which ultimately give living itself a purpose. Of course, as long as we do not live in an ideal world, some writers will insist on the necessity of using writing as a means of describing the problems of social reality and, if they are so inspired, they will be right to do so. But to call this kind of literature "realistic" and any other kind escapist is to sacrifice the pursuit of permanent values for immediate and pressing ones: and there is danger of the sense of that which endures being lost in the exigencies of the present.

If there is any such thing as "escapism" in poetry, it is the tendency of poets sometimes to assert that experiences contained in certain poems have some kind of consoling application to other experiences of a different nature. That a sunset, a rose, or a landscape can be evoked in language which compensates for poverty, social injustice, or war, is obviously a false proposition. To maintain it is to escape from the greater evil into the lesser prettiness. Poets, even such a poet as Keats, have occasionally misled themselves and their readers in writing about poetry as though it were a housing project for happy dreamers. The mistake perhaps arises from confusing the objective standards by which poetry is made and judged with the subjective experience it provides. For the fact is that poetry is an art employing an objective medium and technique for the purpose of communicating the subjective insight of the poet to the subjective sensibility of the reader. It can express and communicate an experience which may be of great value to the individual reader, perhaps even providing him with a philosophy and helping him in his life. But this kind of individual experience conveyed from one individual to another by means of the objective medium of art, arises only as a possible rather irrelevant reaction of the reader to the subject matter of the poem. Poetry cannot preach social values as effectively as journalism or propaganda or systematized thought, even though it may indirectly have a social effect. Poetry does not provide a kind of reality which can either, on the one hand, console readers for the ills of society, or, on the other, by being "realistic," make people face up to social problems. All poetry may do, as an incidental effect of its use of language, is to provide the reader with an experience which will affect him according to the laws of his own nature. The propagandist view that poetry can save society is just as irrelevant to the nature of poetry as the one that it can provide an escape from the ills of the modern age.

I have dwelt on "escapism" so long because one of the chief prejudices the teacher of students of poetry today has to fight is indicated by the word "escapist." However, I think the teacher should be sympathetic to the student who wants to know how poetry will be useful to him. After all, utility itself, in connection with poetry, is a somewhat complex concept, and there is every reason to consider it. For one thing, poetry is useful to anyone who appreciates it, in enabling him to enter into complex states of mind which should help him to understand his own nature and that of other people. The reader of a poem has the illusion, through the sensuous use of language, of being in the presence of the event which is the occasion of the poem. The subject of a poem is an event individually experienced; its method (sensuous language) creates the form which is the universal form of all experience for everyone of every event. The reader of a poem is made aware that the experience of every event by every individual is a unique occasion in the universe, and that at the same time, this uniqueness is the universal mode of experiencing all events. Poetry makes one realize that one is alone, and complex; and that to be alone is universal.

The fact that one cannot establish the value of the experience of a poem in a hierarchy of utilitarian values, does not mean that poetry is not useful. On the contrary, one can insist that poetry is of use to the individual who appreciates it, even while one may refuse to measure that utility. The teacher who thinks it is part of his integrity, or of the integrity of his subject, to refuse to admit the utility of spiritual values, may be in the position of offering art to his pupils in the form of significantly formed stones, when they are asking for bread. He should ask himself seriously whether there is not a sense in which poetry is indeed bread for those who can understand it, and even, to a lesser extent, to those who partially misunderstand it.

Poetry, as has often been said, reveals the familiar as unfamiliar. The inspiration of the poet is the moment in which he becomes aware of unfamiliarity. The unfamiliarity, the newness of things, the uniqueness of every contact of a mind with an event, is, indeed, everything. But there are certain experiences in life which are always unfamiliar for everyone, and these form a vast subject matter for poetry, the unfamiliarity of the unfamiliar. Such subjects are death, love, infinity, the idea of God, the smallness of man in relation to the vastness of the universe, the unknown. Religion, philosophy, and morals are also concerned with these fundamentals of the human condition, and it is here that the experiencing of life in poetry brings the poetic experience close to the reasoned processes of philosophers, theologians, and moralists. Thus the teaching of poetry leads the student to a discussion of conditions of human life, where man is alone with the strangeness of his situation in time and space.

Poets can only express their experiences in terms of other experiences, which men have experienced with their senses. Sensuous language means that the poet creates his poem from words which have associations, and these associations are of the experience of things with the senses. A love poem can only be expressed in words which have associations with actual loving, and in the same way a religious poem can only be created in the language of religious experience—however remote this may seem. For this reason, the teacher will find that a great deal of discussion of poetry in class will consist of inquiring into the connection between the poet's experience and his poem. Is the poet sincere? Did he really feel this? are questions often asked by students. When poetry goes beyond personal experience to the experience of belief, we are brought up against a more difficult question of sincerity. Can the poet really believe this? Does he know God? Can he believe in immortality? We are soon confronted with problems of tradition and belief which may seem far removed from a particular poem, but which may really be essential to an understanding of it.

Amongst our contemporaries today one finds that directly a poet ceases to write of some immediate human experience of an occasional nature, for whose purposes he can draw on the simple associative language of the physical senses, one is up against the difficulty that a shared language of religious or philosophical experience, with associations which are as easily recognized as those of the senses, does not exist. In reading poetry such as T. S. Eliot's *Four Quartets* with students, one finds that for many of them there is no sensuous language associated with ideas of eternity, God, immortality, heaven, hell, and so on. Eliot's world is for them a world of abstract speculation, his language never, or almost never, strikes the note of an experience of eternity in their own minds. Naturally they think of Eliot's preoccupations as "escapism," because they are about an experience of which they know nothing.

If one wishes to teach such students to appreciate the *Four Quartets* the only way to do so seems to be to build up by intellectual arguments the associations with experience on which the poetry is based. One can show that each of the four poems in the *Four Quartets* is connected with real places which have historic associations with certain disciplines of living dependent on certain metaphysical beliefs. One can discuss the use to which Eliot has deliberately put the influence of Dante in his poem, and one can discuss the time-philosophy and the theological ideas of the *Four Quartets*. All this will not give the student the immediate contact with the metaphysical searching which is as much the sensuous experience of this poetry as the color grey is sensuous experience in the line:

> Towards what shores what grey rocks and what islands.

Consider lines such as:

> All manner of things shall be well
> When the tongues of flame are infolded
> Into the crowned knot of fire
> And the fire and the rose are one.

Here it is far easier to make the student understand the Dantesque imagery than the sensuous mystical perception of the life of the individual within eternity. Can one understand such writing without having had, consciously or unconsciously, a mystical experience which foreshadows the condition described? This is a baffling question for the teacher. All he can reasonably hope to do is make the student understand the traditional belief within which Eliot's recent poetry exists, and to argue against the view of the student who thinks that mystical experience is "escapist."

Teachers of Latin within the system of a classical education have always taught much poetry, partly because this branch of classical literature is supremely excellent, partly because the language of poetry taught the greatest mastery of all the uses of the language, and partly also because within poetry there exist all the ideas of Roman civilization. These reasons for teaching poetry remain in force today. Insistence on the esthetic aspect should not conceal from us that poetry remains the most instructive of the arts, being rooted in myth, being supremely the exercise by the poet of the historic sense within the tradition of literature, and involving often discussion of general ideas.

The most important thing to teach about modern poetry is that modern poetry is simply poetry, expressing what poets have tried to express at all times, but within modern conditions. The problem of the poet has always been to express inward experience in imagery and sound which communicate the significance of this experience to others. He can only communicate to other minds what is significant to him by involving an outward event symbolizing a significance which corresponds to his inner state of mind. If he is an Elizabethan, certain of his inner experiences may have a significance recognized by others when he attaches to these experiences the symbolism of the rose, the crown, or the cross. For a modern man who, as a human being, has an inner experience exactly similar to that of the Elizabethan, the symbol which corresponds to his experience will be one chosen from modern life, if it is to communicate itself in a way which will awaken the living experience of our time to his contemporaries. To select rose, crown, or cross would be for him to detach his experience from the present and place it in a literary past.

Our expansive, restless, materialist, explosive age does not easily provide us in our environment with outward symbols for inner states of mind. For our outer world has little accessible language of symbols to which we can attach the experiences of our inner lives. Instead of our minds being able to invade it with their inwardness, it invades us with its outwardness, almost persuading us that not the inner life of man, but nonhuman, geographical and mechanical events are all that is significant in the universe. However, the fact remains that man's problem is that everything for him is a mental event in his own mind. This includes the whole extent of the universe, and all the achievements of scientists and generals. The external world is man's inner world and his problem is to organize this inner world within his own mind.

Therefore the eternal problem of poetry—to express inner experiences in terms of outer things—remains, although the apparent unresponsiveness of outer things in the modern world makes this appear difficult. Man has learned, invented, and organized his modern world. It is an object of his awareness, inventiveness, and will. He is not an object of it. Therefore the machine and the spatial distances which appear to impose their vastness on him are the material of his own inner spiritual life. Within his mind they are symbols. Perhaps they are symbols of the apparent powerlessness of his inner life. But his sanity depends on his mastering within himself what he has discovered and invented in his outer world. He has power to imagine the inner mastery of his own situation. Modern poetry is an aspect of the struggle to restore the balance of our inner with our outer world.

In view of this, it is a peculiarity of American education that it makes a division of literature into "creative," "critical," and "reading" functions. Some students will tell you that they expect to learn to write creatively, others to criticize, and others to read. An extreme example of oversimple approach was given to me by a student who told me that I could not expect her to be interested in any of the poets she read: because she wished to learn to write poetry, not to read it. This was exceptional: but three other students whom I taught were only really interested in those poets whom they considered useful to them in their own writing.

The creative writing classes in the United States must be

considered a very interesting educational experiment, but their advantages must be weighed against several disadvantages. One disadvantage is that they tend to divide literary studies into creative and noncreative. If this means also that the student thinks of writing as being an activity which has little to do with reading, or which has the effect of limiting the writer's reading to that which helps him in his own creative work, here is a further disadvantage. For one only has to read the lives of writers to see that an avaricious habit of reading everything that comes his way is the atmosphere in which most writers have developed and lived.

There is certainly a good deal in the writing of poetry which can be taught. Readers of the prose passages in Dante's *Vita Nuova* will see that Dante considered himself a member of a school who were inventing and propagating a particular style of poetry. Baudelaire, Mallarmé, and several other poets have considered the teaching of poetry as a theoretical possibility. At the beginning of this century the imagists held views about the writing of poetry, such as that the poet must concentrate entirely on producing a perfectly clear image, and that this can be taught and learned.

Poetry is written in various forms, and there is no doubt that these can be taught, just as musical technique can be. The parallel with music exists in theory, but actually it does not quite work out in practice. Music is concerned with notes measured in time. A sequence of notes producing the same tune can be invented to produce a slow or fast effect simply by lengthening the duration of each note, or variations can be made by sustaining some notes and quickening others, within the rhythm. Thus a musician can take a tune and produce a great many variations on it without altering the original idea. However, poetry uses words and not notes. A poet cannot alter the speed and mood of an idea simply by adding syllables and emphatic pauses with the ease which is possible to the composer. Thus the idea which in poetry corresponds to tune can only be created in one set of words in which meaning is inseparable from the form in which it is expressed. A poet is not like a composer in search for freedom of expression which he can achieve among a great variety of forms: he is in search for the few forms which correspond most exactly to that which he wishes to say. When he has discovered those forms, he interests himself in no others, except insofar as he is feeling his way towards those which may further his later development. Form in poetry is inseparable from thought: and the only form which the poet needs is that in which he can think. Thus, from Walt Whitman, down to T. S. Eliot, one can think of dozens of poets who know far less in general about poetic forms than is taught in the creative writing courses: they are masters of their own particular forms, and probably even avoid thinking in other ones, through an instinctive discipline.

A sonnet, for example, is a poetic form for thinking a thought which is a sonnet. If a poet has no potentiality for thinking in sonnets, to write them may actually confuse him and prevent him from attaining so soon the form which is uniquely his. The poet W. B. Yeats once told me that he had learned to write in an over-literary poetic tradition and that he had spent his life trying to write poems in a simpler manner. To a lesser talent, nothing might seem simpler than Yeats' problem. All he had to do was to leave out some rhymes and prune away his imagery, one might think. But the ornament, the overpoetic style had become his poetic thought, and when he struggled to express ideas which were too bare and harsh for this form, he had great difficulty in adapting his style to his later subject-matter.

Thus, to teach students to write in a variety of poetic techniques would be a doubtful benefit. What one can do, perhaps, is criticize their work, with a view to helping them to discover their own form, teach them to relate as widely as possible the poetry of others to what they themselves are trying to do, teach them to think concretely and with their senses, and develop in their minds a sense of purpose independent of the literary market and literary fashions.

Young writers often forget that a poem should be as well written as a letter or diary or any other piece of prose, that is to say, as well written, considered simply as writing, as they can possibly make it. Perhaps the most reasonable method of writing a poem is first of all to write down rapidly those impressions, that rhythm, that shape which makes it seem a poetic experience, without regard to other considerations. But the second or third stage of writing should certainly be to take out the "bad writing," that is to say, the redundancies, the bad grammar, the linguistic inversions, and write the sense of the poem as well and clearly as possible. A teacher can certainly be of help here, because a good deal of potentially good poetry is lost under sheer bad writing.

A poet discovers his own formal qualities through learning to analyse the qualities of his own sensibility. He must know whether, for example, his gifts are predominantly of the eye or the ear. The visual writer cannot afford to sacrifice his eye to his ear: a preoccupation with rules of rhyme and strict metre could disintegrate the concentration on the image which is necessary to develop his gift.

In relating his own work to that of other poets, the student has to learn to avoid two dangers which have destroyed many talents: on the one hand, the danger of being absorbed into a greater talent; on the other, the danger of shutting out greater talent for fear of being absorbed. One has to learn to relate one's own work to that of others and to learn from this relation by using other work for purposes of criticizing one's own, or sometimes for interpreting the work of other poets in terms of one's own talent. The relation of Keats to Shakespeare, or, in our own time, of Eliot to Dante, is each a classic example of the power of a poet to interpret within his own sensibility the achievement of a past poet. Here it seems to me that the teacher should be of considerable help to the student. For example, I think it would be a good exercise for students to make free translations of poems in a foreign language, interpreting the particular significance for them of a poem which appeals to them into terms of their own technique and sensibility. They should seek in such free renderings, not for accuracy, but to create in their own language the general effect which appeals to them in the foreign poem.

Of course far and away the most important quality of a poet is his power of thinking sensuously in words. The test of sensuous thought is not the occasional striking image or well-sounding line, but the power as it were to *follow through* with the senses, just as in a game a player may have a perception of a whole sequence of moves following from one move, which affect him physically, as though he were at one moment feeling the muscular changes required by all these moves expanding through his blood and muscles. The power of the verbal eye to see the transformation from line to line of the image and sound in a poem: this is the central excitement of poetry, it is the real life, and everything else is fabrication. The teacher cannot of course teach sensuous energy: still less can he explain how this can clothe itself in vital words. But he can at least be an efficient guide; for it is in confused imagery, mixed metaphor, abstract expressions, that by far the greatest number of mistakes are made by poets. Here too one has the chief clue to the student's talent and potentiality. If he is able to see with intensity, even for the duration of a phrase or a line, there is the possibility of development. If he is able to understand the necessity of a certain consistency, a poetic logic in the development of imagery and sound, then he may well be capable of poetry.

Too often in schools for creative writing, the student's eye is directed towards the market of magazines and reviews. Perhaps it would be too idealistic to say that creative writing courses should be directed against rather than towards the standards of editorial offices; but at least it may be said that as far as possible independence from such standards should be taught. The period during a student's life when he is writing only for teachers and friends, is not only in itself one of liberty, but it should represent a freedom which he is able to value afterwards, and to which he should always return. In a sense a writer should always remain a student, should be writing only for himself and his friends. But if, when he is a student, he is already considered to be writing for publication, this standard is destroyed in his own mind. Therefore teachers should encourage students to indulge in that kind of writing which cannot be published: for example, the writing of journals and experiments, perhaps even of erotic and obscene poems. The habit of writing for the wastepaper basket is the most valuable one that a writer can acquire.

Despite the creative writing courses, teaching students to read poems seems more useful than teaching them to write them, for various reasons. Although the true readers of poetry are perhaps as rare as the poets themselves, the reading of poetry does lead to many other things. Poetry is, after all, a nerve center of the consciousness of a civilization, with responses to many of the important situations in that civilization. The reading of poetry within an education therefore justifies itself as a discipline of the humanities.

Learning to write poetry is an interesting experiment and in some years' time a survey of the results of this education will be interesting. Perhaps it will be found that in place of the creative writing courses there should be a far greater emphasis on writing in all literary courses. It would seem that a very valuable development of the American experiment would be if the conception of written work in all English courses were extended considerably beyond the essay, to include poems and stories.

To sum up: the teacher of poetry has always to remember that he is not only a poet teaching poets or even a critic insisting on the purest and fullest appreciation. He is really filling several roles, of which these two are the easiest and perhaps not the most important, since writers and readers with a true vocation will probably find it without him.

His most important role is to teach poetry as a discipline of the imagination; a discipline which reveals the complexity of the experience of the individual human being isolated in time and place within the universe and experiencing everything at every moment of his life, as no one before or since has experienced or will ever experience it; which, when it has revealed this terrifying uniqueness and complexity, shows how the unique, which is also the universal form of experiencing, can be related through the understanding of poetry to the experiences of other men who have been able to express a similar sense of their isolation within time and space, at other times and other places; which shows that complexity and awareness only become creative when they can be disciplined within a formal pattern.

The student who is unable to attain complete appreciation can learn a great deal from the discipline of poetry. Modern poetry can teach above all that the poetic problem is the same, at all times, though it has to express itself in different forms; the same, because the problem of the poet is to relate his inner significant experiences to the outward world which impresses itself on him. The world of modern phenomena is as much a product of man's spiritual condition as the world in the past has been and the world in the future will be.

American History in College Education

BERT JAMES LOEWENBERG

Why do we study American history? What parts of the American record are more important than others? What relationship does American experience bear to the experience of the rest of mankind? Who should teach American history and how should it be taught?

These questions, and many more of the same kind, are asked constantly and anxiously. Legislators, national and local, have drafted laws concerning American history based upon assumptions of its role in education and the method of its presentation.

Newspaper editors have written of the need for a deeper knowledge of the American past as a guide to the perils of the future. Radio commentators have lectured the greatest audiences yet assembled on the arresting parallels between great historic events and recurring crises of the present. Even comic strip artists and quiz program conductors have undertaken to aid Americans in understanding their past. And corporation presidents have added their voices to the spokesmen of civic, military, and fraternal organizations who have traced the course of American destiny.

American history, we are told, is the method of teaching democracy, and the inculcation of democratic precepts is the supreme goal of education. To understand the American way of life, we must study the American past and distinguish it from other cultures. A knowledge of democratic theory and of the "American way" is thought to generate patriotism in the young.

Democracy, however, is a series of concepts and values. The American way of life is a phrase which is meaningless without specific historical content, and "loyalty" without precise referents exists in the oratory of patriotism alone.

Claims made for American history suffer from lack of concreteness. Undergraduate studies in the history of the United States are in fact undertaken in order that democracy may be more fully understood and more fully lived. To comprehend the American way of life is one of the chief ends of historical investigation. Both are pursued in behalf of human values among which the value of loyalty is of prime significance. Yet democracy is in part a sequence of historical facts which must be analyzed; it is not an epithet with which to silence criticism. Democracy is a method of living together rather than a charm to be invoked, a cluster of values to be perceived and felt rather than a ritual to be memorized. The American way of life is composed of those parts of our culture which are unique. What is peculiar to America cannot be appreciated without comparison with other cultures and older parts of our own. What students ask of teachers of American history is precisely this: What is democracy? What is "the American way of life"? How does America differ from other societies? What values does America represent?

But the academic history teacher is one of the most rigid of student stereotypes. Of course, students are eager to learn about their past, to understand their present, and to find some guide to the future, but only rarely do they expect to find it in the history classroom. To them history is a series of dates and battles to be memorized and a record of events others have accounted great. They are surprised to find a class discussion interesting or to find a "history book" stimulating. They have learned the collegiate clichés well. Students believe that historical scholars inhabit a world of unreality remote from the concerns of life. Historians are believed to be unconcerned with anything other than documents and libraries. History books are thought to be written by gathering together parts of obscure books few have ever read which are then made into other books which students are forced to read and sometimes compelled to buy.

Since myths do not grow in a vacuum, some justification for the stereotype obviously exists. One reason is that the training of each young teacher is concentrated on a work of doctoral research. Historians are trained to investigate the details of history, not to investigate its meaning. The tariff of 1828, for example, is a fascinating study, but it is something less than a key to American life. The private life of Alexander Hamilton, purple enough for his day, tells less of eighteenth century America that one of Crevecoeur's nameless farmers. The ardor of experts accordingly carries them into the crevices of history; the overspecialization that sometimes renders them unfit to teach undergraduates is difficult to remedy.

Whatever the justification for specialization, American history in college education requires a broader emphasis. There is a place for the many branches of historical study—for economic history, for military history, for diplomatic history—but if history is to yield an insight into the meanings of democracy and American life, it must be concerned with society in its broadest sense.

The adequacy of historical instruction is measured less by how much students know than by what they know. American experience has a chronology, but it does not begin with Christopher Columbus. American life, in other words, does not begin with America nor indeed does it end there. If American history is approached with this in mind, we avoid distortion. Students perceive as much of the totality of American life as their growing knowledge and the depth of their imagination permits. The challenge for the teacher is to convert the abstract meanings of history into instruments of analysis by which the student can create his own meanings and interpretations.

Every historical situation begins with a context. In each historical situation certain factors are given: the physical mold, population ratios, relations of population to resources, the organization of learning, economic fact. The establishment and investigation of the social context opens up the total social process: of stability and change, of institutional development, of cultural modes of behavior. In the interrelations of the several parts—of, for example, population to natural resources, of resources to modes of behavior, of behavior to learning—outlines of "the totality" gradually take shape. The result is neither economics nor politics, technology nor art; it is history. By studying the parts in relation to evolving wholes, students are able to discern the limits of the possible in any given situation, to trace the arc of social malleability, to graph the areas of probable change. Such a factual basis yields theoretical insight: how human events are conditioned by geography, how intelligently directed human thought and action can control the malleable areas of a social context, how accidents or "intruding events" alter the contours of society.

The more thoroughly the interplay of these factors is understood, the more students are likely to grasp the meaning of change, of history as process. Indeed, the most searching questions which students ask about ideas, movements, and values in American life cannot be answered except in terms of a full analytical exposition of the cultural context. Why, for example, is so important a part of the history of democracy coincident with the history of the United States? What is the connection between democracy and the rapid development of natural resources following the industrial revolution? In what sense is modern democracy dependent upon the mass production of goods by machine processes? What is the significance of the distinction between democratic aspirations in the pre-industrial age and democratic potentialities in the age of the machine? If democracy is majority rule and majority rule is inconceivable without party government, how are the parties described by Hesiod different from the "factions" described by James Madison? And why are the parties of Jackson's day different from our own? The history of democracy is in part the history of the democratization of a concept because of changes in the organization of learning, population ratios, natural resources, and capital formation.

Democracy does not stop at the national border, nor is the history of democratic man the history of the United States. Thomas Jefferson and James Monroe claimed a uniqueness for the United States in these matters of democracy during the early decades of the nineteenth century. America was the home of the free, and as contrasted with Europe, offered the best opportunity for the continuation of the democratic experiment. In the twentieth century it is no longer possible to make such a claim.

The teaching of American history has nevertheless been provincial in outlook. Students are invited to examine "the European background of American history" by glancing at the Crusades. They are offered a glimpse of the riches of Cathay as seen through the eyes of Marco Polo and are rushed back to Europe in preparation for the Columbian voyages. The expansion of Europe thereafter remains an empty phrase, for once the new world is discovered, attention is focused on Western Europe. Portugal and Spain receive casual notice, but England has already become central. Once Columbus has made a landfall on October 12, 1492, there is a frenzied rush to reach 1607 and Jamestown. Historians from New England are often more anxious to reach 1620 and Plymouth. The expansion of Europe becomes lost in the discovery of America and the age of exploration in the settlement of the thirteen original colonies. Europe progressively recedes from the historian's perspective except during periods of recurring crises when excursions into "the European background" are necessary to make "diplomatic history" intelligible.

At best the teachers of American history have been concerned with the development of American culture along with the culture of Western Europe; at worst with chronological and geographical fragments of it. Only rarely have teachers of American history gone beyond Western Europe in their thinking, and now that the frontiers of Europe have in effect become the frontiers of the United States, there are some who urge that we stop there. Professional patriots, whose devotion to country seems to be largely geographical, are able to assign cogent reasons for beginning American history at Jamestown or Plymouth and ending at the national boundary. Those reasons, however, are inadequate for democrats. Teachers for whom the significance of the United States lies in the development of democracy begin their account long before Jamestown, and are interested in watching developments everywhere in the world for signs of democracy's success.

Moreover, the map of Europe and America has changed physically as well as culturally. The Europe of Stalin is not the Europe of Charlemagne, the Europe of Bismarck is not the Europe of de Gaulle. Nor is the America of Harry S. Truman the America of Abraham Lincoln, and as a matter of important fact, the America of Harry S. Truman is not the America of Franklin D. Roosevelt. Advocates of the view that American interest—political as well as intellectual—should be confined to the Atlantic Basin might redraw their maps, as others have suggested, to show the Western hemisphere as an island in a global world and Western Europe as a somewhat diminutive peninsula of the Russian-African-Asian land mass. Those who do so will find a significant key to the shift in power relations incident to the geographical revolution, as well as a key to the forces making the problems of man and society in 1950 different from what they were in 1939. Students born less than two decades ago are already immersed in the living of life defined by this newer physical and social context, and fearfully scan the future. Educational theorists with curricular blueprints for the salvation of youth do not impress them. They are much more likely to find themselves in virtual agreement with the assertion of Alfred North Whitehead that the whole tradition of Western society "is warped by the vicious assumption that each generation will substantially live amid the conditions governing the lives of its fathers and will transmit those conditions to mould with equal force the lives of its children. We are living in the first period of human history for which this assumption is false." Like Whitehead, who discovered a new universe in which older aphorisms simply do not apply, the modern student has grown up in a world which bears a scarcely recognizable relation to the issues ordinarily discussed in the history classroom.

Stresses in modern society making for global emphases are apparent enough, but America was an integral part of the world from its very beginnings. The discovery of the Americas resulted from the commercial upheaval of which Columbus was the symbol and the Western hemisphere an incident. The Americas were peopled by successive waves of immigration from older centers of population which had European causes as well as American results. European ideas, institutions, and values were transplanted to Plymouth, Boston, and Jamestown as well as to Mexico City, Darien, and New Amsterdam. The new world was Europeanized before European ideas, attitudes, and ways of behavior were altered to suit new conditions and new human wants. Every major change in the fabulous territory which, until the age of railroads and airplanes, blocked the path to the Orient registered on the minds of the citizens of Europe. From Peter Martyr, scholar of the fifteenth century renaissance, to modern scholars creating the renaissance of Jerusalem, America was a cultural fact that could not be left out. Nor were the ties of America with Europe ever broken. If the Declaration of Independence is an American document, it is also a European one. Actually, it is a human document in which there is no reference to race, creed, or nationality. It is significant that the Declaration, as well as the Atlantic Charter, became the hope of millions, not because of their national origin but because both documents gave expression to the perennial yearnings of man.

A major task of the college course in American history is to demonstrate the essential unity of the period from 1492 to 1950. American history as a separate discipline exists for scholars, but history itself takes place in America. There are certain fundamental cultural categories in which students and teachers must think. Otherwise history in America is studied in a vacuum.

American history, for example, begins in the delta of the Nile. Civilization commenced in the river valleys of the Tigris-Euphrates and the Nile, and moved by way of the Aegean islands to the Mediterranean. When civilization reached the Atlantic Ocean, American history specifically starts. Each area of the early world presented a different geographical and cultural mold: the riparian, the thalassic, and the oceanic. European history and hence American origins followed a westward course: from the river valleys of the ancient Near East to the peninsulas of the Mediterranean Sea. Greece precedes Italy and Italy precedes Spain. Spain, however, faces both the Mediterranean and the Atlantic, and with the rise of Spain a new epoch in the history of man commenced. America was discovered, settled, and developed entirely within the oceanic stage of human existence. Until our own day, America and the American way of life matured during one of the major stages of cultural evolution. But, more importantly, within our own day, another stage of human culture began clearly to emerge. The oceanic age has been succeeded by the global age. Recent history, consequently, is the history of a crucial transition. Franklin D. Roosevelt is as much the symbol of an evolutionary transition as Christopher Columbus symbolizes the transition to the new oceanic world.

With the discovery and settlement of the Americas, the history of Europe and the history of civilization altered markedly. Europe ceased to be isolated; European society expanded. The natural resources of the Western hemisphere remade society, and for the first time in human history democracy became a real possibility. Population multiplied; Western culture moved all over the globe. Feudal barons were succeeded by royal despots who were in turn succeeded by parliamentary governments of the middle class. And gradually the new middle class ousted the landed aristocracy from political and social power. Localism was replaced by nationalism; feudal decentralization by the central power of the national state. The Church Universal was challenged by the Reformation; the drama of salvation by the drama of life. The commercial revolutions produced a series of multiple revolutions in politics, in religion, and in culture. New attitudes, new institutions, new ways of behavior, new values resulted. And the revolutions in commerce were preludes to the revolutions in economics which created the machine age. These transformations unify the centuries from Magellan to the Wright brothers, and during these centuries, democratic values, ideas, and institutions matured. During these centuries the history of the United States was in the making.

American history, therefore, has a chronology, but it is not the chronology conventionally employed. If this historical sequence is longer and more difficult, it has the advantage of being more meaningful. But it demands that some items of American history be omitted; that some materials, long considered essential, must be replaced by others; and that more fertile relationships must be established between the great transitional periods of the past and the revolutionary transition which is our own. Specifically, it means that less undergraduate time must be spent on the colonial charters, more on the colonial movement as a process; less attention accorded to the revered monographs of Massachusetts history and more on cultural anthropology; less on the measured pace of the American westward movement, more on the affinities between the critical periods of transformation. The purpose, in other words, is to trace a pattern in bold, broad strokes, to stress similarities rather than differences, uniformities rather than diversities. Nationalistic history has obscured the pattern, and the task of undergraduate teaching is to discover similarities where nationalism has created differences. Nationalism is no better for being sublimated in the language of learning, nor is pride of race any better for being academic and polite.

Patterns, nevertheless, are not to be sought at the expense of the revelation of diversity. But which set of differences are most important for undergraduate learning? Differences between Massachusetts and Rhode Island in the seventeenth century are unquestionably significant, but the differences between Puritanism and left-wing sects are probably more consequential. It was as the cultural carriers of individualism that religious "enthusiasts" distressed the Puritan "elect." The manufacture of textiles in Rhode Island and Massachusetts exhibits interesting differences from the manufacture of clocks in Connecticut, but the connection between the commercial revolutions (from the twelfth century to the eighteenth) and the revolutions in economics (from the eighteenth to the twentieth century) are probably more vital from the standpoint of college education. The American character, due to the American way of life, developed out of the circumstances which conditioned it, and these conditions lie outside the formal scope of American history as well as within it. Oliver Cromwell had a hand in shaping it as did Jefferson; Imhotep as well as Watts.

Teachers have been satisfied with a provincial view of time just as they have been satisfied with a limited view of culture. By dividing time into rigid categories of past and present, historians have deprived contemporary culture of a past while robbing earlier cultures of a present. History is a temporal continuum. The past exists in every present while the present, yesterday's future, has already in some part influenced what is yet to be. The study of history contributes to a sense of the past, to an appreciation of the process of becoming, to a feeling for age. Students who perceive the genetic relations between Eli Whitney's principle of interchangeable mechanical parts and the principles of mass production have begun to acquire a feeling for the past. They have begun to acquire historical mindedness.

The existence of the past surrounds us completely. To demonstrate the ubiquity of the past students need simply to be reminded of those essential daily practices which show the operation of history in the present. The American businessman, archetype of modernity, honors punctuality and strives to capture time, but he measures it by means of a clock and records it by means of a calendar, methods of measurement achieved by the peoples of the ancient near east long before the mariners of Crete had made their way to the Greek peninsula. Awakened at the proper hour to catch the suburban train to town, the businessman breakfasts on cereals and processed food derived from practices discovered by the Egyptians. The train that transports him to town runs on wheels, a device upon which men labored when Egypt was young. And when finally he reaches his office situated in a building erected on principles of engineering known to the pyramid builders and often supported by columns which are Greek, he settles down to the business of the day. He deals in commercial paper—notes, bonds, mortgages—but is probably unaware of the fact that early progenitors of current forms may still be found written on tablets of clay in the mud of the Mesopotamian plain.

Yet in a real sense all history is contemporary history, for the past can never be wholly recovered. Any past is at best but partial, and whatever portion of an earlier age is recovered is selected, selected in response to contemporary issues, contempory standards, and contemporary values. Consequently, the past recreated by historians is never a literal past but a past conditioned by principles, goals, and objectives rooted in a given social context. Historical scholars can never truly evade the present by cultivating a past. On the contrary, while engaged in the cultivation of a past, historians are inescapably immersed in the present. The past is truly the living past, living precisely because vital parts of it are implicated in contemporary relations. "There is no material available for leading principles and hypotheses," writes John Dewey, "save that of the historic present." The meaning of any past then derives its significance from those seeking to understand it. Men are impelled to understand history *for* something, the resolution of a contemporary dilemma, the validation of a contemporary judgment. Comprehension of the past is a function of living rather than a methodological goal. Human beings *reconstruct* the past just as they reconstruct other types of data. And the importance of historical reconstruction becomes apparent when it is recalled that any interpretation is invariably selective.

Selection is unavoidable. But if selection is unavoidable, criteria are implicit and if we are faced with the necessity of choice, we are faced with the problems of value. Nor will reliance upon the "elemental fact" rescue the embattled historian from the necessity of coming to grips with measures of importance and standards of choice. Every fact—no matter how elemental—was once a theory. A fact becomes a fact only after prolonged investigation. One order of knowledge precedes such analysis; another order of knowledge follows it. the data of experience are subjected to a series of conceptual operations before factual status is attained. Even at this point, knowledge does not stem from particular facts, but from the relations established between them and other classes of facts. From this point of view all the so-called primal facts of life and nature are former concepts. And it is the concept, not the brute fact, which lies at the threshold of all inquiry. Concepts, fashioned by human beings for human ends, are charged with human hopes, ideals, and aspirations. Hypotheses cannot be evaded, for without hypotheses the isolated facts of human events like the discrete facts of human nature are barren of meaning or significance. But the priority of concepts in the construction of thought demands that we revise our notions of the relationship between concrete particulars and conceptual knowledge. The historian in any case can no longer hope that in capturing the "brute" fact—the objective data of manuscripts, coins, and monuments; of dates, battles, and documents—he has thereby succeeded in capturing knowledge.

If the past is always with us, it is in the present alone that we can attempt to use it. The present provides us with our intellectual motivation and generates our individual and social drives. Ideas are alive, it is only a convention of scholarship which petrifies them. Ideas are petrified when the present is amputated from the past, when they cease to have meaning for living ends. They then become in Whitehead's phrase "inert ideas," ideas without utility, without roots in life as actually lived, unrelated to the altering hopes and the changing bewilderments of existence.

Events should also be studied as they occur. A living relation is thereby established between past and present in which the student himself is the vital link. But the relationship must be natural and spontaneous, deriving from the experience of the student and the desire of the student to know. It must come out of the student's current learning, from the problems of class lectures, discussions, and reading as well as from the background of experience the student has brought to college. Let me illustrate with the case of one of my students. The transformation of society during the waning of the Middle Ages interested the student only mildly. The expansion of Europe, the era of discovery and colonization, offered revealing parallels to other periods, including the contemporary, which she was quick to note. But the analysis of the transplantation of institutions and ideas led her to wonder what was truly American. After reading Crevecoeur and de Toqueville, she decided to check their impressions against modern studies of "national character," checked in turn against "American types" in a large metropolitan area. For this purpose studies of immigrant groups and the acculturation process together with experimental studies in personality development were used in preparation for converting a part of the United Nations staff into a laboratory. She came to the conclusion that the national aspects of "character types" were transitory, that human aspects of personality were more basic however much they altered in response to tensions, aggressions, and hostilities. What distinguished Americans from others was the tradition of poor men or "common men" striving to be free of restrictions preventing them from becoming what they thought they could be. She concluded finally that the major cultural problem in the United States concerned the possibility of fulfilling the tradition of individual development, a tradition which began to take concrete form in modern times soon after Columbus discovered America.

For another of my students, it was the presidential campaign of 1948 which awakened her imagination and inspired her best energies. Stimulated by the news of election campaigning, this student was led to investigate the origin of the election system. The Electoral College, for example, began to acquire a significance for the first time. The experience of carrying out her own research made possible in her case an understanding of the relations between democracy and majority rule, for it established a genuine relationship between past and present. The student had already studied the operation of parties and the machinery of politics in books and documents, but the distinction between constitutional mechanics and the organic functions of government became real only after she had observed the process of government in action, and had calculated its social effects. The movement for the federal constitution and the struggle over its ratification acquired additional meanings in the light of current struggles between interest groups struggling for power within the two-party system, while the conflict of power blocs in an observable situation later sharpened her comprehension of the many-sided sectional conflicts on the eve of the American Civil War. Thereafter she was able to grasp the notion of institutions as instruments for individual and social ends, and that among these ends, she and her fellow students had a part.

If a presidential campaign provides insights into the dynamics of social relationships, close observation of other functioning institutions offers materials for field studies in cultural anthropology. A student who had done no work in social studies until her senior year came to American history with deeply-rooted anti-labor views. Her antipathy to unions was so passionate that she was confident further research would serve only to confirm them. Since she undertook a study of American economic problems with partisan convictions, government reports and the sober monographs of scholars merely strengthened her prejudice that all she had heard of the propagandist's art was true. She responded to the suggestion that she study labor at first hand with something less than alacrity, and once she had overcome her patrician scruples, she permitted herself to be introduced to a union leader. After she recovered from the shock of finding him both personable and grammatical, she attended a meeting of shop stewards at his invitation. Reporting the event, she confessed that she found the deliberations much more temperate and rational than she had anticipated, but concluded that the statement of workers' grievances had certainly been colored because of her presence. From the meeting of stewards she went to the shop, from the shop to the homes of workers, and from the homes of workers she went back to government reports and the analyses of the specialists. With this as a background, she read the statistics of the distribution of wealth with growing interest and mounting confidence. She was beginning to see how institutions operate and alter, how some institutions fulfill men's needs while others frustrate them. Thereafter she discovered that the meaning of the internal revolution during the struggle for American independence had really escaped her and she reread the class assignments covering that period. "I think," she remarked at the end of a conference session on the Declaration of Independence, "I am beginning to understand the connection between equality of opportunity and democracy." If she did not know what John Dewey meant by the "going concerns" of society, she had gained an awareness of the continuing effect of older occurrences in human history that still shape the lives of living men. She had learned that there was a continuity of social attitudes, of patterns of behavior, and that there was a variety of traditions in America, many of them still operative as spurs to human action. She had also begun to appreciate that no group enjoys a monopoly of wisdom and righteousness, that the general welfare in a democracy is never achieved by victory of a special interest.

When students are educated in this way, they ask themselves the fundamental question: How do I know? They do this, not because they are asked to read a paper to a class, or submit it to a teacher, but because they have undertaken to investigate something of importance to themselves. The student is trying to find an answer to questions he has himself raised, questions which can only be answered by hard work and independent investigation. Here the teacher is presented with a rare opportunity to present the value of scholarly method, to encourage the intellectual virtues of accuracy and precision. By challenging every fact, by exploring each hypothesis, the student comes to learn from his own intellectual venture and from his own private resources what the teacher himself and the volumes of scholarship have been desperately trying to say.

Appreciation of the connections between past and present helps students to locate themselves as individuals within the historical process. In one sense, men control society by understanding it. But the more that students know about themselves and their culture, the more they are enabled to make a fuller use of their own potentialities. To achieve historical mindedness, students must immerse themselves in history. They must know that part of the past which has conditioned the present. And they must study the world in which they live—the merger of present and future—in order to learn how they, as individuals, as well as the society of which they are parts, has been shaped by history. By observing closely how ideas, techniques, and institutions alter, they observe history in the making. This is the beginning of intelligent choice and the testing ground of values. It is not so much that the study of history can tell a student exactly what to do, but a student can learn to make choices by understanding how historical events actually occur. The beginnings of intelligent choice lie in the recognition of the areas where change is creatively possible.

Like all history, the American record teaches the value of the past. Thomas Jefferson is dead, the draft of the Declaration is already yellowing with age, but the philosophy of the Declaration still generates responses in the minds of millions here and abroad. That governments derive their just powers from the consent of the governed is a living article of the democratic creed. The twentieth-century problem is an institutional one: how to determine the needs of the governed, how to elicit their consent to programs designed to meet those needs, and how to mobilize that consent for social action.

American traditions are alive, although the men who once gave them expression in word and action exist only in history. But because they continue to exist in history, men still act upon those traditions. It is in this sense, as Carlyle said of Boswell's Johnson, that history, greater than fiction, is poetry. And it is in this sense, too, that history gives to all those possessing imagination an added dimension of thought and understanding. Men rebel against active oppression or resist the subtler oppression of cultural constrictions. But they resist them only in part because fulfillment yields satisfaction and frustration creates tension. They are also impelled to do so because the tradition of democracy proclaims that man should be free, free to develop his humanity. We call upon the past to vindicate our urge to create a democratic society first because we are human and are moved by the urge, then because, being democratic, we are heirs to a tradition. The tradition goes back to Roger Williams and John Wise, to Joel Barlow and Thomas Jefferson, to Jackson, to Lincoln, and to Whitman. But in the texture of the tradition there are other strands. Whitman is an American variant of human aspiration in the formulation of which Kant, Hegel, and Darwin commingle. Jefferson is an American symbol of Cicero, of Locke, of Rousseau. Democrats in America have always dissented from threats to democracy in their times because every evil in American history produced a social retort, every violation of human rights created a crusade.

American history, like every other, also teaches the value of the present. It is in the present that the past comes to life; in the present that the forces of change and the forces of stability clash to form the issues which give meaning to thought and action. Likewise, it is in the present that the American heritage is constantly redefined by a union of the traditions of the past and the insistent needs of newer generations. It is in the present that processes of history become continuous.

Comments on Art and Education

KURT ROESCH

Experience teaches us that every expression is the result of one's own life experiences. It would be easy to assume a variety of possible experiences, common to all of us, which would necessarily be followed by expressions understandable and common to everybody. This is—as we all know—not possible, so many of our experiences have not arrived at adequate forms of expression, and are neither communicable nor have they touched the conscious self of the person involved. We call them experiences in spite of ourselves, though what really occurs is that a reality is falling upon us; it is a passive situation which we endure without form. Such a situation of receptivity or formlessness may be enjoyable to some, but others may experience distress. "It is only when the distress is upon us that we can be said to strive, to crave, or to aspire. When enjoying plenary freedom either in the way of motion or of thought, we are in a sort of anaesthetic state in which we might say with Walt Whitman, if we cared to say anything about ourselves at such times: I am sufficient as I am."*

The striving for adequate expression can never complete itself in an absolute form: different forms of expression are way-stations to adequacy. It is a part of the dilemma of men that only partial communication is possible, since nothing we think, do, or explain can be completely understood, even by ourselves. When we think of the exactness of the mathematical sciences, we contrast them with the arts. People let mathematics *be* mathematics when they try to learn that science, and make no special demands which can stand between themselves and the symbols. In connection with the equations of the mathematician, most of us are not inclined to ask that the mathematician show us the "beautiful equation" he has made. We assume that the mathematician had no wish to express

* William James, *Mind*, July, 1879.

himself, though the result of his work is an expression: an expression of equality between two magnitudes. We suspect that his equation has to be understood, and not merely be "felt." In contrast to this attiutde we seem to "think" that a work of art—one we like—can be felt, but does not need to be understood. We assume that an artist expresses himself, and forget that his work is an expression of an artistic idea in the same sense as the mathematician expresses a mathematical idea. Of course, both men's work is based on sets of experiences; but people do not let art *be* art, and many things stand between people and art. The occasion for removing a few of these "many things" is an education in seeing.

The diversity of the visible world around us is tremendous, and no one perceives this manifoldness more strongly than children. How many leaves has a tree? A child draws the tree, and instinctively it reduces the numbers of leaves and draws a simplification of a tree which we take for a child's simplicity of seeing. Children's endless questions are also nothing else than a constant craving for a simplification of their experiences, whatever they are. Children can hardly avoid looking at, and touching everything in sight. It is a way of meeting the shape and texture of the different objects they observe, because without touch, a child would only experience a part-impression of an object. A child wants to *acquire* the visible world, and takes an active part in doing so. The perception obtained by merely looking at an object is not enough for the child, it longs for complete identification. We try to help children to satisfy this need. We simplify their experiences by answering their questions in a simple way, using an inherited form, our language, but allow them only in a limited way—limited to ready-made toys, and limited to unobserved moments in the house —to use their hands to feel and touch the things they see.

We divert the child's interest in touching everything, and direct its interests. We give the child a picture book. There is a picture of a cow. "This is a cow," repeats Mary after her mother has read it and explained it to her. The picture of a cow does not mean a thing to Mary, because she has never seen or touched a cow; it only suggests—by some lines, and some blotches of color—the idea that mother knows an animal which produces the milk the child likes to drink. It means two visual conversions. First, that Mary's first experience of a cow has been received in the same way as the word-symbol: a linear symbol, made by an artist, has been given to her. In other words, the word-cow and the picture-cow, given to Mary at the same time, have become identical. Second, in case Mary ever has a chance to look at a cow in real life, she will not see her any more, because it will be sufficient for Mary to recognize a cow in comparison with her first impression. This example could be easily multiplied, and varied in relation to where people live and grow up, in the city or in the country.

Think of all the pictures in children's books of little girls, and ladies, and grandmas, and little boys, supermen, and horses, and dogs—all drawn and painted as they are supposed to look, in order to standardize millions of Mary's experiences. Funny papers, movies, and similar visual abracadrabas will do the rest, and provide the children with "experiences," promising to twist and hinder the real experiences of seeing. When the children have collected this "visual reservoir of forms," and they can recognize all the things, living or dead, by comparison with the printed productions of our time, they do not feel the need to see them anymore. We say, "The child has now grown up."

Our satisfaction is great, but we seem to be unable to recall that the young person now misses the real experiences of seeing, which means that he misses a great number of experiences altogether. The "experiences," which are constantly delivered in all those different and abbreviated sketches, furnish a child only with a rudimentary sense of recognizing things. Muddled thinking, seeing, and feeling is the result of such a passive reception which our society inflicts upon its children. A totality of so-called experiences is suggested to them before they can be consumed, and this fact alone complicates the chances of growing up.

One positive and important fact appears: all this nonexperience, and inability to touch everything in sight, sets an activity into motion in young children which is, in a limited sense, an artistic activity. It arouses a wish to go beyond the saying "yes" to the purely recognizable in a ready-made fashion.

At this stage most young people begin to show signs of what

parents like to refer to as "creative ability" or "talent." I should prefer to call it simply an energy, in contrast to inertia; the energy which young people feel which makes them want to use their eyes, and hands, and to play with colors, or with clay, or with any other material which by itself represents nothing, but lends itself easily to making something out of it. Once in school, these children want to study one of the different arts.

Those progressive educators are sentimental who like to imagine the children's vision as being unspoiled, pure, and innocent. On the contrary, children are filled with unclear and trivial notions, unelastic, they think primarily with words, they are inhibited in their capacity to see.

The most important characteristics of children who present themselves to the teacher of art is their energy, their wondering, and their desire to impose themselves upon reality and to make it take heed of them. An education neglecting this energy and wondering would be purely rationalistic. It would be inhuman to insist that man has permission to use only his practical and rational faculties at every stage of life for the sake of his survival. Occasionally we allow him to interrupt his rational activities to glance admiringly or irritatedly at other people's artistic expressions. But the gifts of the human being include unknown qualities and virtues which reach beyond the rational, and are not independent of our own sense perceptions and emotions. The energy within us, and a forgotten, neglected, or undeveloped state of consciousness, drives us to search for clarity and form. Man's desire to overcome the naked necessities of his existence makes him search for, and find, more forms than one, to gain his freedom. The desired and necessary forms can be found in the different arts, in science, and in philosophy.

Rationalistic teaching follows only one idea: that our existence has a definite meaning and purpose, to be gained by reason alone, and for which we have conveniently established norms of order. Instruction in the use of such norms of order, and a student's diligence to accept and follow them, would give him clarity about nearly everything. The idea is static and intellectualistic. It excludes the emotional, the irrational within us. It excludes the dynamic, and the elasticity of the whole being.

Art education should be a legitimate field of education, and art should not be the leisure-time course which offers merely a kind of "creative outlet" with incidental emotional happenings, somewhat useful for different practical or therapeutic purposes. Art education makes sense only if art is conceived to be as central to life and to education as any other activity, and is not merely tolerated as a "cultural ornament."

A student of art must be taught to find the rules for each individual work as he discovers them during the process of his own creative effort. Artistic laws emerge from executed work. There are, unfortunately, many teachers who are satisfied with their students only when a preconceived idea has been completely executed. This has the same effect upon the student as it does upon the artist; namely, that the individual freedom of his work is strangled. The execution of work by students according to the laws of a teacher is the mark of those industrious professionals—teachers who teach the how, or students who employ the trick—who take aesthetic delight in manipulating the "instruments" of the artist with the absence of understanding of what it means to see and think visually.

One of the reasons for assuming basic laws for teaching art is the idea, or rather the doctrine, of the unchangeable character of art. Yet our empirical observation today teaches us something upon which many philosophers have agreed; it cannot be said that things "are," only that they become or evolve. But art is expected to stay satisfied with the ideas of the Renaissance. (There is not a single institution where the sciences are taught with the knowledge of the time of the Renaissance.) Students who are studying art are living today and not in the time of the Renaissance or in the nineteenth century. They see with their eyes today, and not with historical eyes.

A teacher of art must be a student with every student as well as a teacher. If he were only a teacher, he would become that person who leaves all experiences and experimentation to others, imagining himself to be the sum of all others. Then he would begin to teach Art—which nobody can teach. One can only teach students.

In a pamphlet published by the army during the war, it was suggested to instructors of the air force: "Remember, you are not teaching how to fly an airplane, you are teaching students, and the only difference between you and your students is that you did the flying before." This is a good conception of teaching, and though it may sound simple, it is a difficult thing to carry out. Has not a teacher to know everything a student does not know? No, not in the field of art education. The student searches for what is unknown to him and also unknown to his teacher. There is always the unknown formation of an experience which will be a surprise to student and teacher alike.

Students who wish to take a course in art express their feelings by simply naming a goal: "I wish to become an artist," or saying: "I love art, and it always interested me," and so on. Can we recognize "motivation" in such statements? A motivation sufficient enough to make sure that the student won't waste his time? Such general statements express nothing else but an interest of the student. This interest alone should be justification enough to advise a student to enter a studio. The fact that only a certain number of students dare to mention it is partly caused by neglect in the usual academic system, a neglect which fails to recognize the study of art as a proper academic subject, partly by the prevailing notion that artistic talent is necessary for the study of art. Students state that notion this way: "I can't draw a straight line." Here we come across another idea, fostered by academicians of all branches: that art is a technique. If it were a technique it would be very simple, and everybody could acquire it and produce works of art. People should not say "I cannot draw," but rather "I cannot *see*."

We are using our eyes most of our time; why shouldn't we train our eyes to see more clearly? As a famous physician once said to his colleagues who congratulated him on an important discovery which became obvious after it had been discovered: "I am not brighter than you, and my medical knowledge and education are the same, but once I studied art with a good teacher, and I learned to see better." It should be easy to understand that the training of the eye could be of the greatest value to many different human activities, not to mention living itself. What we usually call seeing is nothing else but the act of recognizing something which is already familiar to us, be it a chair, or a class ring, or a mother's face. If we could really see, we would buy, use, or make better chairs, or rings, and also understand our mother better.

Education in our institutions of learning is fundamentally based on language. A society without language is impossible to think of. What we call man's intellectual consciousness happens through this inherited, specific material. Forming of words into sentences gives us a consciousness, familiar to us, and creates meaning in our mind. Even unspoken thoughts are shaped in our minds through word concepts. Sometimes art has been called a language too, but the visual process of becoming conscious is not a language, not even figuratively speaking. Visual thoughts are not thoughts expressed as in writing. Visual thinking happens in forms, color, space, and line, and it should be clear that such thinking can only come about through the forming processes in one of its materials. The hand does not do something which has already been formalized in the mind before, but the combined doing of hand-eye-mind-emotion produces, in an indivisible process, a thought. By going through the artistic (visual) forming process himself, a student studies art and learns to see.

Institutions of learning are founded on old traditions. Classic ideas prevail in respect to art, and we are directly or indirectly brought up with those ideas. The contributions of modern philosophers, artists, and educators have not noticeably changed the old ideas in respect to art and art education, except in the nursery schools. At the base of it all sits the spirit of Plato and his Idealism. Plato wished to save the idea of an absolute knowledge, and he refuted the relativism of the Sophists. Plato did not settle the problem of relativism. Instead he retreated from the sensuous world altogether to another world of knowledge. A large portion of the history of philosophy followed along behind him. Everything became subordinate to word-thinking, which alone could give the idea of reality. Artistic doing was pleasantly accepted as a useful but inferior human activity.

On the other hand, people—primitive as well as civilized—feel that life without art lacks something—a spiritual element. Yet, such deficiency could not interrupt or disrupt our life. Most would still agree with Félibien, one of the first art critics of the seventeenth century: "The light of reason is superior to anything the workman's hand is capable of executing." Indeed, hand and eye would be secondary if art existed only as an added spiritual element, with a few people busy "making profession of dumb things." The primary and most important reason for the existence of art is, that without it our reality and concept of life would be more incomplete than it is bound to be anyway. Many people, however, recognize this reality only after it has passed. The majority of the people, living behind their time, believe that the artist is always ahead of his time. This is not true, the artist lives exactly in his time.

If we are careful not to divide the single individual into different compartments, we should understand that the artistic activity asks the individual to attain a balance of the emotional and intellectual substances he possesses. A student, by going through the artistic processes, will learn about the "nature of things," a "nature" which includes himself. It is not so-called talent which makes this study significant. It is the opportunity to allow an energy, as it was called earlier, to be developed in its pertinent field of study. In this sense one can say that the goal of art education is art; but not a training in how to become an artist, or an instruction in how to create works of art.

It is a fact that art exists as much as science in our time. Its "irrational quality" can be perceived and understood as well as felt, because it takes a form, and this form is the manifestation of certain experiences. Art is not a contrast of beauty with "real" life, to be used as a moderate stimulus during some moments of leisure. Like science, art finally leads beyond the different individual desires and attitudes.

We begin with the subjective in this study, and grow slowly towards the objective, which in the end we like to call knowledge, in this case, a knowledge of art. It will make the further question "knowledge for what" dispensable, because the process of doing the work in art has served us with an answer.

A teacher cannot supply a student with his own experiences or emotions or knowledge. Neither teacher nor student knows about the irrational material which lies concealed, before it appears in the work. The processes of work are as different as there are different persons in the studio.

A variety of materials can be used in visual education. It depends upon the individual student to explore a number of them or to limit himself to one alone. The empty piece of canvas or paper provides the first artistic consternation for every beginner. There is also no library in the background which supplies the student with saving references. The studio is filled with silence, and the teacher has to use words, and avoid them at the right moment. The teacher may ask his students to close their eyes, and hold their hands open, and pass around a familiar object, i.e., an apple, and an unfamiliar object, i.e., a small, twisted piece of iron. After these objects have made the round, and have been felt by everybody, he will ask the students to draw those objects. It is impossible to describe the resulting variety of the drawings; there will be none alike. The teacher may also ask his students to make another drawing: to draw something they have never seen, and never expect to see. And another one: to draw something they remember well, be it their dog, or their couch, or their grandmother. The teacher may ask them to do as their first homework a self-portrait in any material they prefer; one drawing in front of the mirror, and a second one by memory.

All these beginnings may go on for a while until the teacher has the feeling that he is able to recognize the different students' memory, imagination, capacity for observation, manual facility, visual influences, and visual "age level." In the meantime, the teacher must give the students a chance to get acquainted with him and his ideas. He will talk to them about the ideas and concepts of "memory," "imagination," "observation," "facility." He will also have individual conferences with each student. Everything ought to contribute to getting acquainted with each other. Discussions will be held, and not necessarily on art, but rather on, let's say, the "George Washington Bridge," or the different types of chairs, or the shape of the new "Studebaker," or a discussion about advertisements and fashion drawings. Discussions on such topics will help to make clear certain confusions about art. The student must learn to distinguish between the constructions of the engineer and the designs of a designer of motor cars; between the craft of the carpenter and the technique of the commercial artist.

After the first beginning another beginning is made. Soon the teacher will know where creative energy has been suppressed by circumstances. It will have to be re-awakened. If the energy has been disturbed, it has to be re-assured. If it has taken a blind direction, it has to be re-directed. It is the talent of a teacher to discover the quality and quantity of the energy a student has. A teacher cannot fill a student with that energy or with art, but he can do a great deal by emptying him of all the things which becloud his capacity for visual thinking.

Artistic elements have to be studied. They are the material out of which the forms are made in drawing and painting. Some six hundred odd colors which we get by mixing pigments need to be learned, and experimented with; students need to observe their behavior in different situations. Colors are like people, they keep their individuality but change their behavior in different contexts. Lines too are complicated elements. The most difficult element is space. To talk about these elements in words, and to describe how a student is experimenting with them, must necessarily remain unclear to people outside of the studio where the experiments are done. The language used in a studio is traditionally as restricted as in any other field—physics or mathematics for instance—which use symbols for the purpose of translating another material.

Take, for example, the idea of "Perspective." It is relatively easy to talk about the perspective of the Renaissance, or the horizon line, because everybody is familiar with that idea of an organization of space. It has been taught for the last four hundred years. But take a modern idea of perspective. Here we find different artistic elements (volume of color, primary or dual colors, one degree of the achromata, lines, and so on) on and in the chosen space which expands and contracts, according to the relationships between the different artistic elements. This space cannot be measured, and it is not a detail of a composition in proportion to the whole, but rather the sum of many different points which makes the whole.

There is a danger in an art education which pays great attention to the study of form and experiments with artistic elements. Students may think that the experimentation with color, line, and space will enable them to make systematic "abstractions." Unfortunately, such a knowledge, separated from its purpose, leads to nothing more than a kind of empty millinery. Also the drafts of the engineer should not be imitated, or the psychologist's way of thinking mimicked in the student's work. All such misunderstandings can happen, but should be noticed by the teacher in time. Everything becomes visible in art education. A student cannot hide behind his work.

The disciplines which art and its material demand should not be avoided. Such a neglect would lead to a dissolution of thinking. On the other hand, the teaching of techniques is a bad idea. Such training neglects thinking, and the danger is disorientation in art and life. It overemphasizes the *how* of what has to be done, and the much more important meaning of the study will be lost. Students can easily confuse resulting effects with creative force.

It is the teacher's job to teach the student to learn to avoid the limiting chances in his work. Incidental chances do not bring freedom of expression to a work; they only lead to a playful jumble. But since there is always more than one possibility in organizing, it is necessary to discuss the different possibilities with the student, until he has found his rules for his specific work. These self-found rules are always different in relationship to dissimilar experiences, and the metamorphoses of image and memory.

Artistic control is a condition of a ready, receiving spirit which is open to every idea, every feeling and emotion to select the necessary without succumbing to sheer temperament. The teacher should try to lighten the burden of the onrush of the emotions and the irrational. He should guide the student in a loose direction, so-to-speak, following him on all his detours.

The student's work is always unfinished, "unterminated" work in the following sense: the student uses a material, and brings his forms to a conclusion which is on the level of his own experience and understanding. Just as an artist does not know about the outcome of his own work, the teacher should not assume a goal for his student's work. Any forced goal in connection with art education is a persuasion to a dead end, and not a support for a new beginning. Art, as such, cannot be taught, but creative energy can easily be killed. It is an error to understand student's work from a point of view which takes the end-effect for the final and finished result. Teacher and student ought to understand the work from its point of departure, unmolested by possible pictorial effects and results.

The idea of the result, the "finished" picture or drawing, fosters necessarily the idea of "talent" in the young person. Students begin to compare their drawings with those of Michelangelo, and their water-colors with those of Matisse. This either discourages one student or makes another conceited. The easy conferment of the word "talent" makes it difficult for young people to acquire a discipline in their visual thinking because they learn to get accustomed to trust their own temperament, which they like to call intuition. Occasionally it therefore becomes nearly impossible for a student to be open to artistic influences, for fear of losing his "style."

The fanciful notion of "originality" in our time tries to let us forget the origin which every originality must have. The origin of art is always the same: in the tradition of the artist. We can frequently observe that people who are too convinced of their own originality are willing to praise everything (from cooking and mountain climbing, to art and ventriloquism) which they feel technically unable to do themselves—in order to be fair. Yet that which they consider easy to do, they will criticize—on the grounds that it is not original. It is the anarchic taste of the day, as André Gide once said, which lets us forget that an artist is not self-begotten. Applied to education, this means that the idea of the "original talent" hurts the development of the young person who is supposed to be endowed with it.

We find another type of person among students. He is the person who wishes to play aimlessly in drawing or painting. He should leave the studio and play somewhere else. It would be unfair to this student to expose him to "discipline" by suggesting to him the value of making "correct" drawings of vases, or a drawing after the plaster cast of the bust of Caesar, in order to correlate history and art. But the worst of all would be to direct such an aimless student —who presumably loves art—into a class of Art Appreciation. Under this name anything can happen: memorizing of names and dates, or instruction in the trick of knowing how to distinguish between an abstract, non-objective, surrealistic, naturalistic, impressionistic masterpiece. Such a course is perfectly useless from any point of view, be it from the educational or artistic; it contributes to the general confusion about art, artists, nature, and the life of man. Many of the ready-made answers about art, taste, and particularly about "beauty" derive from it.

Who is the person to be in charge of teaching students in a studio? For this, we should prefer the "living" artist. By virtue of his own work and knowledge and understanding, he is apt to guide the young students more comprehensively than a teacher who is not an artist. He knows by his own work the difficulties and the many different ways which are possible and necessary to arrive at seeing. Since there is no objective method or system for teaching "Art," he will be satisfied in teaching students how to see-feel-think more clearly, and make it possible for art to become part of the "business of living."

Delacroix once said that the words of an artist about art are nothing but an explanation of his own work. Indeed, words are not fitting material for a painter to express his thoughts adequately. Of all kinds of material, words are the most risky for him, and very rare have been the artists who have been successful in using them. Hence we have the popular notion that artists utter a variety of artistic prejudices. Yet people who do not practice an art, and teach it, are taking another risk, and no matter how fluently they may use words, their words could be nothing else but an explanation of their own or other people's words about art.

An artist who teaches students must use his words with infinite care. Words should never be the ground on which his students build their own experiences and expressions, a kind of pictorial interpretation of the teacher's words. The best learning happens through the constant exchange of ideas, and the spirit of criticism of the students among themselves, working together.

On the other hand, a student must go to see the art of the museums and galleries. The student will slowly learn to "listen" to them. He must learn to bring himself into a state of thinking and feeling *with* a work of art. This means seeing, and following the action (life) of the forms in the work. Then he will be able to meet the experiences of an artist, because he has received the expression (forms) of that work. It is clear that the student is able to see the expression (forms) because he has learned to know forms by having experimented with forming expressions himself. It is the opposite of agreeing or disagreeing with a work of art. Such a procedure is an arbitrary act of self-expression, and therefore dilletantism. The personal delight of saying "Yes" or "No" to something without understanding it, excludes actual experience.

A scientific work can be judged only with knowledge in the specific field of science to which it belongs. If such a work is felt to be of no value for an uninformed onlooker, it does not mean that such a specific science is worthless. But how is it in connection with art? First, everybody who has aesthetic judgment, and everybody has it, judges works of art. If it happens that the works dissatisfy his aesthetic sense, he will find it easy to refuse a whole group of specific artistic productions. Second, since aesthetic judgment is not based on artistic knowledge, a person will measure the work of art by some other knowledge he has, or thinks he has, be it literature, psychology, or anatomy.

In science, in law, in medicine, and in all other fields—business included—it takes a long time before people "know." People study and practice their respective fields. People learn to read before they understand the meaning of the printed word. But the arts are an open lake into which everybody feels himself invited to plunge. It seems to be the property of all men.

Yes, art can belong to everybody who has learned to see and think. No matter how bewildering and disturbing the forms of our art today may appear to the masses of people, all are influenced by their occurrence, and it should be their privilege—in a modern society—to learn to understand art through an unspecialized education. Specialized training of a special ability in one direction or another may come afterwards.

Would we have medicine if our students had learned nothing about the human body, if people still agreed with Paracelsius that leeches could cure an acute attack of appendicitis? How can the arts be expected to live and continue to exist in a civilization if people have no understanding of the arts themselves? It makes a great difference in the life of a nation whether artists, educators, and public leaders proclaim that people have a *right* to communicate with art, or whether they say that people have the great *wish* to communicate with art. If one insists that people have a "right" to art, one has also to admit they have a right to get "their own particular art." Wherever there are no cultural rights of this kind, there are also slaves. It is obvious in the case of art who would be the slave. It would be the artist. In authoritarian societies we can observe the suppression of one "right" to art, in dogmatic preference of another, for purposes which lie entirely outside of art. Students must learn to understand these things from the point of freedom of expression, not only from a political or economic point of view. Through art, students can learn how artists have gained, lost, and regained what is a common desire to all of us: freedom of the human spirit in form, in a visible order, and not in anarchy. Each generation has to obtain this freedom by its own experience. Art thus sustains that intangible quality of all men, "bringing nothing but profit if we, in our turn, set ourselves to school with it."

Education and the Family

LOIS B. MURPHY

I

Many different observers of family life today have centered their attention on the importance of the mother-child relationship. They have emphasized the significance of the child's emotional experiences in the day-by-day life at home, and the ways in which feelings of security and acceptance, making for strength of personality, are communicated to the child. These emphases are expressed in different terms, but all imply that prospective mothers need help in emotional development. It is not merely knowledge which they need. It is a matter of emotional maturity. Nor is emotional development only the task of women's colleges. Every college must have this as one of its major concerns.

In his stimulating book, *Personality and the Cultural Pattern*, Dr. James Plant distilled out of fourteen years of experience with children two major psychological needs for whose fulfillment women are primarily responsible, either in the family or in the school. Every child needs the sense of belonging and he needs to know *who he is*—the feeling of being wanted, no matter what comes, or what his failures and mistakes may be. This sense of belonging comes earliest from being lovingly held, fondled, and played with. It comes from the sense of intimacy and special closeness that grows in a happy family. This is something different from the education any school can give.

What can the school give? Dr. Plant's answer is that it can help the child to learn *what he is*—what he can do, where he fits, how he can meet the needs of others outside of the family, in just what niche he is going to be most adequate. This sense of adequacy is the school's chief gift, and we may assume that the school fails if it fails to help the child develop a sense of adequacy to the world outside of home, and if it fails to help him find the role, the niche in which he *can* be adequate.

Mothers and teachers set the stage for the child's development. What are the characteristics of the stage-setting that are important? Probably the most important of all are what Plant calls the psycho-motor tensions in the group, or the atmosphere conveyed to the children by the personalities of mothers and teachers. The atmosphere may be one of artificial quiet and anxious authority, or of free enjoyment and relaxed behavior; it may be one of nervous competition, or one of affectionate security. A compulsive, anxious, strained teacher or mother will not usually be able to communicate a sense of genuine ease to her children, nor give them a sense of belonging and of adequacy. Yet the college girl has little preparation of this kind for the role of married woman, or for the emotional adjustments involved in being responsible for a family, or for the flexibility, versatility, and emotional depth she needs in order to be a wife and mother.

In America today, a great deal of effort is spent in training graduate social workers to administer different kinds of therapy to patients who need emotional release and personal insight which they have not been able to attain. Actually these forms of therapy would not be needed at older ages if the emotional growth of the child had been adequate. Every child needs unconditional support and understanding, along with the direction and guidance which it is the adult's responsibility to give him. Every child is entitled to have many areas of release. He is also entitled to know the limits allowed to him while he is learning to channel his impulses. Too often children get the direction and the limits, without the support and release.

College courses seldom deal with these fundamentals of relationships between people, in the family and in other areas of life. On the other hand, mere textbook analysis of the emotional needs of children will have little effect in educating students for family life. What is needed is a direct awareness of how these human problems can be solved, and what the problems themselves are like when they are actually faced by human beings. Students need to see the relation between the emotional needs of children, the responsibilities of the mother, and the whole sweep of family life. At Sarah Lawrence we have tried many ways of developing this

kind of emotional insight and have come to believe that the best
way is by asking students to make close observations in families and
institutions and to report their discoveries to the members of their
class and to their teachers. Here are some reports of students who
have been through this experience.

I was very impressed with the visit to the Foundling Hospital. The main
thing which now stands out in my mind is that I didn't realize how many
small babies are left to the care of nurses and hospital wards. It was de-
pressing to see row after row of these children and to realize that life
starts like that for so many. . . . Many of the children were constantly
in motion—standing in their cribs and holding onto the rail—while they
swayed back and forth, or continually banged their heads against the edge
of the crib or the glass of the enclosing window. Some, however, lay
perfectly still—sucking toes or fingers, lying apathetically and staring at
the ceiling, or with their eyes closed in what seemed a semi-doze. One
little boy was lying on his side with both feet thrust awkwardly out
through the bars of the crib. A few children seemed to be not in the least
disturbed by their unnatural (out of the normal) surroundings. One little
red-headed boy, in particular, stood in his crib, holding onto each side
and shook it so hard that it actually moved, with a great deal of banging
noise. Many did show interest in the outside world, watching us intently
and smiling small smiles occasionally. There were some, particularly one
little girl, who cried violently the whole time we were in the ward—ten
or fifteen minutes—and was still crying when we left.

The thing that struck me most was the atmosphere in the wards. There
was so little noise, so little activity, and I guess most obvious of all, such
a complete lack of gaiety. I know that young babies do very little, but
there is a contented, well-satisfied, well-fed look about the average baby
which was missing here.

Another student reports this for the class record:

The main feeling I had when I left the Foundling Hospital was depression. The rooms were cheerless cubicles filled with iron cribs and dull,
apathetic babies. It was very difficult to tell the difference in ages. The
Sister who was showing us around didn't know, so unless the children
were walking in the play room or were still very tiny infants, it was almost
impossible to approximate their ages. For the most part they would lie
listlessly in their cribs, staring at the ceiling. When I tapped at the glass
nearly all of them responded in some way. One little boy tried very hard
to touch my hand; it seemed to mean a great deal to him and he cried
when he realized it was impossible. Other children would smile at me or
just stare at me, and then there were a very few who made no response
at all.

Seeing the children at the Foundling Home emphasized and drove deeper Ribble's and Aldrich's theory of "mothering" children. I had found it hard to believe that babies could really become seriously physically ill or just waste away because of lack of love. However, that is exactly what I believe has happened in the case of these dull, lifeless little children. Certainly their food is nutritious (even if it is given to them in tin cups); their rooms and cribs seemed clean, if dismal, but as for stimulation of any sort, there seemed to be none.

Not only the scientific facts and theories of human emotions are uncovered here by these trips and the subsequent reports, but also the pathos and tragedy of the neglected people of the world. This experience with babies has many more effects upon the student's understanding of human problems than appears on the surface. It helps in the entire area of human relations and personal insight.

Other ways of reaching the student can be found, even in the conventional baby-sitting job, provided the student is instructed as an observer, not simply a sitter. Consider the following paragraph from a report by a student who spent Thursday afternoons for several months with the baby she describes, and found that her field work with Jane from her fourth to tenth month gave her a feeling of security with her own baby born a couple of years later:

To begin with, it seems to me that if ever a baby was being given a fine opportunity to live and learn to live, Jane is that baby. Perhaps the thing that impressed me most on that score is the way she is handled and accepted by her family. From the dog to the family laundress, they have all obviously followed Mrs. Thomas' pattern of accepting the baby as an individual—someone who likes to be talked to and to be loved—someone who requires care and attention, but not to the exclusion of everybody else. As a result, Jane is a very even-tempered, happy baby.

Actually, children are the most complex products of nature; by comparison atoms, molecules, bacteria, and even rats are models of simplicity. It is necessary that men and women should bring all the depth of knowledge and scientific resourcefulness that can be brought, to the understanding of how children grow and what their behavior really means. Yet other courses than those concerned with the psychology of children are of similar importance. At Sarah Lawrence the students who show the richest response to the implications of their own behavior are apt to be those who have already learned to "see" the things which the painter and teacher, Kurt Roesch, has taught them, or have learned to grasp the meanings of symbols and mythology through work in philosophy and literature with Joseph Campbell. It is a mistake to assume that insight into emotional problems can be isolated in courses of psychology. When the curriculum is constructed so that the meaning of human experience is constantly related to the curricular materials, the total curriculum will have the effect of maturing the student's mind and emotions.

Emotional maturity and warmth cannot grow when feelings are shut out and repressed, and the repressive forces in our culture have been many. The high frequency of frigidity among American college women can hardly be laid at the door of education alone. However, education has not helped much to prevent it—there is a pervasive anxiety about sex, and taboo attitudes toward it which are reflected in both teachers' and parents' feelings. At another level, emotional frigidity in parent-child relations cannot be laid solely at the door of psychology with its behavioristic emphases of the twenties; the responsibility must be shared by all education which assumes that reason and feeling are in opposition, and that the latter must be sacrificed to the former.

In a time of rapid social change each generation of children must find its own way in its own world with a degree of independence not imagined in more stable cultures. In the latter the social habits, the insights, and the notions about life acquired by parents are still largely useful to their children. The Depression years, the war years, and the post-second-World-War years have all made more independence necessary for the young; new ways and attitudes have become essential for their own stability. The independence seldom emerges without some tension between parents and children, since each generation has its own setting, its own experience out of which its ideas grow, its own pair of glasses through which it looks. Each finds it hard to see through the spectacles of the other.

But college can provide experiences which help to make the situation of the older generation better understood. Students who work with children in the nursery school cannot discuss children without discussing families, and when they begin to see the needs and problems of other families, they gradually come to see their own more objectively. Instead of protesting at their parents' de-

mands, they come to see them in their own setting, how parents feel
and why parents find it hard to understand their behavior.

The topic of "human relations" has come into focus in the last
generation in a variety of ways. Courses, departments, professional
journals are now occupied with this theme, where no such area was
marked off before the thirties. How people in different groups grow
and live, their institutions, their cooperative or competitive attitudes to each other, the ways in which their relations are disturbed
by mutual frustrations, are all the subject of careful study. Personality problems, coercive needs for power, dominance, prestige
are studied in their bearing upon conflicts between economic, religious and national groups. The emphasis upon conflict is unfortunately more common than an approach which emphasizes the
development of qualities which might *prevent* group conflicts. The
processes leading to social identifications, empathy for others, insight, intuitions, and the capacity to feel with and relate to others—
these are matters which have not yet been studied as intensively as
have sources of aggression, and patterns of response to frustration.

Here again a variety of opportunities to work with people, and
to have good experiences with people, is needed. Students working
in the nursery school quickly learn that children need adults who
can feel warmly and intuitively with them, that rules and knowledge alone are not enough. They discover that sometimes explosive
feelings can be helped to evaporate by the simple, accepting remark,
"I know just how you feel," when Bill upsets a pile of blocks.
The student learns to tell the child, "Sometimes it makes me cross
when someone spoils what I'm doing too, but he didn't mean to do
it, it was just an accident." Or "You look pretty mad, what can we
do about it?" Through learning to accept the feelings of children,
students can learn both to accept their own feelings, and even those
of difficult friends or of parents. They learn to look at groups as
well as individuals in terms of how they feel and therefore, in which
terms one can deal with them.

As part of this process of educating feelings, students learn to
accept their own feelings about what they observe, or read, or discuss; "objectivity" is not interpreted rigidly as an exclusion of feel-

ings, but rather an awareness of them and an ability to make good use of them.

This can be seen in the case of a student whose report on two schools follows; the writer has learned to see perceptively. She feels strongly, but she can analyze the material with objectivity. Empathy and the development of broadened feelings as well as awareness may be stimulated in dozens of ways, with only this in common: that the student is encouraged to experience fully, and in her own way, the field trip or housing survey, or political interview, or baby-sitting job—whatever she undertakes.

This school, a private one but with some provision for having children from different cultural and ethnic groups, was like many of the so-called progressive schools I have read about. There was a certain permissiveness in the manner in which the group was controlled. Perhaps it would be better to say that the teachers seem to make a conscious effort to say "yes" rather than "no" to the children, to answer questions they asked, to take some criticism from the children good-naturedly, to suggest or offer alternate activities or ideas when they felt they had to remove an already chosen one from the children. . . .

In this school the emphasis is on helping the child to establish himself in his community or world by learning the requirements of that world while also learning the possibilities which it offers to little boys and girls. Thus the child in the five-year old group where I visited who was walking around saying "Sum-un-a-bitch" was not punished immediately; instead the teacher talked with him, asking him if he knew what he was saying, and adding that it wasn't acceptable. She further explained to him that although people at school were willing to let him use that expression, still many times outside of school people were quite displeased with it. In the light of that perhaps he would do well to practice not saying it so often. The teacher punished him not at all. She mentioned to me later that she felt that with most children who experimented with words they picked up from other children, if they were adventurous enough to say them in front of adults, and if they produced a negative reaction, that seemed sufficient impetus to giving the words even more hard use, so she simply wished to point out that some grownups don't like those words and others don't mind so much. This seemed to me to be putting it squarely to the child in a non-punishing way but letting him know that not everyone would be as tolerant of it.

The others had opportunities to talk, even those who didn't really want to. By not forcing them directly but by showing that she had an interest and confidence in one reluctant child, she got him to take the discussion for a while and be a part of the group instead of an outsider. She made a particular effort to see that no child was left on the fringe of things. She achieved this through the whole morning by asking help from children who had not talked to the group, for instance, so that they all had a feeling of being important and responsible to the whole group.

This was a school I liked very much. It seemed to me, too, that the teachers liked it very well, were enjoying the children and their duties, and the children certainly seemed to be learning and enjoying, two possibilities which are compatible nowadays in school situations.

The second report is as follows:

This school caters to a group of people who, apparently, want their child turned out in a particular kind of mold, as it were. It is important, apparently, to the parents of these children that their offspring have certain marks of ladylike polish such as good manners, a perfunctory ability in speaking French, grace acquired through the study of ballet from the age of four years on. This set of requirements is rather an anachronism in this age and the demand for it, I would judge, to be waning to almost nothing. In addition to teaching the social graces, the school is succeeding in forcing the regular, established curriculum of arithmetic, geography, social studies, reading, spelling, writing and science down the throats of its children. This is still a well-established formula for education in this country, and so schools who have the same curriculum as this one are more in number by far than those who don't have this kind of philosophy. Still I think that in terms of what is known about children and their development, this school was an outrageous one. I am not going to describe it, as my blood boils badly when I try to discuss it, but the attitude here was so much an autocratic, competitive, punishing, dominating one that I don't see how a sensitive child could possibly survive.

I will use one example of what the typical teacher attitude seemed to be toward pupils. The first-grade teacher showed me a Christmas card like those which the class made and sent home to their parents. The pattern consisted of a cover on which the Nativity scene was painted, and an inside of the same colored paper with a snapshot of the first-grade children next to the Christmas greeting spelled out in neat letters. The teacher, after explaining that she had designed this card for the children, added apologetically that she hoped I wouldn't take this for the best they could do, for in fact she hadn't let the child, who made the card she showed me, take it home "because it was such a poor and sloppy job." I tried to imagine how a child would feel when told that she couldn't take her card home, because it wasn't good enough. Actually for first-grade work it was excellently done and neat too, although it lacked the originality which is encouraged in schools where children draw what they wish and not what everyone else is drawing that day by the teacher's command. Also this incident indicates how defining and limiting grownup standards are; this was quite a severe demand for six-year old muscles. I decided that this school must often be a pretty discouraging place to children who try their best and produce to the utmost of their developmental ability and still get criticized. . . .

One of the objectives of college education must always be to develop maturity and objectivity within the student. These cannot be taught directly, but have to be achieved gradually. Sometimes buried feelings interfere with clear judgment; resentments, disappointments, and rebellious feelings can be released by listening to and appreciating comments like these made by children with whom the students work:

I wish grownups wouldn't be so impatient because they put children in a bad mood. Also it isn't good for anyone.

I wish grownups didn't act as though us kids were untouchables from India and they could order our lives about. For example, if I have a radio program on at eight-thirty and I'm sitting peacefully listening, they say, 'What, you still up? Go to bed immediately.' And when you go to bed, some of your mother's friends come over and talk in loud voices and keep you awake.

I wish my mother would say I did well sometimes instead of telling me I can do better.

I wish my mother didn't make up my mind for me.

Grownup ladies like little boys better than little girls.

Often, as students report these remarks, the comment is added, "I know how she feels, I felt that way myself." Sometimes this leads to a discussion of the consequences of those feelings, how they affected the student's relation to her family or school and her later development; sometimes just recognizing them is enough to make it possible to discard some of the emotional freight which hampered free growth.

Learning to feel and to express feelings is thus not incompatible with but contributes to objectivity or mature analysis, as we can see from the final summary written by the same student whose intense feeling about two schools was expressed in the two reports quoted earlier:

The more autocratic type of schools require each child to learn an already-dictated body of knowledge which it is unconditionally supposed each child needs to know in order to attain grade status each year. This is really done irrespective of any individual needs or allowance of human variation. We have learned that the baby who doesn't learn to walk as soon as his older sister did will eventually learn to walk at his own leisure, in terms of his own peculiar development. We have learned to be quite accepting and acquiescent and tolerant of that. We understand that. Yet in this kind of school there is no allowance made for different growth patterns in each child which are as important in the learning of fine skills as they are in motor skills. They don't allow for different readiness intervals in different children. Thus they try to fit all children in to one prescribed pattern and the most adaptive individuals get along all right. Sometimes, however, for the sensitive ones or the intimidated or overpowered ones, this becomes a dangerous and highly destructive process.

II

The nursery school at Sarah Lawrence provides a morning program for three groups of children from two to five years of age, with twelve to fourteen children in each group; a group of about ten children stay for lunch, a nap, and afternoon play.

The nursery school is a laboratory in several senses. It provides first-hand experience in observation for girls who are beginning to get their bearings in understanding growth, personalities, child development. It provides raw material for the analysis of new scientific problems in personality development. It provides a situation where students may try out their own abilities in working with children and develop skills needed in this field. Another analogy would be that of the art or music studio, where a student develops insight, acquires facts and theoretical background along with the development of skill in working with her medium. The children in the nursery school are in a situation resembling a studio-laboratory, they are both the artist's medium and a source of scientific data. Many other values, of responsibility, of administrative experience, and of executive skill, can be learned through work with nursery school problems.

One student started a small afternoon play group at the request of parents in the neighborhood. Another had a group of half a dozen children for dramatic play, so successful that the children and their mothers begged to have it continue during a second year.

Some students, who have had work with groups of children—or who are not yet ready for it—may work intensively with individual children; one student at Sarah Lawrence last year made an excellent study of a little boy who was a serious problem at the beginning of the year—excessively withdrawn at certain periods and dangerously aggressive at other times; this year he is an accepted member of a kindergarten group.

The possibilities of project work in connection with the nursery school are almost unlimited. Students have made photographic studies of children; one recorded patterns of behavior in the group play situation which were particularly revealing of two different children; another did a study of children's posture. Students have studied music as a creative activity, and as a type of experience contributing to adjustment of certain kinds of children. Some children who are at a loss in the free situation of group play become more quickly oriented through the forms which music supplies, and find their first satisfactions with the group at music time. Each year there are a few young children whose creativity is expressed through music more readily than through other media and who give plenty of material, if there is anyone to collect it, for original songs for children or for analysis of the process of creativity at its early levels. Much the same thing is true of painting. One little girl who stood around on her heels the first few weeks, utterly lost without the precision of home formality, found her way to real spontaneity when she first confronted paint. Children vary enormously in their attitudes toward the different media of work in art.

Learning to see children objectively may be a major step in outgrowing moralistic and social stereotypes generally. Any adult starting to watch a child comes to his observation with a bundle of preconceptions of various sorts. First of all, the adult is full of typical notions of her own social class. If she is middle class, she believes that a child ought to be self-dependent and self-reliant, able to stand up for himself, and also cooperative with grown-up demands; that he should accept the typical routines imposed by the grown-ups, and also be creative and have ideas of his own. He should be out-going and participating in social activities, be able to handle a wide variety of materials, handle a bicycle, bat, and the other equipment and tools suitable to his age level. He should be spontaneous enough to laugh, but self-controlled enough not to cry; but he should also be well-mannered. He should have a mind of his own, but he should not be arrogant. Above all he should not be a sissy, or a —— or a ——. Whatever the special preconceptions of each adult, his biases will somewhat limit the picture of the child he produces. No child is merely a bundle of habits or of mores or of anxieties or of nervous habits, or of growth indices. Each child is a little self, with its own feelings about itself, about the world around it, its own ways of experiencing life, coping with its difficulties, and growing up. The person who wishes really to understand a child will do well to try to find out how it feels to be that child, to feel things as he feels them.

How do you learn to see a child in this way? It may not seem so mysterious if we ask how do you learn to see a dog? If it is your dog, you watch to see what he does, how he does it, when he does it, and you try to figure out why. Mostly people don't give that kind of attention to a child. We assume that we do know what the child is doing and why. We project assumptions partly accumulated in the traditions of our culture, partly accumulated from the odd selections of our memories of our own childhood, and we think we know. Most of us are moralistic, constantly making value judgments. And most of us don't really see a child with its individuality as clearly as we see a dog. For instance, take the typically adult reaction to a child chewing bubble gum. To many adults it is disgusting, showing a child's inconsiderateness of adults' feelings. The fact is that adults may also be inconsiderate with their cigars and cigarettes and pipes, or more considerate with their liquor than a child with his bubble-gum, which is much more innocuous than either tobacco or alcohol. We can't really understand the child with his bubble gum unless we can recapture what it feels like to be a child. The same applies to a child's noise, jumping around, delight in mud, old clothes, or just plain being silly. The over-serious teacher or mother sees no point in being silly. Of course she cannot see that it contributes to the child's physical, mental, emotional or moral development. If she knew the whole truth, she might know that it contributed a good deal to the child's mental health.

Part of learning to see a child consists in participating with children in their work and play. The more we can live *with*, not just around or near or in the same house with them, the more we can learn to see them and understand them. Good observation, insight, and understanding depend not only upon standardized situations which fit into the psychologist's rating scales, but also upon the habit of looking and listening when the child is living most completely, either happily or unhappily. Good observation depends on trying to understand what the child is expressing, not just what he does, but how he does it and the meaning of it to him. An important source of misinterpretation lies in our own unmet needs in childhood. We are apt to think every child needs whatever we didn't get, whether it was discipline or affection, or freedom, or protection. These egocentric evaluations extend to other people as well and explain why we have feeling for some individuals and groups while we are indifferent to others. Learning to see children's experience objectively can be a step toward appraising other people's experience, in terms of its meaning to them, not to us.

Other obstacles to understanding children lie in the fronts, the masks, and disguises which some of them have acquired even as early as the age of two. Some of them learn that it does not pay to show their real feelings; but if they are polite, and if they conform, if they cover up their fears and their angry feelings, they will avoid trouble with grownups.

The things that children do to us also affect our capacity to observe them accurately. If they embarrass us or frighten us, or annoy us, or flatter us, they disappoint our hopes and expectations. If they frustrate our desires to possess them, or if we are anxious about how they are going to turn out, or whether they are as good as children of the teacher next door, or the family next door, or if they have interfered with something we care very much about, such as the tomatoes in our garden, or pulled the tail of our cat, we may find it hard to understand how the child really feels.

This is the raw material for other work in the college as well, —intensive studies in personality, in advanced courses in psychology, or social work, or literature, are all deepened as a result of such experience. This is an aspect of work in college which fertilizes work in other fields, just as learning to observe in an art course, or to analyze the relations between symbols and experience in a litera-ture or philosophy course enriches the study of children and per-sonality development.

But the nursery school is not only a laboratory, or a place in which a student deepens her perception of personality and the needs of human beings through learning to see children intelli-gently. Students have taught us that the nursery school is a place where children and adults live together for part of the day, enjoying each other and growing in security, ease, and happiness in social relations, and that this growth can be just as exciting to the col-lege student as it is to the four-year old.

Some students are afraid of children when they come to college. Children are unpredictable and dangerous, you can't tell whether they are going to like you or hate you. They say dreadful things and sometimes do worse things. For college students it can be a great relief, or even a thrilling experience, to discover that it is possible to get along with children, that they can set limits which children will respect, that they can talk to children and enjoy the freshness of childish thinking, and that children like them. As the students learn to talk to children and understand their ways of thinking and feeling, they get a new sense of children as people, individuals like themselves with individual needs, problems, ways of approaching their problems. When this happens, the desire to help and support the child's efforts to handle his own life comes to supplant the stu-dent's fears; and she finds new insight released, new possibilities in her own behavior with children.

Other students are "used to" children, but are sure the only way to handle them is to punish them sharply whenever they do "bad" things. Their general feeling is that since they learned how to be-have by being punished, why shouldn't these children be punished too? Sometimes these students are rigid, inhibited people who do not realize the serious consequences for themselves of the regime they want to perpetuate. But sometimes, like the student who wrote the paragraph below, they are girls with great sensitivity and capacity for growth:

The Sarah Lawrence Nursery School is very different from the type of school I have always thought of for young four- and five-year olds (and the complete antithesis of the one I attended). I at first disapproved and criticized it strongly. I rather expected children to learn how to obey, how to be polite, I even expected them to learn what I realize now can only be expected of an older child. But slowly I began to give much less importance to these rigid academic standards as I began to see benefits in this kind of nursery school set-up that I truly hadn't thought of before. I feel that the children here are unusual in a sense. With one or two possible exceptions, they are the most interested children I've ever come in contact with; they are completely "alive," questioning, eager. The world all about them is constantly enlarging and growing, they are all on their toes to examine everything that comes within their reach. They are looking, seeing, feeling, and observing!

Another group of students feel vaguely ill at ease or troubled about relationships in their own family. They feel dominated or dependent or bullied or rejected without quite knowing what is wrong. Often they want too much to be independent to allow themselves to talk these things over with dons or teachers. Students like this are apt to be drawn to children in the nursery school like themselves; through learning to understand the child's feelings, they come to understand their own; and through understanding, they become more relaxed. If they can also understand the child's mother and some of the reasons why she has treated the child as she has (for she always has her own difficulties, too), the student may become more objective and understanding about her own parents. When this is followed by an improvement in her attitude and relations with them, she often receives more acceptance and reasonableness from them.

Finally, there is a group of girls who are not completely happy with the academic life; generally, they are not girls who are working in an art studio, in music or dance, or in a laboratory. They need something active, a contact with real life, relations with people who are working. If this kind of girl does not find a satisfactory field work job, she sometimes finds what she needs in the nursery school; after a few months of sharing responsibility with the teachers, of helping, playing with, and laughing with children, this student is a "new person." She seems confident, poised, perhaps radiant, where she seemed tense and unhappy before. She has "found herself," and gained a security in relationships which can give her a basis for new independence and wholeness.

III

There are other ways of deepening the quality of experience in which college students become involved. When we speak of education at the college level we generally think we are talking about the courses which make up the curriculum. We continue to do this in spite of the fact that students who discuss the college they plan to attend, and graduates who discuss their college after graduation, seldom mention the curriculum. They talk about college life and its character. This is not just a question of having friends. Many students comment on how much their intellectual interest was stimulated by round tables, lectures, bull session discussions in the dormitories. Students not spontaneously drawn to science, or dance, or music, find their interests aroused through participation in special programs in which their friends were active. Colleges put too much emphasis on the curriculum as the educational medium and not enough on the total situation of college life. We who teach at Sarah Lawrence write reports on how students are getting along in their courses, but are also interested in the use they are making of the college as a whole. Many alumnae comment on the importance of their friendships with faculty as a central part of their college experience; they speak of being treated as adults, of their friendships with intellectually and emotionally rich personalities, of help in learning to work through problems, and of learning to see things maturely. From the point of view of the alumnae, college is seen not as an educational curriculum but as a place and way of living, where they found student and adult friends, a chance to mature, to expand, to reconsider their basic feelings about life, to learn how to work with and to understand people.

The kind of group living which exists in a college needs a certain combination of common interests and aims, of range and variety, of opportunity for easy contact between groups. It is important for the college not to become so big that groups split off and lose contact with one another, so that scientists, artists, social scientists, and others do not have contact.

This means that we must also look at the college environment as a whole to discover the number of opportunities for group partici-pation which actually exist; how many of the students can find the chance to work, with and for the college, through government, political organizations, campus and community activities. The identi-fication which the student develops through working for the college, or through strong relationships with members of the college group, can be an important bridge from childhood identification with family, to adult identification with the community.

The opportunity for close association with adult men and women, in small discussion groups, and in conference, has other values for students, values which they cannot always state for themselves, but which are noticed by those who work with them. In one case, a stu-dent of divorced parents may never have seen much of her father and his friends and in college may have her first experience of a close understanding relation with a man; in another instance the chance to talk things out with a mature adult may give an oppor-tunity to get over negative attitudes toward authority, or come to terms with conflicts about authority which could not be faced in an overstrict family and school.

At Sarah Lawrence, both in conference and in class, the constant free discussion involves a spontaneous interplay of appreciation and criticism, accepting and disagreeing, coming to understand others' points of view and experiencing the acceptance of one's own inde-pendent opinions. This helps the students to get over the feeling of needing to be right all the time, or of needing always to be approved.

Another experience of responsibility is extended in field work jobs, where the students simply do not "look," but work with people, establish warm relationships and learn to know how it feels to have someone counting on you, to be needed, to be compelled to carry out assignments by the fact of an employer obligation.

Growing boys have often had part-time job experiences from the age of 12 or 13 on, and these have helped to initiate them into the ways of adult life, the problems that different personalities confront in working on the same job, the ways in which men learn the steps and processes involved in better jobs, the ways in which stores, pro-ducers, or trade unions maintain their relation with the public.

Realities like this are behind a closed door to most girls. Yet if they are to participate intelligently in their communities they need to know what makes the wheels turn. At college, field work jobs, doing clerical work in a trade union office, or helping to pass out leaflets, or assisting with interviews, can open up a world of realities to a student who has never participated in any activity outside of school or home. One student at Sarah Lawrence who expects to work in her father's industry after college is working now with trade union leaders in that industry, going with them to settle grievances, reading proof on collective bargaining contracts, assisting them on organization. Her teacher started her off with this kind of beginning: "Let's see how things work; these are human beings, with their own motivations, their own needs. Sometimes they are idealistic, sometimes they aren't. Let's find out how they *feel!*" By working with them and participating, she does find out how they feel, why they do what they do, the kinds of problems they are coping with, the backgrounds of some aspects of labor legislation. Incidentally she is also learning how to get along with different kinds of people, how to record her rich observations and to organize them. And she is learning that her opinions, which formerly seemed to her to be of no value, have cogency when based on her own firsthand observations.

Even helping to send out announcements of meetings can open up some of this reality world to students alert enough to read what goes into the envelopes, find out what went before, what comes next, what the other people in the office are doing, the politics of the office and the aims of the organization; they can learn something about the way in which organizations work simply by alert observation from any chair in an organization office.

Few upper-middle-class families open their account books or exhibit their income tax records to growing children even in adolescence, long after they have acquired the grasp of arithmetic needed to handle the figures. Girls come to college, and leave to get married, without any adequate knowledge of what it costs a family to live—any family—or how the parents allocate portions of the money available, to the various needs of the family. In economics courses students may find opportunities to remedy this lack. One group at Sarah Lawrence assisted with a study of housing needs.

The students rated the housing facilities in a designated area. This required a careful inspection of the inside arrangements of each house. While doing this, they added an interview with the parents regarding income and how the budget was divided, which gave them a chance to learn something about the costs of food, clothes, medical care, and other basic expenses for different kinds of families. From this, they could extend their thinking more realistically to other levels of family costs. They learned in addition something about the variety of ways in which people live, the variety of their family problems.

Other students working as case work aides, collecting children for appointments at clinics or family consultation agencies, going into homes in the role of helper, have a similar chance to see realities of family life first-hand. Working with a social worker to help make out supplementary budgets, they learn to think about family needs —what kinds of clothes the children need in order to feel socially secure at school, what kinds of toys they need to provide adequate activity and satisfaction of needs to build, explore, create. They learn something about what people can do with the money they have, and how much money it would take to meet other needs. In this way a student who complained, "I haven't any idea what it costs my family, or any family, to live. I don't know how to think about money," began to learn something about what it costs to maintain any family decently in a democracy.

Students sometimes come to college with intense feelings of rebellion against their fathers; full of good intentions and fine ideals, their ideas about minority groups, or labor, or political leaders are sentimental and naïve. Everything for them is black and white, and their values are a reaction against the particular black-white pattern they learned in their families. In such instances, a more realistic, flexible, approach can emerge from experience with the groups they idolize: by interviewing Negro students and a professional Negro couple, visiting different areas of Harlem, such a student gradually learned to see Negroes as individuals rather than as symbols of a cause, and her views are getting a rational foundation, related to convictions about the meaning of democracy, and objective facts about human beings. Instead of needing to defy her father she is now really thinking for herself. Students vary greatly in their awareness of political responsibility, and in the kind of experience they need in order to get clearly oriented to political problems. "I am politically lost," complained one alert sophomore, who did not find that reading alone helped her to clarify her thinking. She felt that going to meetings to hear both sides of the issues supplemented what she could learn from books and periodicals. She knew that she needed to learn a great deal before coming to conclusions, and that hearing arguments and points of view tested in debate helped her to test her own.

Many women who have attempted to work with an architect designing a house are frustrated by the architect's apparent preoccupation with design, especially external design, and his lack of sensitiveness to needs of individual families, or such questions as how the adults can have the privacy and quiet they need at times and still have the children's rooms near enough to let the children feel the security and closeness to their parents which they need.

Women going into such vocational fields as architecture, apartment house design, city planning, can help make buildings meet the needs of people, if they have been trained from the first to look at structures in terms of the needs they attempt to meet. One such student is working with the City Housing Planning Commission on a field work assignment, both for her course in design and her course in community. She learns about what people want and need, what buildings mean to people, the satisfactions they should be able to get from the spaces in their homes, the facilities—schools, churches, stores, recreation areas they need to have accessible, the provisions for safety, air, beauty and how space has to be handled to take care of all these. Working on blueprints, spot-maps indicating sites and the resources available to them, she puts to use the awareness of needs and values as well as the technical knowledge she is acquiring in her course in design.

In these and other ways, field work helps to introduce women students to real situations, puts them into effective contact with realities from which they have been shut out before reaching college, but with which they will be coping after they leave. Concrete experiences give them material to think with, three-dimensional images as background for abstract concepts, and a feeling of security about the results of their thinking. Their emotional relations with people are broadened and grow more realistic.

IV

It is important to ask whether or not these values which education believes it can accomplish—by field work, nursery-school work, psychology, art, philosophy, science, community life and so on—are actually accomplished in terms of what values our graduates take with them to later life. This is, of course, a difficult thing to measure, and requires a sensitive and exhaustive analysis of many other factors than those of college education. We can, however, refer to the comments made by graduates about the things which have stayed with them, and which they feel were the responsibility of the college. It is interesting to note that the emphasis in the replies to a questionnaire distributed to a representative sample of Sarah Lawrence alumnae was more in the direction of values and attitudes than in terms of courses taken or information obtained. Consider these examples:

College taught me how to plan my time.

It taught me to be conscious of new ideas and works . . . developed my curiosity.

College taught me certain bold questioning habits.

College did not teach me how to do housework, but it taught me to use my common sense on everyday problems.

People are often afraid of emotions; college teaches you to understand them, your own as well as other people's.

College gave me a social conscience.

I learned to look beneath the surface.

I learned to look for excellence myself instead of waiting to have it pointed out to me.

I learned to be self-reliant . . . and to plan . . . this was valuable in homemaking.

The deep insight . . . of my professor . . . gave me a desire to understand other people.

Coming from a protected southern home, my ideas were not what you'd call liberal. I often wonder whether I would have participated at all as a responsible citizen were it not for my contacts at Sarah Lawrence ... now my prime concern is to live as a responsible citizen ...

Literature and philosophy helped me to mature emotionally.

I developed a personal sense of importance.

I learned to *listen*.

The family feeling in my dormitory gave preparation for dealing with emotional aspects of human relations.

Women are appreciative of what college can do in providing these basic orientations and attitudes toward the tasks involved in either a job or a home. They are also appreciative of the wealth of knowledge which is available to them in their courses in college.

In this chapter we have not meant to imply that work in such fields as child study or the community can do all that education of women needs to do, or that real experience with real people in these areas of work is all that college work involves. Rather we have tried to show that emotional development, the development of insight, empathy, warmth, at-homeness with people, ease in dealing with reality, can be a legitimate part of a woman's education and can be furthered by experiences at the college level. Such experiences are most conducive to learning when they are well integrated with the analysis of scientific research and of literature which gives the student material to document her hypotheses and set them in a broader perspective. Women's education cannot omit any of the main areas of culture and science, which women need quite as much as men do, in order to understand the world they live in. But women's education may extend the field of education, perhaps for men as well as women, by demonstrating the possibility of adding another dimension of emotional depth to the kinds of intellectual development more widely fostered. In the fine arts this dimension is taken for granted; creative writing, musicianship, or the work of a painter are counted incomplete without evidence of feeling integrated with perception and skill in performance. In the field of human relations this criterion is even more urgently needed.

Music in the College

NORMAN DELLO JOIO

Music is an expression of something real in human life. It is not a retreat from life. Nor is music a soothing agent. If a segment of society enters the concert hall to escape the painful truths of the present world, that is a function assigned to music by those who understand only its surface and not its content. Either that, or it is a function assigned to it by cultural hucksters who simply use music as a way of making money and employ artists, conductors, and composers to fill the largest halls with the most people. I need only mention the hack programs conducted by artificially glamorized conductors to show what I mean.

If music has to do with reality, it is a special reality for each person who listens and creates it. We cannot say what it means except in terms of what each person experiences through it. But to know music is to become greater in knowledge and insight and to know many things other than music. It is to develop a sense of values about art and to learn about another dimension of reality previously hidden.

My approach to education is through music because that is the way I became educated. Everything else but music was merely an accompaniment to the central part of my life. But it was music which taught me about aesthetic standards and about standards of honesty, integrity, craftsmanship, scholarship, and taught me to love the work of artists and of honest men, whether in literature, politics, education, or music. I think that those people who like music and like to hear it, or play it, or compose it, should study it as a central part of their education in school or in college. This is not simply because a knowledge of music is helpful to a listener or one who will take part in music after college, but because it is an important way for people to become educated. The prime reason for teaching any art is to establish an attitude towards contemporary life, one that not only assimilates but also rejects. It is possible for students who have no talent for music (as composers or performers) to gain an intelligent understanding of music, and to gain insight into the implications of the subject-matter for contemporary culture. Thus they will learn to counteract the questionable and supplement the desirable practices that have shaped and are shaping our musical world. This, in effect, must influence the course of the future.

I am aware of the risk one runs in using the words questionable and desirable in determining standards of value, for they are relative. Their meaning depends on the persons who use them. For example, in cultivating musical taste, concert bureaus employ a staff of art salesmen. In cultivating musical taste in students, the teacher has, in some degree at least, a knowledge and a professional experience on which to rely. The motivation of the concert bureaucrat and the teacher are different, and their aims conflict. Music and its use mean for the educator and the concert bureau contrasting things, although both influence the development of music.

Recently, for example, a metropolitan newspaper printed the following publicity release from a college. I quote in part: "A unique four-year curriculum in MUSIC BUSINESS, designed to prepare students for work in the music industries will be introduced . . ." Aside from the worth this course may have in a vocational sense, the main interest it holds for me lies in its apparent acceptance of a prevailing condition, namely, that music, a profitable commodity, is inextricably bound to the industries that flourish out of its use. We may list radio, recording, concert management, and publishing among the cultural corporations. The hired specialists of these enterprises, the scientist, engineer, and businessman, are the ones who receive most material benefit.

I recall, too, the story of the commercial sponsor of a radio program who was scandalized at the moments of silence in a composition his program director had chosen for broadcasting. The sponsor reasoned that if one bought a half hour of time, one purchased a full half hour of sound. The resultant executive order handed down from the sponsor stated that for the half hour a week when the program held the air, there must never be music with pauses. The existence of these attitudes by men in control of the arts is a constant threat to music, and a challenge to the teacher. If the teacher accepts conditions as they exist, he compromises his office and helps to perpetuate the material structure alone. He allows the betrayal of the purposes for which art is created.

At the present time the cultural hucksters are winning and the teachers are losing. Because of the tyranny of the concert bureau, the public still is in the unhealthy stage of approaching music on the basis of who is playing, not what is being played.

The extent of the educator's responsibility for the arts has thus become enormous, since the colleges and universities have grown to be the last strongholds of a cultural morality. The men in education should look upon the classroom as a clinic that probes into the bodies of these morally bankrupt musical institutions. At times we seem to be struggling against hopeless odds, but if the teacher relinquishes his task, there is no one else to take it over, and society fails to shape the values upon which the young can build a more enlightened future.

The creative man, in re-examining his relationship to society, is now turning to the areas of education as a release for his activity. More of us are growing aware of the futility of assuming the role of unconnected artist, with allegiance to none and liberty for oneself alone. In our society, we as artists need a sense of connection between ourselves and a group in the social order who believe in our work, who believe in the values of the arts for life, and who make up that body of critics whose enjoyment and interest it is to keep track of new works and help to prepare the ground for their reception. The contemporary artist has no patron except the State or big business. In America, this means that the younger artist has few ways of getting started, no source of support while he composes or learns to play, unless he wishes to take a job in some part of the music business. Even the music schools provide little musical culture. They produce instrumentalists who join the fierce competition for places among the scattered few who are recognized in the big cities, and who pay their rent for Carnegie Hall as a tribute to the world of commercial art.

In a sense, it is by default that the liberal arts colleges are now in a unique position to provide the connection of the artist to the social order and to give him the enthusiastic support which he needs. In the ideal situation, the college provides a community in which the composer may write and where his works may be performed, one in which his students may also write and perform, where experiments of any kind will be made and appreciated, where a man can grow in his art and where his art enriches the life of his community. Here in the colleges is the music patron for our age, supplanting the church, which seems completely to have lost interest in this significant part of the church's former life, supplanting the patronage of the aristocracy, supplanting the private patron, and perhaps eventually supplanting big business.

As yet, there are too few colleges which think of themselves in this way. They are more interested in other parts of the curriculum than the arts. Or if they include music as a regular subject, they teach it by use of conservatory methods. The colleges have not yet learned to think of the study of music as one of the best ways of becoming generally educated. The student and teacher in most institutions follow the line that if the student sings or plays an instrument with a minimum of wrong notes, and maintains a steady rhythm, the goals of music teaching are being met. Any exchange of ideas between student and teacher is limited to discussing the mechanics of projection.

On the whole, the standards of instrumental teaching in America are high. But the standards of education in music and through music are shockingly low. Whenever people mention music in college, they mean either instrument-playing, history of music, or the incredible music appreciation course. Even when the teacher of music appreciation is successful, little is accomplished in the liberal education of the student. When he is successful, the music appreciation teacher plays something like the role of hypnotist and persuades the students into a vague state of manufactured emotion. Students come to no conclusions for themselves but merely absorb the prejudices and opinions of the teacher. People usually forget that music is like other sections of the curriculum—it can be used unwisely to tell students what to think and to give them information and general feelings which they accept as the correct ones to have. It is just as bad to lay down the rules about music and painting as it is about politics or philosophy. Unless music means something more than listening to records and being told what to hear, the experience of the student is vicarious—the student's knowledge is secondhand and involves no personal conviction. The phonograph and the blackboard serve as instruments for learning a tonal language in the same way that the students learn the language of botany or French. There is no individual analysis of the experience of music by the student himself.

I have found in my own experience as a teacher of composition that there are certain fundamental and penetrating questions which students constantly raise. They are questions which transcend the technical, and to try to answer them means that the teacher has to conduct a full examination of the nature of music and to investigate, with his students, the properties which give it meaning. At the same time, in order to keep in touch with the reality of the students' ability to learn and their existing notions about music, it is necessary to find out as much about *them* as it is to have them find out about music. Otherwise the teacher has no idea whether the materials of music are anything more than a set of sounds which the student can identify. There are varying degrees of capacity for absorption of musical knowledge. Yet a common basis can be found in the student's curiosity and love for music, and the general level of awareness can be gauged for a given group of students.

Here it is necessary to say something about talent. Most people believe that no child should study in the arts unless he has a talent amounting to genius. We all know the little boys and girls who have either had the misfortune to draw or play the piano quite well at the age of five, or had the misfortune to draw badly or show that they are tone-deaf. In either case, parents and teachers make mistakes, they make too much commotion about the talented and too much handwringing about the untalented. This means that the middle group, where most children are, is treated more like the untalented, and since obviously none in this group will become a great concert pianist, a sculptor, or a painter, it is assumed that there is no point in going on with the arts in their case.

This is a misconception about the whole idea of the arts in education. The existence of great talent for an art is not necessary for the full realization of the arts in the education of the young. Most children *like* to draw, like to paint, play with clay, play a tune, dance a rhythm. This is enough. If the child, in school or in college, has sufficient ability and interest in music to learn through it, as a medium of his own development, this is sufficient. We are not making performers or composers; we are helping our students to grow up, to know the place of the arts in their lives, to appreciate the finer feelings and the more elevated experiences.

The resistance of students to the study of music theory is very great. To most of them the study of music is the study of an instrument or voice, and they begin by protesting about the practice time they lose in studying theory and continue looking upon it as a necessary evil. Students have the same response to the study of formulae in statistics or in chemistry. The formulae have no connection in their minds with the quest for knowledge. Students also object to a dreary study of grammar without reference to the language. Their objections can easily be understood. All good teaching must transcend the idea that the so-called "tools" of any art or discipline must be learned before students have any direct contact with the art itself. At Sarah Lawrence, beginning students of French or German start using the language at once in the classroom; students of mathematics learn that mathematical formulae are important as they symbolize meaning; and students of music are helped to see what happens when they translate the music on the printed page to music on the piano, or when they write a musical idea on paper. These musical acts become more meaningful as the students understand the principles behind them. This is the function of the study of music theory, and it should go on as part of playing an instrument, as well as part of writing music. In the classroom our students play an instrument and talk about the works they have played with their teacher. The study of music theory should be at the same time a study of the literature of music. The connection between composition, theory, and performance has to be maintained continually.

I have found that anyone with interest in music is willing to go deeply into it, as soon as it can be made clear that dabbling accomplishes only a little of the possible. When we attempt to make real to the student the reasons why he is asked to apply himself to specific tasks, we are making him realize that in the practice of learning, he is founding a personal aesthetic, and for this, no one can give him definite rules. At the same time, there is one specific rule for the teacher who wishes to educate his students through music. It is that each student must experience the music for himself, and it is up to the teacher to find the ways of making that possible. Few of my students have technical training beyond the simple knowledge of scales, and few of them know much about music. Therefore, it is up to me to teach them to make something for themselves. I must teach them how to recreate the experience which the composer has when he writes his music. It is not necessary to work in terms of the past, or to teach students how to write like Mozart, but it is necessary to allow students to write in terms of their own ideas about what is right and fitting.

For example, when I work with a beginning class of music students in my studio, I know from my previous study of their remarks about music and their previous training that most of them have stereotyped ideas about what is good. Most of them cannot read a score or tell what it is they are listening to when they play a record or hear a symphony orchestra. I try to introduce them to the materials of music and to show them that the composer has a certain number of sounds from various instruments, a certain number of notes and combinations of notes to use, and that he works at his materials in the same way a painter uses his brushes and colors. Just as in the painting studio, students must learn to use these materials of the art form before they can understand art from the point of view of the creative artist. This is necessary in order to become a creative listener.

One fundamental pattern of notes at the disposal of the composer is the triad. I often ask a beginning class to use the combination of three notes to make something for themselves. They write in their manuscript notebooks a variation of the three notes which they have chosen. I ask them to sing what they have written. If this is impossible, I play it on the piano for the whole class. Sometimes the student writes his pattern of notes on the blackboard, and we all sing it together. Then I invite another student to write a harmonic line to accompany the first line, and divide the class up, with one half singing the first line, the other the second. The mistakes in the writing become quickly obvious, and we can then go back to the reasons why a theory of harmony has been developed, and the students can see that the theory was developed to save the trouble of having to make these mistakes every time.

At other times, if the students, or their friends, play instruments, the class writes for whatever combination of instruments we happen to have. Other students write simple settings for poems, or set the poems their friends have written for other students to sing. Every month or so, we have a small recital in the studio at which the students sing whatever songs have been written, not as a performance so much as an exposure of the music to the class, so that the student may hear what the work sounds like. Violin and piano music are handled in the same way. This is not for the purpose of developing composers, but only to make the musical experience real to the student. Sometimes, of couse, the student develops faster than I expect, or comes with previous experience in composition and music study. One of my freshman students wrote a work for piano and full orchestra and played the piano part in a rehearsal-performance for the college. Others have written chamber works, choral pieces, and so on, still in the spirit of learning to listen and to understand the music of others, as well as their own. The point is that each student does as much as he or she can and goes as far as possible. In doing so, the student is forced to learn the technical details and theoretical parts of music, as well as its history and its variety of styles.

With more advanced students, it is possible to do more in the field of history and style. We can specialize in the work of two or three composers, or a student may be assigned a project in the work of a particular composer. I remember one student who began a project because she kept telling me how much she hated Wagner. She could not say exactly why; few people can. But in this case, I asked her to study Wagner in order to find out what he did which she considered bad. This meant the study of his letters, his biography, the history of his period, the opinion held by the critics who were his contemporaries, the predecessors in music who influenced him, and the aim he had in writing the way he did. It also meant studying intensively some of Wagner's scores, through listening to records, and through playing parts of the score on the piano. The completed project gave the student a vastly increased understanding, not merely of Wagner whom she continued to dislike, but of the whole field of music, and the whole field of the arts and criticism. She discovered that to dislike a work of art means something different when you know and understand it than when you simply refuse to listen to it.

I think it is important for students to go to the original sources in the work and writings of the composer rather than to read books about music and the kind of expanded program notes which most colleges give their students as an aid to understanding and appreciation. A student can learn more from one letter by Mozart than he can from reading a whole book by someone else. I also think it is important for students to learn to read and to analyze the composer's score, not by having it analyzed on the blackboard before the class, but by playing parts of it themselves on the piano. Often I find that it is best to take the score and work at the piano with it before the class, stopping to talk about parts of it as we go along. After we have spent some time together learning to understand its structure, we can turn to the record and listen together to the full work. I think that unless the teacher works in this way, the students hear little of the composition itself merely from listening to the record, since the habits of discrimination, and remembering, and analyzing, which make the appreciation of the listener so sharp and heightened once they have been learned and have become automatic, never have a chance to get started. When the approach to the teaching of music is taken in this way, I find that students discuss the philosophy of art, the history of art, the relation of music to the other arts, quite naturally, and that all the other things which go to make up a good liberal education come into their lives as they learn to relate music to the other things in which they are interested.

When the student acquires a basic knowledge of the methods of the craftsmanship in music, he experiences the exhilaration of being able to notice those factors in the music by which the right thing happens at the right time, whether it is in his own work or in someone else's. Music no longer remains a source of vague emotion. The tonal language becomes an instrument for aural clarity. It is less possible then for the student to indulge in uncritical statements about music and exhibit the "I know what I like" attitude.

Another possibility for the teacher lies in the use of music as a center for many of the other arts. The history of the various art forms has been one of specialization. Painters have isolated their subjects and have done easel paintings to be hung in drawing-rooms and in art galleries. Sculptors have made monuments and objects, sometimes have been commissioned to aid the architect and the town-planner to enhance the value of the human environment by his work. Poets have written for a special audience, or have written plays for a wider public. Dramatists have brought their talents to theatre audiences. Each one has worked in his own medium for his own audience. But the musician has many more opportunities for uniting the arts, rather than separating them, than any other artist, since his work for the dance can set the dancers moving, his music for films, for plays, for opera, and for concerts as well, suggest a deeper integration of art forms than any yet attempted.

During the last few years in America, a new way of developing the various art forms has appeared for the composer. In place of the older ideas of the opera as a musical vehicle for dramatic performances, in which the emphasis is upon the music and the use of song to carry dramatic action, a new conception has been substituted. Composers have been commissioned to write for the ballet and the modern dance. In the modern dance, there has also developed a movement towards the dramatic arts, with their integration of the field of stage design, modern art, mythology, and the theatre. Many of us have speculated about the chance here of unifying the arts of music, theatre, and dance into one medium which exploits them all—that is, the opera which thinks of itself as the opportunity for using the dance drama and the theatre for the presentation of a story.

At Sarah Lawrence College, this speculation resulted in a commission of an experimental opera which we have now carried out. Our problem was to find a way of using all the talent which was available in the work of the theatre, music, and dance students. The work had to be written in such a way that inexperienced performers could come together in a joint production—dancers, actors, stage designers, chorus, and singers—and under great handicaps of space and stage facilities, and financial backing, make it possible for these various elements to coordinate. In carrying out the commission, my problem was to write what I wanted to write, yet at the same time, remember at each stage of the work the physical and personal limitations of the production. I chose the theme of Joan of Arc, her struggle and her victory, and wrote a work which I called a lyric drama. The part of Joan was sung and acted by a music student who was studying voice and who had had training in the dance. The other members of the cast were chosen from the regular students of the arts, in theatre, music, and dance, in addition to others from various parts of the College who sang in the College Chorus. The barest equipment was available for performance. We had only a plain assembly hall with an inadequate lighting system and little possibility of scenery, since there was no stage and the audience just about balanced the cast in numbers of people who could be accommodated. It was therefore necessary to produce the work in arena style, with a cast of sixty-five in the chorus, twelve in the dance group, six in the theatre group, four singers, and about fifteen in the stage production crew. There was room for only one hundred and twenty-five people at any one audience.

Rather than run the risk of producing a thin and anemically orchestrated score for the small chamber music group available, I wrote the work for two pianos, and conducted from one of them. Yet with all these difficulties, the work itself was a success. It involved nearly a hundred students in its performance, and gave to the various groups involved a good chance to do creative work of their own. The theatre students, for example, rehearsed their parts under their own student director, who worked with me in discovering the intention of the libretto and in carrying out the dramatic action which I had in mind and which was indicated in the musical score. The dance students had a completely free hand in doing the choreography for the whole production. This meant that an entire section of the curriculum was integrated in one effort of a creative kind, and an opportunity was provided for a new experiment in college theatre, music, and dance. I hope that similar experiments may be tried in other colleges, not necessarily following the same pattern as the production at Sarah Lawrence, but one which takes as its basic aim the use of music as a means of inducing the students to exercise their imagination, their separate capabilities, and their previous training. This can teach everyone concerned something about the field of knowledge and aesthetic values which lies all around them, yet has not been explored.

There are many other ways in which the student who is in college can become liberally educated and can achieve the qualities of mind and of emotion which mark him as an educated man. I have tried to show how music gives us a way. Far too many colleges treat music as if it were a separate professional skill to be learned by those who will eventually become performers. Or they treat it as an academic subject which has to be learned in order for the student to receive a degree. Neither of these ways is appropriate if what we want is a kind of knowledge about art and life which can make a difference to the standards of taste and the quality of living which it is possible to develop in young people. What we are trying to do at Sarah Lawrence is to make use of the arts to help our students to become sensitive, informed, and discriminating members of American and world society. I believe, and I believe it not only as a musician and a composer but also as a teacher and a citizen, that the student who learns music in this way has thereby been enabled to become an important and interesting person in the modern world, a person whose influence in the community can bring good to it.

Learning in Biology

MADELEINE P. GRANT

I

The task of teaching students who hope to go into the world as trained biologists in a special or allied field, has been a challenge which American college teachers have met with notable success. This work in teaching science must continue to increase, for we desperately need more physicians, nurses, medical social workers, laboratory assistants, and research biologists. On the other hand, the use of biological material for the education of a much larger group of students who are interested in history, literature, philosophy, poetry, or art, and who need to make parenthood or citizenship their profession, is an even greater challenge. It seems greater because, so far, our teaching of science has had little success in helping students become better human beings, wiser parents, and more effective citizens. Some of these failures are due to the fact that we have tried to help students become more effective members of society by the same means we have used in training specialists.

Today most educators believe that everyone can profit from work in one of the natural sciences, and few colleges or universities in the country are willing to allow a student to graduate who has not completed at least one course in this field. The reasons for these requirements may be stated quite simply: the study of science is expected to give everyone some knowledge of natural phenomena and some experience in critical thinking. No educator will hesitate to endorse such objectives. Unfortunately the factors which determine learning are far more subtle than any such solution implies. In fact, to make science a general requirement for all students not only fails to solve the problem, but tends to intensify it. Laboratories and classrooms are overcrowded with students who are there to meet the requirements, and a situation is created which makes it impossible for teachers even to try to discover the different uses which science may have for different students. As a result, too many students emerge from a required course in science with few, if any, educational experiences which have gone beneath the surface of their minds.

The study of science at Sarah Lawrence College is not required of all students. This does not mean that we fail to recognize the value of education through science, but rather that we know we must understand what makes an educational experience genuine for each student. Our responsibility as a college is to discover what students want to know and how they may best acquire this knowledge, and further, what additional scientific information they are likely to find most useful in the art of living. We also recognize that we must make full use of the special opportunity which the study of science offers for critical, unbiased thinking. In this connection, however, the important point is that we must somehow try to help the student develop the desire for critical thinking which will help him solve those problems which he meets outside, as well as inside, the laboratory. These are ambitious objectives, but it is necessary for teachers to view the study of science in these terms before they are ready to study the role of science in general education, or before any faculty member is in a position to make the study of science a general requirement. We intend that the study of biology should stimulate and free the mind: it can enslave it. We intend that the study of biology should help the student recognize his own biased attitudes wherever they may lie: it can ignore this problem. The chances are greater that our best objectives may be reached if we watch what is happening to the student as he works; if we talk with him about his practices in the laboratory; and if we select and emphasize the human aspects of the biological sciences.

The human implications of biology include more than the study of the human body and how it functions; they include the psychological and social aspects of human physiology. It is not enough to know some of the facts about the biology of the nervous system; we must in addition study the role of the autonomic system in fear, worry, and anxiety, common day-to-day experiences for all of us. The study of health and disease must be viewed as a psychological and social problem as well as a biochemical one. Any consideration of the types of diseases included in psychosomatic medicine offers the opportunity to introduce the idea of the oneness of man's mind and body, a concept which the liberally educated person of today may find congenial to his own system of philosophy, and useful in contemplating some of life's deeper mysteries. In brief this is what we mean by humanizing the teaching of biology.

The successful physician knows that different persons respond differently to the same treatment. He consequently searches for clues which will suggest ways of promoting health in each patient. Similarly, the teacher who knows that the study of biology cannot have for all students the same meaning which it has for him, will search for ways in which this work will have the most meaning for those who study it. Physicians often fail, but those who treat the patient as well as the disease are more likely to promote health. As teachers we often fail, but if we study the student as well as our subject, we shall be more likely to promote learning.

Further, if we try to discover what is enduring in the process of education, we gain some insight into learning. If we consider what students recall in later years as important experiences from their courses of study, or if we ourselves turn back to our own associations with different teachers, and state the significant experiences which are immediately recalled, we discover what has in one way or another become a conscious part of us.

Experiences which take on major importance for the student, and thus remain in his memory, are matters which were originally of concern to the individual. They reveal the emotional aspects of learning. They often have to do with habits of thinking, ways of feeling, methods of working: in short, with habit formation or character development. Detailed facts from a body of knowledge, which we as teachers may have labored so hard to impart, are seldom recalled. The emotional content of an experience endures longer than any of the specific facts relating to it.

One of my students in biology, who had made some original observations on the process of bone formation in the embryo chick, revealed the importance this study had for her when she later commented: "The experience I value most in college was having to finish a study of bone development which I was scheduled to exhibit at a meeting of the Anatomists' Association." Although the teacher can recall the intellectual excitement this student experienced during the progress of the study, it was the student's own struggle with discipline which remained uppermost in the student's mind. Another student once commented: "That was the teacher who taught me really how to work, and that I got on better when I used my own head." Another student said to a teacher of comparative anatomy, years later when she had become a successful physician: "I shall never forget the criticism you once made of my attitude toward my own abilities." And in my own undergraduate experience nothing stands out more vividly than the enthusiasm of a biology teacher about an independent study I had made.

It is of some significance that many of the episodes which students remember most vividly are often not recalled by their teachers; they appear to have developed as by-products. The core of teaching in the modern nursery schools and primary grades consists in forming habits of effective thought and action in the student. College teachers seem to fear that the dignity of scholarship is threatened if they emphasize such aims. But the scholarship which can be achieved when interests and needs of the student are considered; when independent thinking is encouraged; when the integration of ideas, rather than the accumulation of facts, is emphasized, goes much deeper than conventional scholarship. The questions which students raise give their teachers ideas about the things the student needs and wants to know. The integration of ideas increases comprehension and is intellectually exciting. Independent thinking is hard work. It results in discipline for the self.

It is not my purpose to minimize the value of the acquisition of a body of knowledge, but rather to try to understand the role it plays in character development. A body of knowledge is, of course, the medium out of which intellectual and personal attitudes grow, and without which they cannot develop. But attitudes are habits of thinking, feeling, and working; and the quality of these habits contributes to the character of the individual. The teacher of science should give constant attention to these aspects of learning, for whether he is aware of it or not, the attitudes a student acquires in the laboratory will have more influence on the development of his character than the scientific information he gains. It is more important that in some way a student develop the desire to observe accurately than that he merely complete a required number of accurate microscopic observations.

II

If we encourage students to talk, to ask their own questions, and if we listen to what they have to say, it is not difficult to discover some of the things which concern them. In biology students ask: Does John inherit his father's quick temper? I want to know about meningitis. If all these things are due to heredity and all these others to experience, what then is me? What is a blue baby? Is this animal we are working with dead, if its heart is still beating? What are test tube babies? Can hens lay eggs without roosters? I can't bear the thought of a physician looking at me when I give birth to a baby. What is the Rh factor? Is there a safe period? Do Negroes inherit a tendency for tuberculosis? Is cancer inherited? What are contraceptive devices? What causes cancer? Can a white woman have a black baby? Isn't there some course we can take in biology where we don't have to dissect anything? You can't tell me my asthma is imaginary. Can scientists bring a dead animal back to life again? I want to study biology because I enjoy seeing how animals are made and how they work. I want to study biology because I enjoyed all the drawings we did in high school.

By whatever standards we may choose to appraise these questions, at least they give us clues towards what biology means to many college students. The human interest which the questions reveal is obvious. Some of them may be traced to an experience in the life of the student. The radio and press are responsible for others. Some questions have to do with confusions and fears about the human body, and about sex; some with heredity; many indicate an interest in the unusual or the drama of disease. They all show a genuine attempt to comprehend realities of life and indicate how the teaching of biology may serve these needs for understanding.

Most of the questions which students raise as they begin the study of biology appear, on the surface, to be asking for simple factual information. However, if we consider these questions more fully we sometimes find that they carry social and philosophical implications of which the students may be entirely unaware. If the biology teacher is not confined by a restricted factual interpretation of what students say they want to know, he finds that many students show a lively concern for discussing the nature and origin of life as revealed by knowledge of the virus and gene; mechanism, vitalism, and organic evolution; the relation of science and religion; the biological aspects of death; the meaning of cause; the process of man's search for truth.

The teacher uses students' questions in those ways which are most appropriate at different times, and tries to organize the material so that students gain sound information along the lines indicated by their questions. Sometimes a student must be led to see that any satisfactory discussion of a particular question must wait the development of a knowledge of certain facts or of particular techniques. Sometimes this knowledge must develop slowly through a year of study. But the important point is that questions must be used for all they are worth because *they*, not a body of factual information, form the core of the work. Sometimes fears need to be arrested; sometimes a student needs to take a broader outlook on life; often categorical thinking must be criticized or the need for definite answers challenged. The teacher who has come to appreciate the psychological value of discussing problems of human reproduction, death, and disease, will not only impart knowledge but will help to resolve minor anxieties by helping students to recognize and face them. Discussing fully the question of tuberculosis and the Negro means introducing the discussion of the social aspects of illness; the question about the Rh factor needs to be dealt with not only by a clear description of the biological mechanism of antibody sensitivity, but also by recognizing that the facts need to be presented in a manner which will not arouse fear. Suggestions should also be given showing how married couples can make use of this knowledge. There is psychological value to be derived from the study of body functions, and if we could understand better some of the unknown variables which condition the process of learning, we might come to see why an objectivity toward the human body—an acceptance of it—can be gained from work in biology by some individuals and not by others.

If, as often as is possible, we select the biological knowledge which students' questions raise, and then, gradually throughout the year of college work, emphasize the philosophic and social aspects whenever the material warrants, students' understanding of life is likely to broaden and deepen; their personal philosophy may become enriched. To some persons a scientific understanding of life's processes increases the sense of the mystery of life. This aesthetic value is one of the strongest emotional satisfactions enjoyed by the research biologist. One of our poets once told me that no poem ever moved her as much as the experience she had the first time she saw the beating of a frog's heart. I am certain that many students who find work in biology satisfying, respond in similar ways. A student who discovers that knowing more and more about living processes increases the sense of the mystery of life may be the one who will continue in research work in biology. Einstein once said that science meets some personal need in the scientist, and I think the deepest of these needs is more often than not an aesthetic one. The satisfaction of the need releases the emotional energy which drives the research scientist through his daily routine and fires his imagination during his waking hours of the night. These are some of the factors which contribute to a genuine experience of science.

Most biology teachers have found that the study of their science meets some such need in them. However, if our interest is to explore the role of biology in liberal education, we must recognize that a great many students do not and cannot gain any such experience from this material. If the study of biology is to serve any function for them, it must meet other needs.

III

A course in one of the natural sciences is required of all students in many colleges because it is believed that the way of thinking which these disciplines demand should be understood and acquired by every liberally educated student. There is little doubt that critical and independent thinking is needed today more than ever before. But, what is the scientific way of thinking, and what special claim does the natural scientist have to that way?

The natural scientist legitimately treasures the fact that he deals with knowledge which is open to a high degree of measurable verification. This is true as long as he asks the "right" questions of nature. For instance, when the biologist asks: What is this organ? What does it do? How does it do it? he is raising questions open to observation, measurement, controlled experimentation, and concrete verification. On the other hand, when he concerns himself with the nature and origin of life; the nature of mind; the process of organic evolution; the inevitability of aging and death; he raises theoretical questions equally important, if not more so. These, however, can be only partially verified, for they reach limits of verification beyond which they cannot be pushed in the light of present scientific methods.

It is important that the student of science should not only have frequent opportunity to use different methods of verification, but that he also discuss these methods as he uses them, so that he may become aware of their role in establishing ideas. In other words, he should know when he is observing, when he is accumulating data, when he is interpreting, and when he is drawing a conclusion. However, we must not be so zealous in our teaching of these matters as to give our students the notion that science is infallible; that it has no limitations; or that intuitive methods are without value. The human mind gropes for knowledge of nature and of man. Science is one expression of this groping; poetry, art, and philosophy are others. The span of man's intellectual experiences includes some ideas which can be verified and others in which verification is as yet difficult, if not impossible.

Science deals primarily with questions applied to materials which lend themselves most readily to quantification, controlled experimentation, and verification. However, a true understanding of science should include an appreciation of the degree and the limits to which even scientific questions may be verified. For example, knowledge of the activities which take place inside the living cell have as yet been only partially verified. We can observe what goes into a cell and what comes out of it. From these data and from knowledge of how these changes take place within the test tube, we deduce what has occurred within the living cell. Knowledge of cellular activity has been, therefore, only partially verified. Similarly, our knowledge of atoms is based upon the effects they produce; the atom is a *concept*—it has never been seen but its behavior can be measured. Our knowledge of the gene is based upon similar degrees of verification.

Recognition of the fact that the scientist must often employ working hypotheses not yet verified will help students realize that science is "knowledge in the making." In this way, they learn to appreciate that theories not verified today may be verified tomorrow, and that the yet-unobserved phenomenon may suggest a new theory. In short, the nature of the question asked determines the degree and limits of verification which are possible at any given time. Such attitudes help science students carry congenial points of view to other disciplines where verification is even more difficult. In this way biology students have not been alienated from studies in other areas of knowledge where the type of question asked necessarily makes verification not only difficult but frequently of a different order.

The question of verification leads to another basic point. Those who work in scientific fields believe that the truth they seek is vested in the properties of matter. This is scientific truth, but not the only truth by which men live. In other words, authority is where we place it. The natural scientist places it in the properties of matter. To the biologist, authority is vested in living plants and animals, including man. Two biologists may observe the same phenomenon, yet their interpretations may differ. But each believes that the *phenomenon* holds the answer.

This means that when a student studies biology he has the opportunity of dealing with authority in a concrete situation. It matters little what the teacher thinks, or what the book says about the eighth nerve in the dogfish, for instance. The student has the dogfish before him and the dogfish holds the answer. Furthermore, the student is free to explore the animal. If such emphases are preserved in laboratory work, and if the student is able to capture this attitude, an atmosphere is created which stimulates him to ask his own questions and work out his own answers. The opportunity which biology offers for this concrete type of independent inquiry is one of its most valuable characteristics. When the emphasis in the laboratory is, "What do *you* see?" a stage is set for experiencing the adventure in learning.

About a century ago, Louis Agassiz fought for the values of independent inquiry in the study of biology. He had the art of stimulating in others the desire for free inquiry, both because this was his way of working, and because this method of study was what he valued most. He urged the "study of nature, not books"; but no one recognized better than Agassiz that this was the method for only those who are able to turn to nature for inquiry.

Today, the beginning student, required to go over a large number of experiments at a speed which would challenge even the most experienced worker, naturally develops the feeling, "What am I supposed to prove?" For days, or weeks at a time, Agassiz left his students alone with plenty of material, always returning with the attitude, "What have you found out?" It is true that as we look back upon the days of Agassiz, we imagine a sense of leisure hard to capture in our time, but Agassiz taught at Harvard during the days of the Civil War when social unrest was as great as it is today. What is it which has caused the difference between the spirit of free inquiry which dominated Agassiz's teaching, and the practice of hurrying over volumes of required work which characterizes the teaching in some college laboratories? It certainly was not that Agassiz regarded the study of nature a privilege to be enjoyed by a chosen few, for he "would talk of glacial phenomena to the driver of a country stage-coach among the mountains, or to some workman splitting rocks at the country roadside, with as much earnestness as if he had been discussing problems with a brother geologist; he would take the common fisherman into his confidence telling him the intimate secrets of fish-structure or fish embryology, till the man in his turn became enthusiastic and began to pour out information from the stores of his own rough and untaught habits of observation."*

What has happened since the days when Agassiz pioneered for direct communication with nature and sought to liberate students

* Lane, Cooper. *Louis Agassiz as a Teacher.* Ithaca, N. Y., Comstock Publishing Co., 1945.

from the paralyzing effects of learning by memory then in vogue? For one thing, memorizing is still in vogue, and to make matters worse, the number of facts to be memorized has grown to staggering proportions. The accumulation of knowledge has indeed reached the point where we are at a loss to know what to do with it, either in teaching or in society. So, what do we do in biology? I am afraid that some of us write detailed laboratory directions of, let us say, the circulatory system of the frog, from which the clever student is able to produce accurate drawings without ever having looked at the frog.

If we can keep our attention on the values derived from independent, free inquiry, and if we can give serious consideration to the philosophy which Agassiz held as a teacher, we will go a long way toward preserving the spirit of science in the science laboratory. As a member of the Harvard faculty, Agassiz crusaded for the "individual's right to choose the courses which developed his natural inclinations," and he "championed the broadening of the elective system . . ." Today, many college faculties appear to be returning to the pre-Agassiz period when the list of required courses was long and free choice difficult. Under such a system many students are required to take a laboratory course in science and some of them, with little interest in biology, find their way into such a course. When this happens, and when the classes are large, teachers find it impossible to preserve the Agassiz tradition, and many students are there to meet a requirement with no interest in meeting the frog or any other animal.

IV

I have mentioned the danger of over-stressing the virtues of scientific verification and thus alienating students from other life sciences where verification is more difficult. But surely we can try to achieve something more positive than merely preventing alienation from other disciplines. We can emphasize the contributions from biology to general human problems whenever possible. The biology teacher need not possess detailed knowledge of these other life sciences, but he should hold a liberal and objective attitude toward the social scene, and have a sympathetic awareness of the kinds of problems dealt with by other teachers. His competence must lie in biology, but he must search his field for topics which have relation to social or psychological questions.

Whenever topics in biology are chosen for the contribution they can make to social and psychological problems, the teacher must keep in mind the importance of the feelings and attitudes created by the discussion. For example, many teachers in different fields deal with race prejudice. The biology teacher has something to say on this matter: he can trace the mechanisms for emotionalism, but unless he acknowledges the complexities of emotional behavior and suggests ways of recognizing and dealing with it in any of us, he has not succeeded in humanizing the teaching of biology. The biology teacher can discuss mechanisms of individual and race differences in different species including man, but unless he has indicated the positive values of these differences, the spirit of science in human terms has not influenced the discussion.

If a teacher discusses the social implications inherent in biological material in order to indicate the many ways in which biological research has benefited society, well and good: it will form a dramatic way of recording history. However, if the principal aim is to guide the student toward more liberal and flexible views of society, a different emphasis will be given, and for some students the work will take on added meaning. It is conceivable that for a particular student, this day might be the time, this idea or this teacher might be the one by whom social awareness is aroused. Whether or not the biology student is to become a specialist in the field, he is living at a time when he must face social responsibilities. He is unlikely to have his interest in social problems quickened if he has to wait to quicken it in a course in sociology, completely out of relation to the chief interest his own field of biology holds for him.

The problem of maintaining and improving health is another natural way to reveal the social implications of biology. It is obvious that research in biology has reduced human suffering and lengthened the lives of hundreds of thousands of persons. But it is equally clear that hundreds of thousands of others have not received these benefits. One might anticipate that the United States, a country rich in natural resources, advanced in standards of living, and endowed with a large national income would rank high in national health. It does in some areas, but not in others. The very size of the country produces disturbing inequalities in the distribution of medical service. The good spots are very good, but the bad areas are black indeed. If the low infant death rate which Connecticut was able to establish for the year 1942 could have been realized in all states, thousands of infants would have been saved throughout the continent in that year alone. Similarly, the national health picture would improve if the low tuberculosis death rate for Utah, the low infant mortality rate for California, the low typhoid rate for Massachusetts, or the low diphtheria rate for New York could be made to apply throughout the country.

I recently finished writing an essay on tuberculosis in which I tried to present the wholeness of the problem. The material was treated from the bacteriological, the immunological, the social, and the educational points of view. A young student, recently graduated from college as a major in social science typed the manuscript and upon returning it she said, "I never realized before that tuberculosis is a social problem." When I was her age, I am certain that I did not either, and I was trained to diagnose the tubercle bacillus under the microscope. Today none of us can afford my former ignorance, or can afford to be unaware of the social aspects of illness; we do remain unaware if the tubercle bacillus is studied only in a course in bacteriology; if public health problems are delegated to advanced courses for health officers; and if the economic and social aspects of illness are ignored by social science teachers.

I know of no better illustration of what education for social action in public health can accomplish than the record of recent events in Colorado. In 1945, the political machinery in the state of Colorado regarded its Division of Public Health as merely another spot to force political appointments. Furthermore, the municipal government of the city of Denver had had a record of successfully defeating health bills. Two years later, through a local election, the picture had radically changed. A new candidate for governor, Leo Knous, campaigned for a health program and was elected in 1945. In 1947, in Denver, a new mayor who ran without support of the old political parties was elected, and likewise indicated a desire to modernize health activities of the city. In 1945, the new governor appointed a Health Committee. A health survey of the state was made and through wide publicity the citizens were informed of the findings. Health bills were formulated, state-wide educational programs were conducted and finally seven of the eight health bills were passed by the State Legislature. As one legislator expressed it, "We all knew in advance that this time we had to pass the health bills." And in the words of Dr. Florence Sabin, retired research biologist of the Rockefeller Institute in New York, "The people of Colorado had willed it so." As a matter of fact, Dr. Sabin had been their leader. Episodes such as these are case studies of social science, and have an equally legitimate place in the classroom of biology, or bacteriology, or sociology.

V

There is one major criticism of science teaching in America which we must face. Professor Edwin G. Conklin of Princeton University, who has been outstandingly successful in humanizing the teaching of biology, states that criticism clearly:

A principal fault, I think, is the general lack on the part of science teachers of a constant social and ethical aim in teaching. We have been obsessed with the idea of "science for science sake." Like the famous Cambridge toast, "Here's to mathematics, may it never be of use to anyone," we have felt that the dignity of our science demands that it be taught and pursued for the sake of abstract truth. When we have emphasized use, it has almost always been external, objective use; the harnessing of the forces of nature, the increase of human power and comfort, the conquest of disease. These objective uses of science are vastly important, but they are not the most important service of science which in my opinion is the cultivation of the spirit of science in the student.*

In day-by-day living we look for the spirit of science in each other. Those who possess it are easily identified. We think of such a person as having a mind which is emotionally free to listen to many sides of a question. We see him trying to avoid prejudice, to detect propaganda, to learn about matters of which he has little knowledge before he voices an opinion. He appears to possess the

* Conklin, Edwin G. "Science in the World Crisis," *American Biology Teacher*, Vol. 1, 1939.

ability to make an independent decision, the desire to be fair in judgment and the courage to act upon it. He expresses an intelligent reasonableness in dealing with human problems. However, when we try to discover how these character traits are formed, there is no denying the fact that their acquisition appears to bear little or no relation to whether or not the individual has ever studied science. Furthermore, some men of outstanding achievement within the science laboratory often show least command of these traits in other fields. In short, students may be scientifically informed, yet may not have learned the spirit of science which can guide them in their daily thought and action.

If this is true, we need to understand many factors which make it so. Since no special study has been made of this problem, we can only offer tentative suggestions, and it seems to me that one contributing factor may be found in the fact that, generally speaking, the natural scientist has little or no personal bias against what appears in the test tube or under the microscope. His needs are satisfied when he has the opportunity for imaginative thinking, for suggesting a new test, for formulating a new hypothesis or devising a new and crucial experiment. These experiences meet his creative needs. It is hard to imagine that Galileo held any vested interest in what the law of falling bodies might prove to be. Intellectual curiosity drove him to devise an experiment, and his emotional satisfactions came with performance, discovery, and comprehension. However, when man's task is to solve a social problem, or to try to understand another human being, vested interests and prejudiced attitudes block clear thinking. In such instances, biological reactions within the human body which accompany emotional thinking—including changes in heart rate and blood pressure—have not been stimulated by the discovery of some natural law, but by the desire to defend a prejudged opinion.

As individuals we must learn how to recognize these biological reactions which can give us clues for emotionally-driven, biased thinking within ourselves. Unfortunately, the study of natural phenomena offers too little opportunity for this type of self-inquiry. Honest thinking in the laboratory is easier than in the home, the community, or the world at large. The trained scientist forms the habit of speaking with authority, and society only serves to rein-force this concept of himself. Much as we need specialists who can speak with authority, science teachers in a liberal arts college need more to recognize the weakness in emphasizing such objectives in introductory science courses. Unless the *desire* for unprejudiced thinking is developed in the laboratory, and unless the study of science is related to the realities of life, little is done to cultivate the spirit of science in the student.

The remarks of Professor Conklin challenge each teacher to become aware of these weaknesses in science teaching and to dis-cover ways of dealing with them. He himself develops the general thesis that the spirit of science becomes a habit in the science stu-dent as a by-product of science work, if that work has been "con-ducted in the spirit of real science, by teachers who are themselves the exemplars of this spirit." This may actually be the crux of the whole matter, but if it is, it leaves us with the problem of discover-ing how the study of science may be thus conducted, and how science teachers may come to acquire this spirit.

Although answers to these questions escape us, I am reasonably certain of one thing: this spirit is an attitude which is learned. Furthermore, I doubt if it is learned merely by the execution of critical laboratory experiments, however great may have been the scientific spirit in which they were originally performed. Actually, we do not know whether there is any transfer of habits of thought from one discipline to another. It seems more likely that we ap-proach human problems with reasonableness only when we have learned to think about human problems in these ways. When bi-ology is viewed in this light and taught with these ideas in mind, it has a better chance of developing the spirit of science in the student.

The development of the scientific attitude in both teachers and students is so complex a problem and so important, that it can not be the concern of any one teacher, but must be of concern to all of us who teach. Recognition of these aims develops when teachers work together. When the environment makes it possible for teachers in different fields to do their teaching together, the scientific spirit stands a better chance of developing; and biology stands a better chance of being rescued from a position of isolation. These, it seems to me, are the real reasons for integration of separate disciplines. The problems we must now handle are much too important and far too complex for any one teacher to deal with alone. By working together, teachers learn, knowledge advances, and the scientific attitude develops, through the joint effort of those who are trying to see the whole world of man and nature as a process which we can partly understand.

Western Values and the Individual

CHARLES TRINKAUS

The main problem of higher education today is to bridge the gap between the individual student's experience and the objective needs of society. The goals and values of the individual and his conceptions of reality have at all times failed seemingly to correspond to what a particular age, culture, or society demanded. There has always been the educational problem of socializing the consciousness and attitudes of the maturing members of these cultures. We know from history and anthropology how varied this process has been. At no previous time or place has the problem been more complex or crucial than it is today in mid-twentieth-century America.

One way of bridging this gap is to study the relationship between individual and social values as it has developed through the course of the history of our own Western culture. Many college courses, and in some cases even entire curriculums, seek to teach the essential values of Western Civilization. There are various degrees of success in reaching this objective. Consider, for example, those courses in the humanities which rush the student from Cheops to Communism in a thirty-two-week school year, with the aid of a text that spares a page or two to Plato, a paragraph to Julius Caesar, arrives at the Renaissance by examinations in January and whizzes down the home-stretch in time to include the latest pre-convention presidential election campaign. Whatever educational purpose may be concealed behind this procedure, it clearly does not accomplish the aim of making the student feel any more closely identified with the values of Western culture. Nor does it show the student any relationship between his own life and the nature, conditions, and historical trends of the world in which he lives. History, civilization, society, become a series of "flashes" in the manner of the newsreel, of assorted pops and gratings and explosions culminating in the biggest explosion of all over Hiroshima. There has, of course, been a reaction against the shallow habits and customs of the survey course, although occasionally even now, one is startled to find a college here and there in which the newsreel approach is being used as a way of replacing the discredited departmental introductory courses.

Other colleges have been turning to the study of the texts themselves of the Great Books, or at least to excerpts from them. The flash-back method shows history as a collection of discrete happenings somehow occurring in one century instead of another. It leads usually to the rote memorization of course outlines, and the useless system of "objective" true-false testing. The Great Books theory, on the other hand, seeks to teach its students to respect and venerate the philosophical monuments, and the history and content of the great thoughts. It is assured that a grasp of classical ideas will equip the student to enter a world of social conflict.

In practice it is possible, in fact likely, that the American student has an intellect and personality active enough to become aware of the job of translation necessary in moving, for example, from Plato to the Report of the President's Commission on Civil Rights. It is also possible for even a progressive educator to say that there is nothing educationally inadvisable in studying Plato. The real question is that of the relevance and content of any such study. Is there not the danger of abstractness and unrelatedness between the ideals of the classic writers, and the striving of men, individually and collectively, for self-realization—a danger that this could perhaps lead to an analogous disjunction of principle and practice in the student's attempt to deal responsibly with the public problems of today? Is there, perhaps a parallel danger that a sense of discrepancy between the public problem out there, and his private life and interest, will often lead the student to conclude that his own individual gratification or gain doesn't square with what seem to be the requirements of public social justice? Shall he participate in a restrictive covenant excluding Negroes from purchasing property in his neighborhood and thus maintain a higher realty value or rent, while at the same time he becomes indignant at the threat of a filibuster by a Southern Senator against antilynching legislation? The trouble, of course, is that such conflicts are the daily fare of life today. The question is, what kind of education can put the student in command of these problems so that he can solve them constructively and responsibly.

It may be doubted that any education in the great thinkers, however important the thinkers actually were for their time, can aid much in this process, as long as their works are presented as a series of thoughts hovering somewhere above reality and individual experience. When this approach to education is fruitful, it is because the student himself frequently has been able to assimilate these values into his own life, either with or without the aid of the teacher. We must try to devise an educational approach closer to the reality of the student's own experience and to relate these values to the life he must lead today.

Insofar as traditional ideas and values can be understood in terms of the life experience of the men who expressed them, they can have meaning for students today. Apart from such understanding in the context of their creation and functioning, such ideas and values can only have an abstract dogmatic meaning, a meaning which may reinforce contemporary abstractness and the separation of theory and practice, or may seem utterly ridiculous, archaic, or superstitious. An understanding of these ideas in their actual context, however, may indicate both their reality then and their lack of relevance now, or the extent of relevance in the now different context. In all events it will tend to encourage a closer integration of ideals and reality, of theory and practice.

In what follows, one approach to the tradition of Western civilization will be presented. Operating on the premise stated in the preceding paragraph, a course in the history of Western values called, "The Individual and History" was developed over a period of years at Sarah Lawrence College. The plan at first was to study a series of historically significant autobiographies or confessions or self-analyses, and then in each case to examine the general cultural and historical environment of the particular thinker. In this way, it was hoped, the prevailing ideas of a certain phase of the history of Western culture could be examined through the eyes of a contemporary and as a part of his own life. By seeing what the thinker felt to be the meaning of these ideas to him, we might have a case history of the personal meaning of these values. The idea was, if possible, to develop a clinical approach to history.

The first figure hit upon was St. Augustine. Here seemed to be an eminent proponent of the fundamental ideas of Christianity who had left a justly famous account of his movement toward orthodox Catholicism through various pagan philosophical positions and Christian heresies. Here was a man who in his own life had run the entire gamut of changing and conflicting ideas in his own epoch and finally come to a personally satisfying conclusion.

The reactions of students to the study of *The Confessions* could not be predicted. Neither could those of the instructor in this educational experiment. It was not so easy to show, at first, how Augustine's ideas had a functional importance for his own times. It was necessary first of all to understand them. Barriers that existed in the minds of the students suddenly became noticeable. The major one was the anti-clerical and anti-religious prejudice of a generation who had either known Christianity through their parents' indifference to it and dismissal of it, or as the result of enforced attendance at Sunday Schools. The occasional Catholic student always reacted initially with favor to Augustine. But the reactions of all had only the most superficial connection with the actual thoughts of Augustine as he set them down. They were attracted or repelled by his frequent and fervid mention of God and his imploring, imprecatory style of writing. They had somehow to be taught to look at this passionate history more directly.

At the same time it soon became evident that although Augustine was a professor of classical rhetoric and a devotee of skepticism and of Neoplatonism at different periods of his life, the full meaning of his rejection of Classical for Christian values could not be understood without a more direct examination of both. The clinical approach seemed to be breaking down—educationally at least. The impediments to seeing at all, in actual terms, what was the life experience of Augustine, had to be eliminated. It was necessary first, to look at those very ideas apart from their relationship to a living experience. Yet we were reading Augustine in order to see his ideas as a part of his experience!

The fact was that practically no knowledge, let alone understanding, of the most elementary information about either New Testament Christianity or the classics could be assumed to exist among students. This is a reflection both of the weakening of the classical, linguistic tradition in preparatory schools, and of the decline of church-going Protestantism in America. Such a fact alone should condemn the various attempts to claim that an education in the ancient Greek and medieval scholastic philosophers best fits students, in America at least, to cope with the modern world. These ideas, until they have been given real meaning, are about as exotic and strange to students as those of the Buddha, or Ikhnaton, or the inhabitants of Easter Island.

Nevertheless, it was not possible to find meaning in ideas without first looking at them and allowing students to draw many erroneous conclusions about them. So we began to read one of the synoptic Gospels, the Acts of the Apostles, an Epistle of Paul's and the Epistle of James. The class was also previously asked to read some chapters describing life in the Roman empire. From our discussions we first sought to arrive at an elementary knowledge of the tradition of Christ's life. Then we tried to reach a more historically accurate feeling about the way in which the early Christians moved about in the Roman empire, winning converts among the Jewish communities and the lower classes. All of this was as a rule completely new to the students, but possible to understand well enough on a descriptive level. The ideas and religious import of Christianity still remained to be gained.

For this purpose the students were asked to state what differences they saw between the teachings of James and those of Paul. Which seemed to be closer to their understanding of what Christ himself had been saying? Which did they themselves believe to be true? In this comparison the students were introduced to one of the fundamental controversies of Western thought—a controversy which has manifested itself in a variety of forms and still remains at the heart of almost any contemporary discussion of values. In the theological way of expressing it, the argument was over whether man was saved by his own natural efforts to comply with the moral law, or whether the gift of supernatural grace was necessary to enable him to overcome his attachment to his physical and social nature and thus to be capable of willing and acting according to the Christian law of love. Among other implications of this dispute was, that in the former case the objective, external, social relations of men were considered in ethical terms and man, himself, consequently, could be considered morally just, only insofar as he conformed to an objective definition of justice and social harmony. In the second case, conversely, the emphasis lay not on the objective manifestation of one's morality but in the subjective fact of having overcome the flesh and the world through divine assistance.

The Epistle of James with its emphasis on outward realization of inward motive: "If a brother or sister be naked, and destitute of daily food, and one of you say unto them, Depart in peace, be ye warmed and filled; notwithstanding ye give them not those things which are needful to the body; what doth it profit? Even so faith, if it hath not works, is dead, being alone," (3:15–17)—and its equally vivid excoriation of the man of wealth cannot fail to make its point and confront students very sharply with the issue of whether principles are to be practiced.

Paul, on the other hand, although he presents certain barriers to understanding in the obscurity of his writing, can, with careful elucidation of his language by the teacher, make the other conception of values just as real and poignant. Nowhere have the conflict between good intentions and the inertia of a preformed way of existence, or the claims of man to possess a self-determining, spiritual individuality that can transcend the bonds of tradition, been more discerningly exposed. "For I know that in me (that is, in my flesh,) dwelleth no good thing: for to will is present with me; but how to perform that which is good I find not. For the good that I would, I do not: but the evil which I would not, that I do. Now if I do that I would not, it is no more I that do it, but sin that dwelleth in me. I find then a law, that, when I would do good, evil is present with me. For I delight in the law of God after the inward man. But I see another law in my members warring against the law of my mind, and bringing me into captivity to the law of sin which is in my members. O wretched man that I am! who shall deliver me from the body of this death? I thank God through Jesus Christ our Lord. So then with the mind I myself serve the law of God; but with the flesh the law of sin" (Romans, 7:18–25).

Educationally, two major objectives are achieved through this comparison. The student comes to realize that if within Christianity itself, even within the New Testament, two such opposed conceptions of life can be asserted, then he must examine his own conceptions anew, since authority and tradition give him, not one simple answer which he can either accept or rebel against, but a living search, a controversy, and a struggle to solve genuine difficulties. On the other hand, these two opposed views by their inherent content have an immediate relevance to the student, and introduced him to the consideration of those very issues in his own daily life.

The objective, however, is not limited to the above two goals. The study of the controversy over values in earlier times cannot be automatically applied to the present. A third and more sophisticated lesson has next to be absorbed by the student, and that is, that whatever standpoint, James' or Paul's, may seem correct to him, he is arriving at this conclusion on the basis of the problems of his own life and his own lifetime. His own conclusion need not have been true for the first centuries of the Christian era in the West. His choice of these values as they apply today may also need reconsideration in the light of a new conception of historical relativity.

This third objective cannot be reached by direct didactic teaching, since to attempt such teaching would be dogmatic, unhistorical, and, in the end, would not result in any conviction on the part of the student. It is doubtful whether any moral value can be taught directly in conventional didactic terms. Abstractions, moral or social, have meaning only as the student actually thinks and feels his way into them, and as the abstractions are seen to be relevant to concrete situations of significance to his own life. For the student to choose between the ideas and values of James or Paul, it is necessary for him to move from the direct examination of the philosophy of each, to a consideration of them in the historical and cultural context of the world in which they appeared.

Obviously such a task, if it were properly done, would require a thorough study of classical civilization. But what is needed here for the student is not so much a definitive exposition as a demonstration, and this can be achieved by again contrasting the opposing Christian value-systems with a sharpened version of classicism. While it is true that classical thought may suffer through the exaggerated features of it that are used for the demonstration, yet the student may, as a result of such arbitrary simplification, gain a method that can lead to a more proportioned understanding of the ancients if he turns to them in the future for fuller study.

For demonstrating the relation of classical to Christian concepts, the *Meditations* of Marcus Aurelius have been used with relatively productive and lively student reactions. An alternative of even greater dramatic value has also been used, Plato's *Phaedo*, the most otherworldly of his dialogues, which takes place at the death-bed of Socrates. In both treatises the highly acceptable modern value of "reason" is presented in a context that reveals a very different meaning from its obvious one of the use of human intelligence for the mastery of the world. It would be manifestly unfair to the Greeks, who used their intelligence to master so much of nature, to consider this selected usage as the only one known to them or practiced by them, but in these works both the aristocratic-philosopher and the philosophical-emperor use reason for inducing a human attitude of indifference and withdrawal from the world, rather than for its mastery in any other than a politically-authoritarian sense. (Of course Plato expresses other views in other dialogues.)

The usual student reaction is, in the first instance, to consider these treatises as an admirable defense of nature, of being natural, and of using one's head, in opposition to asceticism and superstition. They reveal clearly the dangers that are latent in a too literal classical educational program. Their further reaction and more considered insight comes as a result of discussion. They come to see that these two highly-charged ancient and modern words, "nature" and "reason," when used by Marcus Aurelius, have the meaning of a world of fixed structure revealed by reason that underlies the visible changing world of experience. A rational life is to live according to the rational structure of nature, but this "nature" is not our material world, but a hypothetical eternal order to which we are being urged to seek a purely intellectual attachment and thus to give up caring about the emotions, senses, and involvements of experience of our historical and daily existence.

Against this essentially dualistic and, by implication, ascetic attitude the student begins to protest. He begins also to see that the two Christian attitudes he had already examined were also both protests against the classical despair about experience and attempts to go beyond the social and psychological defeat which classical reason concluded was written into the very nature of the universe. But then the question arises as to which attitude, the Jamesean or the Pauline, was the more historically significant and effective.

The basic objection against classical revivalism in education today lies in the metaphysical card-stacking that takes place when it is assumed that eternal values are to be found in Plato, Aristotle, and Thomas Aquinas, and that they can and should be a universal guide to life in this day and age. It is unquestionably true that the proponents of this pedagogy are perfectly sincere in believing that there are eternal truths. But the fact that they are unaware that the deck from which they are dealing is stacked, does not make for a fairer game. These educators make, through the classical authorities, a series of persuasive and cogent arguments on behalf of seeing the more permanent values beneath the flux of appearance, of seeking an objectively rational basis for ethics and a mature and responsible attitude toward the more transient whims of human desire. Nevertheless, into such studies there are often interpolated notions of the superiority of contemplation over practical productivity, in fact, many of the prejudices of the highly-cultured, leisured aristocracy who lived on the labor of the multitude in the ancient world, whether free or slave, Hellene or barbarian.

These ideas and their metaphysical basis may at one point in history have meant a step forward, humanly speaking, at a time when their early Presocratic proponents were writing on behalf of a thriving commercial culture which needed for its continued progress, a more calculating approach to reality and a discrimination between appearances and deeper truths. Such ideas have had proponents in some of the classical revivals since that time, proponents who had much the same impetus for discovering new modes of controlling nature and extending commerce. The enlightenment of the eighteenth century, for example, was partially of this nature. But classical Greek thought very quickly exhausted the possibilities of progress latent in these early philosophies, and turned them inside out to make of them a bulwark for a system that on principle rejected the right of mankind to happiness or the hope of ameliorating the human condition. These implications for conservatism are contained in the classical curriculum—a curriculum whose function in the past has been to teach students once and for all what is the truth. Unless the social role of these ideas in their own day are shown to the students, they may well find them to be dogma.

Students, however, when asked to see the growth of ideas and the conflict of values as they functioned personally, socially, and politically within a given historical setting, are aided to think critically and to reach the insight that what matters is not reason as such, but the use of reason in the service of human goals. The protest of the students against the Roman imperial philosophaster Marcus Aurelius is apt to be both social and psychological. Why is it either "rational" or "natural" to consider the peasant and the slave as akin to a stone in nature whereas the aristocratic philosopher is akin to the universal, unchanging, superterrestrial platonic ideas, or if not ideas, as Marcus also allows, the elemental atoms? How is one to suppose by mere assumption that to be true to one's truly "rational nature" means to yearn for this kind of inanimate universality and thus arrive at the state of *apathea*, or indifference to desire and fear? These two questions, which students are provoked to raise, by reading the Greek and Roman reactions to their society, find an answer, in the one case in James, in the other in Paul.

But then the new question arises as to whether the Christian protests against the inadequacy of current thought meant any real difference in the actual living situation of men. According to James's teaching it should. According to Paul it could not. An examination of the obvious facts of social history is enough to convince students that the Jamesean view of social equality could apply only to small sects corresponding to the early Christian communities that practiced a communism of consumption, sharing their incomes, as described in The Acts. What was needed in that age was not so much a program of impossible material reform as a new and more hopeful conception of man's position in the world.

The real significance of Christianity, and of Paul's interpretation of it, can now become evident to the student. He can also begin to see the meaning of a religion as opposed to a philosophy or a science or a political platform. He is able to grasp that the suffering masses of the Roman empire, first, and later on the cultured classes as well, turned to Pauline Christianity as to a promised world, to be accepted on faith, in which men could achieve the victory of their individual spirit over the bondage of what seemed a given natural state of affairs. The Pauline conception of sin as the acceptance of the natural, in contrast to the classical *hubris* as the defiance of the natural, comes sharply into focus.

At this point—if the original plan to use the autobiographical method beginning with Augustine's *Confessions* is once more taken up—the students are prepared to understand the tensions and triumphs of Augustine's life, not merely because they now have a new familiarity with the classical and Christian ideas and sects he discusses, but primarily because they now understand the various ways of finding an adequate individual relationship to history that Augustine actually lived through and lived to describe. The students can know not only what Augustine meant by the heretical Manichean dualism and the classical doctrine of opposition between body and mind, which he rejected, but they can also understand why he was called upon to reject them in favor of a new theory of the world. That theory is of a world unfolding historically from an original possibility of goodness that turns to evil, in the face of the genuine difficulties man has faced in his efforts to make a home on this earth.

What Augustine adds to the development of the student's understanding is an explicit and carefully worked out explanation of the very thought processes which the students have undergone in their efforts to reach their own conclusions. Augustine shows the way in which men have struggled to come to terms with history, and in doing so, shows to the students some of the factors in his experience which coincide with theirs as they have been passing through the process of their own education. Here, attention is necessarily focused on the famous discussion of the goals of nature and of mankind in the Tenth Book of the *Confessions,* and on parts of *The City of God,* which the students also read.

In this manner students come to find a basis in the writings of Augustine for a viewpoint that sees human values as part of a long and living process. They are able to accept his general approach to the problem of value without accepting his own specification of ultimate value. Although for the most part they cannot accept his mysticism or his asceticism, they are not repelled by these apparently inhuman attitudes but see that they can be regarded in the same way as Augustine regarded the older classical attitudes. These he considered as efforts to discover a satisfying relation between the individual and the world, efforts which had to be superseded because they elevated a partial, relative solution into a final one.

The students may then consider Augustine's three forms of incomplete happiness as the illusory form of accepting for truth one's private joys rather than the discovery of "joy in the truth." The latter unites the gratification and fulfillment of the individual with the reconciliation and recognition of the objective, superindividual, wider reality of truth. Where Augustine, speaking in eternal, unhistorical terms, designates the pseudo-happiness of subjectiveness as the three lusts of the flesh, the eyes, and power, in the *Confessions,* the students are able to follow his analysis of classical society and thought, in *The City of God,* as a society doomed by its acceptance of these partial values for the whole. Sensuality, naïve reliance on the rationality of the mind, the enhancement of the ego through its domination of other men, are then also regarded in the more universal framework of their omnipresence through history, and, in the contemporary world, as increasingly dangerous psychological and social substitutes for deeper satisfactions and a humanly adequate social order.

What is important, however, is that they are seen in the perspective of the fifth century A.D. as values that are in process of being superseded and transcended, just as Augustine also saw them. The values can also be regarded in contemporary society as in transition, and as the consequence of an originally valid human motivation. The conclusion very likely will be a hopeful one, for today as it was

for Augustine. Evil, real and poignant as it may be, is the consequence of an initially good impulse that can therefore be converted
to accepting its own incompleteness and need for further development.

Trinitarian Christianity, as Augustine held it, can also be seen in
the perspective of an early version of a philosophy of process and
progress, that in turn has been, and must be, superseded as an inadequate statement of the most fruitful approach. The goal of a
heavenly reconciliation of man with man and with his world is no
longer acceptable to most men, but it is significant as a necessary
phase of human projection of the ideal relationship between man
and man, and between man and nature. Equally inadequate for the
contemporary world is Augustine's notion of a City of God consisting of those Christian men of good will who dwelt as pilgrims
in the Roman Empire of the world and sought the purely protective peace that would allow them to consecrate their hopes for a
future good society in a future world. Students can find a basis for
a continuing evaluation of the relation between men of insight and
the slowness of insight to become universal in studying this situation in Augustine. They find most of all a way of thinking about
social change and the relation of projected personal and social ideals
to the contemporary existing conditions that opens up vistas and
possibilities rather than closing off the problem in the impossibility
of an irreconcilable dualism between the personal and the social.
The historical view is seen as a more valid view, because it did in
actuality correspond with historical developments in the movement
from Classical Culture to Christianity.

With these insights planted through the seed of St. Augustine,
students are able to survey the succeeding centuries of the unfolding
of the ideals of the West in their shifting relations with actual history. At the time that they encounter these insights, the insights
seem to make sense in relation to Augustine's past, but students
rarely see at this point how valuable they are for studying Augustine's future, or their own past. They remain for a time as seeds,
and grow only later in relation to entirely different views of man
and history and society. Not only are students at this point ready to
study history, but they need to.

If we continue to observe the flow of events and ideas which

makes up the history of Western Civilization, the next phase following the Augustinian period is the attempt to turn the ideas of the
early Fathers into an existing and present way of life through the
institutions of the medieval Church. It is peculiarly hard for mod-
erns, with their acceptance of religion as essentially a private affair
and their experience, in America at least, of the separation of
Church and State, to comprehend an era in which the difference
hardly existed and where the Church in many respects was replacing the old Roman state. The latter, of course, had a very different
place in men's minds and in society than the modern state has.
Whatever the real function of the modern state, it tends to conceal
at least the degree to which it is an instrument for the protection
of a privileged few. The open acceptance of this function and the
doctrine that man exists for the state, rather than the state for man,
prevailed in the ancient world. Modern conceptions therefore owe
more to the medieval Church, which sought to implement its belief
that care of the spiritual well-being of individuals was its prime
function, and that it was the duty of secular power to protect and
ensure that well-being. The medieval Church, whatever its actual
shortcomings, was, in its conception of its role, the first institution
frankly dedicated to human well-being. The difference today is that
we no longer have the same conception of well-being and hence are
unwilling to entrust this public function to a Church.

Without entering into the detailed contents, it may simply be
stated that it was here found to be extremely valuable for students
to look at such seemingly exotic ideals as monasticism through the
eyes of St. Benedict, or the penitential system of the medieval
Church. In these they find both the intent to live a life devoted to
the well-being of all men's souls, and the danger of a lapse into the
ascetic retreat from the reality of experience, or of manipulating
the power of the Confessional and the Keys to Heaven and Hell, for
sake of material advantage. They find also, in the writings of Pope
Gregory I, a long sustained attempt to consider the well-being of the
individual as linked with the well-being of society, and to reaffirm
this conviction whenever the forces of feudalism had drawn the
clergy into its net of blood-relationship and territorial domination.
They find that what has repelled them from medieval institutions

was not their ideals but their deterioration and corruption. Much to their surprise, frequently they discover passionate concern for men and practical wisdom about the psychology of interpersonal conflict and harmony.

From this the student turns to the great shift in human consciousness that was made necessary by the beginnings of modern commercial and capitalistic society in the twelfth and thirteenth centuries. The older view, inherited from Augustine, regarded men as engaged in a continual spiritual struggle against the power of their own nature and of worldly society. By and large, the earlier Middle Ages facilitated the survival of this view of the relation of the individual and the world. Commercial society, however, offered far more immediate rewards and a promise of a good life, at least in material terms, in return for a kind of social relationship that utterly denied the teaching of mutuality and community and the organic interrelationship of each functionally different class of medieval society. Now all accrued to the aggressively competitive person who was able to subordinate his own feelings and whims to a hard-boiled adjustment to the economic conditions so far as he could discern them.

This new condition prompted, on the one hand, a rejection of the supernatural elements which turned out to be useless in gauging the possible profits of a commercial venture. On the other hand, it rejected the confidence of Christianity that brotherly love and a mutuality of interests between neighbors was both possible and desirable. At first no new assertion of moral values corresponding to this more systematically busy kind of daily life developed. Attempts were made instead to attack and discredit it or to incorporate it somehow into the older Christian world view.

Students were asked to examine these contrasting reactions to the developing modern social order through the ethics of St. Bernard of Clairvaux and of St. Thomas Aquinas. They find in the former the delineation no longer of a theory of the good individual versus evil nature and society, but an examination of two ways in which the individual can function within society. The first emphasizes an ethic of love based on a genuine acceptance, and therefore love, of the creative potentialities in oneself which makes possible genuine

love of the creative in one's neighbor and of the creative in history and the universe represented by God. This, which at first glance seems to be a reassertion of the old Pauline-Augustinian view, becomes in the new social context a vision, thought possible only mystically by Bernard, of a way of life corrective of commercial society. Bernard also describes the psychology of a competitive man who establishes social relations on the basis of a continuous comparison with his neighbor to discover who is superior and to reassure himself. The first ideal of cooperation he of course favors, and the latter of competition he condemns for its willful "singularity" and consequent cutting off and alienation of the individual from his fellows. Since students are very sharply confronted by just such alternatives in contemporary ethics, this study helps them to see the relations of these contrasting ideals to the modern world which originally provoked their formulation.

In Thomas Aquinas students find that the so-called medieval synthesis was actually one which contained the older Christian doctrines and the new empiricism favored by the men now living in a commercial society. Following him they turn to the later medieval and Renaissance writers who were more impressed with the gravity of the crisis facing medieval society. Through a brief study of William of Ockham students find the first of the long series of modern thinkers who separated man's practical and social life from his imaginative and private life. They find here the basis for the great revolutionizing development of modern science which stemmed from this new tendency to regard the world outside the individual as knowable only by the most rigorous distinction between fact and fancy. One could no longer move from man's empirical knowledge of nature and his social experiences through a series of steps to the other world and God. Aquinas' work was split apart; Augustine's, except for the possibility of introspection, forgotten.

This severance of the inner experience from the outer, of the individual's subjective attitudes and impulses from the objective laws of nature and society, is thus introduced to students, but they need, as in the case of the earlier intellectual crisis at the end of the ancient world, then to be able to trace out these new attitudes in the life experience of an individual. Fortunately they are able to find

in the writings of the humanist, Francis Petrarch, material that plays this function for the Renaissance and the birth of modern values in the way the *Confessions* of Augustine had for medieval Christianity. Petrarch offered no solutions, but showed vividly, utilizing all his poetic and rhetorical powers, the conflict between a desire for spiritual fulfillment and the distracting and devastating impact of the modern urban social life. He always leaves a deep and lasting impression on his readers, especially when they have been prepared to understand the significance of his self-analysis by a previous study of Bernard, Thomas, and Ockham.

Pursuing this educational procedure, the class continues to study the attempts to find some solution of the apparent contradiction between the spiritual needs of the individual and the personal qualities necessary for economic and political success in modern society. The impression of Petrarch was a surprisingly contemporary one that reflected his own sensitivity and keen vision of the difficulties, and his utter bafflement at any way out except through the rural retreat and the private cultivation of the arts—a situation that students readily identify with their own. Some of them do not find this state of affairs satisfactory however, and turn with interest to Machiavelli's early foreshadowing of political democracy or of a service-state ruled by a benevolent Prince which would undertake a purely secular and mechanistic adjustment of conflicting economic interests, to his equally modern emphasis on social and psychological science as the only way to become a master of the objective external world and so realize one's individual visions through it.

They recognize in the Lutheran theology a counterpart of the modern reactionary politics of despair which, in contrast to Machiavelli, merely yielded power and authority to the rulers and absolved them of any spiritual or human responsibilities. They study in Calvin the attempt to solve the problem of the individual and society by subordinating the individual's wishes and concern with his subjective experience of life to a conformity with those predestined laws of nature and society that the new mathematical and empirical scientists were proclaiming. And all of these solutions, liberal, authoritarian, democratic, and utopian-Christian-socialist, they examine in the cauldron of conflict in the exciting political theorists of the Puritan Revolution. Here they find that these conflicting ideals have reality not only in personal lives but in the historical struggle of men to make over social reality to the measure of their philosophy.

None of these early modern attempts to resolve the apparent conflict of individual and society, however, adequately considered the individual and his psychological needs. Nor did they consider anything like a real harmony possible. Either man had to be content to live in two worlds, an inner private and an outer public one, or he had to repress and give up the former for the sake of the latter. It is this situation that underlies even today, or perhaps especially today, the quest for personal fulfillment through the analytic couch and the psychiatric consultation. The work of Freud and others can be seen as evidence of a continuing lack of integration of the social and the personal in the social thought of the most influential modern thinkers and philosophers.

Between the seventeenth century and Freud, between Hobbes and modern socialism, the students examine several significant attempts to remedy this lack and to find, at least in theory, the requirement and insight that Augustine and Bernard once had that personal fulfillment becomes the very fabric of the social process and that the developing attempts to reach this goal may be seen as part of a world-historical process. The steps by which this thought, and this way of thought, re-emerges in the nineteenth century are followed through the ironic Englishman, Bernard de Mandeville, through the sensitive Jean Jacques Rousseau who felt again that the moral regeneration of the individual and society were possible and compatible, until the range of thinkers whose ideas are of most contemporary significance to any student's attempt to find his own answer to the problem are before him—Hegel, Marx, Mill, Nietzsche, Freud, the Existentialists.

The methods used and the insights gained from earlier writers make the understanding of modern thought, and the personal solution of the problem of making an individual life both satisfying and responsible, less of a mystery to the student. His conceptions and his decisions remain his own affair, but they are inevitably more valid and more human.

The philosophy of education that underlies this course of study is a part of this same tradition of Western values. For just as the modern educational transcendentalists find support for their position in those ancient and medieval philosophers who sought absolute values apart from and above human experience, the philosophy expressed here has also its predecessors among those theorists of process and progress of the past who, in a series of advancing and unfolding ways, taught men not to look away from their daily private and public lives but to seek for the things they believed in the immanence of historical experience. The course described above seeks to enable students to discover this aspect of the tradition in its evolution. In so doing it incidentally uncovers the dogmas of the opposing aspect of the tradition. In addition the course seeks, through its own series of experimental steps, to find a way of conveying the content of Western discussions of value to students, not dogmatically as from above, but through helping them to find links between it and their own experience. In this way the various sides of the tradition might acquire reality for the students and their own world might be widened by them in the actual process of study in which they are engaged.

There are many ways of achieving this end, through the study of thinkers in the past, or in the present, who have many other things to say than the ideas of the thinkers mentioned in these pages. We who are teachers must remember too that the student's world is bound to remain a limited world in spite of any method of education, until each one attempts, in life itself, the more arduous task of fulfilling these values in contemporary existence. No education can help such fulfillment in more than a limited way. But an educational program which considers the values of the Western tradition in terms of their psychological, social, moral, and historical setting, and demonstrates vividly the nature of the search for these values, can develop in students some of the insights and understanding necessary to respect their tradition and to recreate it in the modern world.

The Individual Student

HAROLD TAYLOR

I

In the United States we have the largest educational system in the world, with more students in colleges and universities than all other countries combined. On either coast we have the world's largest universities, with nearly 50,000 students in each. The educational system will become still larger in the coming years. The extent and speed of the expansion in the colleges has meant not only a radical increase in the scope and number of educational problems, but a radical extension of the idea of mass education. As a result, the individual student has become an anonymous unit in a huge educational enterprise. His education as an individual has become less important than his membership in an educationally standardized society. The dominating idea of mass education is uniformity— uniformity of program, uniformity of method, and a central administration. Its most obvious counterpart is mass production in industry. The raw material is processed by the most efficient means, and the methods are standardized. Its most obvious application outside the institutions of formal education is the use of the mass media of communication. One of the most important tasks ahead of us in American colleges is to restore the individual student to the center of the educational process, to work against the pressures which would standardize our society, and to create a design for education which will release the uniqueness and the individuality of each human being we are called upon to educate.

Two conflicting philosophies in American life lie beneath the surface of contemporary educational change. On the one hand, our instinctive response to life is one of individualism. We are jealous of personal rights, we reject authority, we rebel against restriction, we value the new, the fresh, the spontaneous, we think and act constantly in terms of the right of the individual to be free and to make his own way. On the other hand, we are quick to insist upon uniformity of belief, we have invented a standard American personality to which we expect the human race to conform, we have an inordinate respect for size and quantity, and we believe that almost any human problem can be solved if only an efficient and large organization is created to deal with it.

This conflict of philosophy comes to the surface as soon as we mention mass education, or refer in any way to the *masses*. We all feel that we do not belong to the masses, and have no intention of joining, since the term implies that we are units of no great importance in a collective whole, and that there are others who do not belong to the masses who are superior to the rest of us. This attitude toward class stratification can be counted among our national virtues. When the word *masses* is used in America, it carries a vaguely insulting overtone, and contains within it the notion that whatever is presented to the masses must be watered down and thinned out so that everyone may be able to swallow it. Yet while we refuse to admit to personal membership in the masses, our national culture, as expressed through the greater part of the press, the radio, the motion pictures and television, reveals a pattern of paternalism and mass-attitude towards the people who make up the American public. The role taken by the publisher, and the radio and motion picture producer, is to simplify matters so that everyone may understand them without the necessity of doing independent thinking or judging. The press and radio played this role to its full in the last presidential election, only to find that the individuals who compose the *masses* had been quietly doing their own thinking without benefit of supervision.

More and more of the ideas of mass education have crept into the colleges and universities with the increase in numbers. Small colleges which should have remained small have doubled in size, and in doing so have lost the intimate community which is so essential a part of their educational program. But more than this, the larger size has meant a separation of the students from the faculty, and the faculty from the administration. When colleges are small, most of the administrative work can be done in an informal way, by talking with people at lunch, by telephone, by conferences, committees, and conversation. With the increase in numbers, communication from faculty to students and from administration to faculty immediately takes on the form of memoranda, letters, mimeographed sheets, printed booklets, and public statements. In place of the conversation and discussion normal to the life of the college, decisions are made by committees, or boards, or administrators who send out statements. The statements are not actually addressed to individuals who make up a student body or a faculty, but are addressed to a generalized Student body, or Faculty, from the Administration. For convenience, decisions are made by deans, departmental chairmen, governing officers, rather than by groups or committees within the faculty, because there are simply too many things to be done. In the case of the curriculum, it is made by members of the faculty, as the most suitable collection of subjects which all students should take, and again, it is made, not for individual students, but for an abstract student body in which every unit in the mass is assumed to be identical with every other. All these factors in the enlarged university have strengthened the tendency towards centralization of authority and the use of mass teaching methods.

Here again we meet the contradictions of two philosophies. As a basic element in democratic thought, we believe that each young person who has the ability should receive all the education his talents require. We have also been concerned that the unique talent of the individual be provided with the particular kind of education which will suit his need. At the same time, the methods by which individual needs are being met have become those of standardizing the curriculum, and the introduction of mechanical devices which can solve the problem of educating individuals by giving to all of them the same education. We are urged forward by a democratic impulse to give to everyone the education to which his talents entitle him, but have adopted ways of doing it which concentrate on administrative efficiency rather than on educational quality.

To a certain extent, this may be unavoidable. The habits of mind developed by the use of standard programs in the education of the armed forces during the war, particularly in the preparation of officers in the colleges, have remained during the post-war period.

To be able to count upon certain units of study in required areas of knowledge was a great aid to the training programs for the technical specialties of the armed services. The practical problem of coping with twice the number of college students by the use of the same facilities as before, meant that a standard program was organized along conventional lines simply to administer the greater numbers. It was therefore natural to double the size of classes, retain the lecture method, use textbooks, provide standard examinations, score them with mechanical equipment, and continue a marking system of letters and numbers. But this way of solving the problem was due only in part to the severe over-crowding. It was due, rather, to a dominant conception on the part of those who administer and plan the large universities, as to how higher education should be conducted. The conveyance of subject-matter by mechanical means was the standard pattern of teaching before the overcrowding began. I suspect that if adequate funds were to become available to universities tomorrow, most of the money would be spent on buildings, equipment, and devices, with only a fraction devoted to providing more and better paid teachers for the universities. Yet we know that when there are too few teachers for the number of students, there is no time for conferences, discussions, seminars, research projects, essays, personal relationships, or any other necessities for proper teaching.

There are a good many people who believe that the way to solve the problem of increased numbers is to prevent further increase. They point to the fact that many students now in college are wasting their time and the efforts of their teachers. They object to the assumption that a college education is the right of any person who wishes it. They point out that the high schools have not prepared many of the students now in college sufficiently well to make it profitable for them to enter. When it was first proposed that government money be used to give scholarships to thousands of veterans, some of whom had had very skimpy preparation for entering, Mr. Hutchins, and many who thought as he did, were alarmed at the prospect and scornful of the possible results. Mr. Hutchins predicted that "Colleges and universities will find themselves converted into educational hobo jungles. And veterans, unable to get work and equally unable to resist putting pressure on the colleges and universities, will find themselves educational hoboes." Fortunately this has proved not to be the case, and instead, experience with veterans has caused many educators to question whether or not the usual standards of admission to colleges are adequate in selecting those best qualified to enter. There are others who now say that in the present phase of the post-war period it is dangerous social policy to educate too many college graduates, since we would thus be confronted with a large group of discontented men and women for whom there is an insufficient number of suitable vocations.

Yet it is clear that the solution does not lie in attempting to reduce the total number of capable students who are to benefit from higher education. We know that there are many more young people who should be in college than are attending at present. If there are students now enrolled who do not have the ability to work satisfactorily, this is another problem, to be solved by the application of better methods of selection, and better ways of teaching, and better ways of deciding who should continue and who should not. We have a continual increase in the number of men and women needed in each of the professions, and we have the means of selecting the appropriate number of candidates throughout the country from all who apply for professional training. Nor can we have too many people who are liberally educated, unless their liberal education teaches them to believe in a class society in which they occupy an upper class. In any case, the pressure of numbers will continue, and it is the responsibility of the country, its citizens, and its educators, to find ways of meeting the needs of an increased student population. The question then becomes one of how to meet these needs.

II

The best analogy to the large university of 1950 is not that of the colleges and universities of the past, but that of a modern town, with a president in place of the mayor, the faculty in place of the municipal government, housing and hotel services in the hands of private employees, and the students in place of the citizens. The students in the universities of the past were educated in a small community where everyone knew everyone else, and where the bulk of the education came from the experience of individuals who lived together and taught each other. They were a homogeneous group of the well-to-do and the moderately well-to-do, white, young men of families from the business and professional classes, their home life had a similar pattern, their interests a similar cast. In the large modern university, with a population of twenty-five to fifty thousand students, there is an immense variety in the economic status, home life, ethnic and cultural roots, religion, personalities, motivations, interests, and intellectual capacities of the individual students. They differ from each other as do the members of a cosmopolitan city. What they need is an education which takes account of differences in capacity, interest, and aim. Otherwise, students prove unable to make connections between the elements of the academic curriculum and the experiences of their own lives. At present, the major part of educational planning for the colleges and universities is toward more mass education, more uniformity, and less concern with individual differences. This is part of a reaction against "progressive" ideas, and a movement towards conservation in philosophy, politics, and education.

In this situation, Sarah Lawrence College, which takes as its aim and practice the education of the individual, finds itself in opposition to the dominant trend of American higher education. Instead of a radical expansion in numbers, we insist on remaining small. In place of settling down with one of the standard curricula, we prefer to keep on experimenting. In place of the methods of mass education, we deal with individual students. In place of uniformity in subject-matter for all, we put a diversity in the choice of study for each. In place of large classes and too few teachers, we insist on small classes and a faculty large enough to keep them that way.

How can an institution of this kind justify its existence when the demands which American society is making are for more places for more students at the least cost? You are extravagant, we are told. You squander the time of first-rate scholars on only a few students. Your largest class is twenty in size. You give too much to too few. The individual becomes too important. Your faculty has too much freedom. Your students have too much freedom. Three courses a year are not enough. The students never learn to compete. They become too intellectual. Your college is full of social reformers. The College is an exclusive place for rich girls. You have too many students on scholarship. The students have no respect for tradition. You have too much of the arts. You have too much social science. There is too much psychology. There is too much literature. There is no discipline. The students are over-stimulated. The students do not work hard enough. They work too hard. The curriculum is too loose. There are too many Negro students. There are not enough Negro students. Your policies are too liberal. You waste time on women who are simply being prepared to be married. You make your students unfit for marriage by the intellectual stimulation they receive. You heighten their social awareness but it leaves them as soon as they go home.

The comments reveal basic conflicts in what people expect from education, and a confusion about what a modern philosophy of education tries to do. Comments of this kind, however, seldom come from students. Whenever the ideas of the College are discussed with students, whether it be the liberal admissions policy, the autonomy of student government, the place of the individual, or the planned curriculum, there is an immediate response, and the discussion usually centers upon how these ideas could be worked out in other institutions. I believe that the immediate response is due to the fact that young people move naturally and intuitively toward a philosophy of liberalism. In their social and political thinking, as well as in their attitudes to other people, students are warm-hearted, generous, open-minded, humane, and responsible. On most social questions, they are much more advanced in their thinking than members of the faculty in their colleges, and, as I am often told, much farther advanced than their parents.

It is because of the gap in social awareness between the older generation and the students, that most of the extravagant statements are made by members of the older generation about the dangers to democracy which exist in the colleges, and the necessity for a return to fundamentals. By fundamentals, most conservative critics of modern education mean the studies which they undertook themselves while in college, or the studies which they have always felt they should have undertaken there. It involves a textbook course

value of the Harvard approach lies in the flexibility of choice by the student within a general area of study, and the flexibility allowed by individual faculty members in the construction of a course. Although a great deal has been said about the Harvard Report on General Education, the success of the general education courses at Harvard is due, not to any fresh insight into educational theory and practice which the formal statements of the Report have brought, but to the fact that it has given stimulus to the faculty to think about teaching, and that the installation of new courses has given an opportunity to the students to work with some of the best teachers at Harvard at things of mutual interest and of general importance.

The way in which the authors of this book have described the work they are doing and their ideas for teaching is the result of their own experience in dealing with students in small classes. If their classes were larger, I do not believe that their methods and ideas would change essentially, but different ways of communicating these ideas would be developed within a similar framework of educational philosophy. Mrs. Lynd would continue to search for those questions in the minds of her students which are most urgent in terms of their need for answers, and would discover, whether by written statements, or questionnaires, or a series of round-table discussions, what philosophical questions should be dealt with in a philosophy course to be constructed by the students and faculty together. Mr. Loewenberg would retain his attitude to teaching American history in world perspective, and would seek for contemporary examples of social problems which relate to their antecedents in American history. If examinations were necessary in order to discover the amount of thought and energy being devoted by the students, these could be devised in such a way as to help the students to clarify their own ideas about what were learning. If Mr. Gregory were concerned with one hundred students rather than with fifteen, he would undoubtedly match his own ideas of what constituted an important poem or novel with the stage of intellectual and literary development which the students had already reached. He would do this by conferences with groups of students during the first weeks of instruction, and by consultation with representative students throughout each year of work. Similar accommodations to the enlarged situation would be made by each of these teachers. The central fact is that they are conscious of the stage of development in which the students find themselves, and their aim in teaching is to use the materials of knowledge which they have at their personal command to render deeper and more mature the thinking and acting of the students they teach.

In choosing the appropriate materials of knowledge, these teachers would turn to original sources in philosophy, history, and literature, since they and many others have found the use of textbooks, commentaries, and secondary sources to be intellectually barren rather than productive. They would also choose to work in depth and breadth in a few works and topics, rather than attempting the survey of a large number of items. A great deal of time is needed to teach students the richness of meaning and cultural content of works of literature or events in history. In my own experience as a student, it was not until I had spent two years in studying David Hume that I began to understand the philosophy and cultural content of other figures in philosophy, history, and literature of the Eighteenth Century. I believe this experience is confirmed in similar ways by most other students.

If we apply this philosophy of education still further, we are bound to decrease the number of subjects or courses taken by students at any one time. It is impossible to do justice to five or six subjects, each taught for short units of fifteen weeks, in an effort to cover the ground. For the faculty member, as for the student, the excess of courses is self-defeating. There can be no continuity or depth in teaching and learning under such circumstances, since the faculty member hurries from course to course, and lecture to lecture, while the student does the same, each trying by short-cuts and abbreviated ideas to meet the requirement of coverage.

III

The large universities have just as many opportunities for experiments in teaching as do the small colleges. Once the role of the student in the educational process has been taken seriously, arrangements can be made to involve his energies more thoroughly in that process. In a class as large as three hundred, which is a good size for a small college, it is possible that the conventional schedule of three lectures a week can be exchanged for one group meeting and a number of discussions each week. The place of the lectures can be taken by printed or mimeographed material distributed to the class, and some of the discussions may be conducted by the students themselves under an elected committee for each group of twenty-five. This method of teaching has proved successful in many experiments by faculty members throughout the country. Dr. Russell Cooper, of the University of Minnesota, where a new and interesting program of curriculum reform has been under way for some time, has described additional ways of involving the students in their own education.* The Yale Law School, by its emphasis upon case study and individual research, and by the responsibility it has given to students for organizing conferences on large social issues, for which each student must be prepared, is another instance of enlightened reform.

In the large university, where there are usually graduate students attached to each department, a faculty member in charge of a course for three hundred students, in social science, psychology, or literature can organize a group of graduate students into a teaching faculty which works closely with him in planning the materials to be used for the course, in meeting regularly each week as a teaching faculty, preparing the material to be distributed, attending whatever lectures are held, and conducting some of the discussions with small groups of students. Very often junior and senior students chosen from among those most talented in the field can be put to work in the same way, and can be encouraged to take a serious interest in going on to graduate schools to become teachers in their turn, provided they show the capacity for teaching which their initial selection presumed. Another advantage in this kind of reorganization is that graduate students learn in a natural way the kind of teaching which they will be called upon to do after their graduate training is complete, and the conventional separation between research work under a faculty member and preparation of the student as

* "New Trends in College Teaching," Supplement to *Educator's Washington Dispatch*, September, 1949.

teacher is broken down. A creative attitude toward teaching will develop within such groups of young instructors, and a morale generated which will carry over into the class itself.

This suggestion would replace the present system of the use of graduate assistants, in which lectures are given by a faculty member and discussions conducted by the assistants. In a new system, it would be possible not only to bring the assistant to the center of curriculum planning for the course, but to give him the opportunity to work in original source materials with his own group of students aside from the general work of the larger group. The individual instructor might find that for his group of twenty-five students, it would be more fruitful to read and discuss works which were not studied by the members of the other groups. He could then adapt his material to the work of his class, and coordinate it with the general course work by discussion and written assignment.

It has been our experience at Sarah Lawrence College that the involvement of the student in the entire life of the College is the key to improvement in the quality of individual education. This is a key which can be used in any institution, regardless of size. The fact is that students behave as responsible members of their community if they are given the responsibility for doing so. They can organize conferences in philosophy or race relations, they can administer dining room services, curricula, fund-raising campaigns, literary magazines, newspapers, book stores, and student government if they are given a free hand to do so and some sympathetic assistance on the part of the College. It is usually assumed by college authorities that if students are allowed freedom and the responsibility for their own affairs they will abuse the freedom and shirk the responsibilities. The experience of those institutions where student responsibility has been made the basis for community organization has been that many of the administrative posts formerly thought to be the province of faculty and university personnel can be carried out in better ways by the students themselves. The example of Antioch College is a case in point. At Antioch, the community is organized entirely by students, under the direction of a paid student manager. Bennington College, with its student committee on educational policy, and its community government, has done pio-

neer work in this field. Other colleges could extend these examples.

It is only when this conception of the role of the student is taken seriously by the college or university that the gap between the curricular and the extra-curricular can be closed. Very often the political education of the college student is developed in clubs organized on the campus as an extra-curricular activity. It is in this area, where there is freedom from the restraints of academic learning and classroom lectures, that the student places most of his energies. There is no reason why the same amount of energy should not be devoted to the work of the classes in political science or sociology, if the material for study is chosen with a view to encouraging the latent interest in social issues which most students possess.

This is simply to say again that the content of the curriculum must relate itself in a meaningful way to the social and moral issues which disturb world society and the people here in America. From start to finish, it is the relation of knowledge to life which must dominate all other considerations in the education of the student. The lives of many American students have not contained the pleasures and satisfactions of aesthetic experience with literature, plays, history, or the arts. Nor has their life in America given them insight into the existence of social questions which demand their thought or action. To relate knowledge to the lives of these students means, in one sense, to make a new life for them. But unless the student is given a chance to ask questions, to discuss with his peers, to read and to think in terms which he can understand, he cannot establish the basis in his own experience from which to move towards the higher forms of learning. I have found students frightened of the word metaphysics, but anxious to discuss the existence of God or the nature of thought when given a chance to talk. If the students are asked to join in planning a curriculum, the kind and extent of their ignorance and knowledge will quickly be revealed. When they are asked to help in the construction of their own education, they accept the responsibility with enthusiasm and with fruitful results for the curriculum itself. We have the results of experiments by colleges around the country, and the results of our own experiments at Sarah Lawrence College, to show the effects of this attitude to students.

Similarly, the individual student will break down the barrier between the classroom and the rest of his life if he is given a chance to work in the creative arts. At Sarah Lawrence and elsewhere, this educational fact has been proven, but, too many colleges and universities still keep the creative and performing arts segregated from the rest of the curriculum. This usually means that the genuine aesthetic enjoyment and the deepest satisfactions in learning are gained by the student not in the classroom, but in theatre work, singing, playing, writing, painting, and in many other art forms. Experiments in the performing and creative arts at Bennington College during the past eighteen years have demonstrated their significance in liberal education. We know with what depth of understanding the student can learn to know a great play if he is somehow involved in its production, or if he has to choose from among the members of his class the various actors to play the roles called for by the playwright. The experiments in this direction, in music, sculpture, painting, design, architecture, theatre, dance, and literature, have proven successful wherever they have been tried. The limitations caused by the necessity of working with large numbers of students can be met by cooperative planning.

IV

The reason for the existence of an experimental college is to push educational ideas to their conclusion in practice, and to test a variety of hypotheses and suggestions by an appeal to experience. At Sarah Lawrence College we are fortunate in having a situation in which new ideas and suggestions can be acted upon and the results can be appraised. In such a situation it is often tempting to assume that when a new idea is tried and proves to be successful, we have invented it, whereas, for every idea which is suggested at any experimental station, there is a counterpart either in theory or in practice in existence in many other institutions. This is true in the advancement of knowledge in any field of human effort. The new courses administered under the general education program at Harvard are in structure similar to some of those developed during the past twenty years at Sarah Lawrence College. The work in social science in the two-year program of the College at the University of

Chicago resembles in some respects the work of faculty members experimenting with social science teaching at our institution. Many of the classical works celebrated by their inclusion in the curriculum of St. John's College are studied with at least equal enthusiasm and benefit at Sarah Lawrence. Mr. Meiklejohn's concern for the pursuit of Hellenic studies by young Americans is shared by many of us here. The principle of the tutorial system, honors work, and individual projects has been in operation for many years at Oxford, Princeton, Swarthmore, Yale, and elsewhere.

What is of particular interest to us, however, is the design of a total educational experience for each student, without regard to academic respectability and precedent, by which the greatest development of individual talent can be realized in fact. We have pushed farther in the direction of educating individuals than most other institutions, and we are more conscious of individual differences, we take more pains to know our students well, we allow more freedom for individual development, we make more concentrated efforts to develop democratic attitudes, than is the case in most other colleges. Whether or not our emphasis is correct can only be verified by the results in terms of the kind of human beings who have worked with us, and by the quality of the lives they lead after they leave us. This is a very difficult matter to determine decisively, since the effect of a college education is only one of a great many other social, economic, personal, and cultural factors in the life of each person. On the other hand, there are conclusions we have reached about education which we have established empirically. In the short list which follows there are suggestions which may be of use in turning education away from its conventional forms toward a deeper concern for the individual student. They are set down, not as our discoveries, since they are not, but as conclusions we have demonstrated as true to our own satisfaction.

(1) The most successful way of committing students to a serious concern for their own intellectual and personal development is to set them to work at things which they want to do. Therefore, a program of studies adapted to them as individuals will set their intellectual energies in motion with more chance of fruitful re-

sults than a program of required studies which takes no account of individual differences in talent and in aim. For large institutions this means, not a free elective system, but a serious program of guidance and mutual planning by students and faculty together. In terms of the content of courses, it means a careful selection of those materials which show most promise of enlisting student energies by the relevance of the material to the stage of development of the students themselves.

(2) Education, considered as total development, rather than as intellectual training, must concern itself primarily with attitudes and values. A positive attitude toward learning is the first necessity for continued growth in the direction of maturity in each student. Therefore, in any institution, large or small, a great deal of attention must be paid to the intellectual and social atmosphere which surrounds the student. The atmosphere is created by the teachers who either treat learning as a joy and a rewarding experience, or as a duty, an obligation, or a dreary necessity. In its social dimensions, the atmosphere is created by the quality of human relations which exist between the faculty and the students, and between one faculty member and another. This implies a social organization of a democratic kind, with full participation by the individual student and faculty member in making policy for the institution. It involves social policy constructed by the community to provide equal opportunities for everyone to share in the community life.

(3) There can be no intellectual and social vitality in a college or university unless the faculty and the students have not only the right but the encouragement to form their own opinions, hold their own beliefs, and assert their own convictions. For any institution this means that academic freedom must be an incitement to think boldly, not simply a right to have tenure. The freedom itself must be assured by the loyalty of trustees or regents to the ideals of free thought.

(4) The ability of students to learn in depth the meaning of knowledge provided for them in the academic program is in-

creased immensely by giving them first-hand experience with social situations and the every-day working of society. This means an extensive use of the community as a laboratory for student research and related study, running from actual employment in child-care centers or factories, to research projects in unemployment or rent control. The extensive use of the community is more difficult in the case of large universities in small towns, but has been shown to be possible and desirable in most communities where it has been tried.

(5) The college or university is a cultural center for its own wider community, and students, as well as members of the community, benefit from mutual exchange of ideas. This means that the large or small institution must make its facilities available to as wide a variety of groups in its neighborhood as is possible, whether in workers' education, adult education, lectures, motion pictures, forums, political meetings, or theatre performances.

(6) The evaluation of student ability is not a matter for formal tests, true-false examinations, or memory-work connected with textbooks. It is a matter of providing opportunities for students to show their ability by whatever means can be devised. In large institutions, where grades must be assigned, examinations can be developed which put the emphasis upon the exhibition of talent, upon the revelation of ability to integrate various forms of knowledge into independent judgments, rather than upon catching students in the details of their ignorance.

(7) Learning in the social sciences, the arts, the humanities, and natural sciences becomes much deeper and more significant when original sources are used, and it is educationally and aesthetically destructive to use a continuous stream of textbooks, anthologies, surveys, digests, condensed histories, outlines, and cook-book experiments. This means that for any institution, the choice of original material, its presentation by faculty, and its discussion by students, is an essential part in the development of a general education.

(8) Knowledge, when artificially separated into units of sub-

ject-matter, will seldom be brought together by students, but will continue to be isolated in their minds as units of information. Our experiments with exploratory courses, built around the consideration of particular problems and matters of interest and concern to faculty and students, have shown that it is possible to achieve remarkable results in introducing students to a variety of new ways of learning, without restricting their work to the subject-matter of a special discipline. Whether Thomas Hobbes is studied as a philosopher, a psychologist, a political scientist, or an essayist is not important. What is important is that students learn to interpret his insights in any of the fields, in a way which can help them to understand their own society and the bases of human behavior. We have found that the absence of formal departments, as well as the absence of rank, frees the College to teach students without the inhibition of departmental prerogatives and seniority privileges.

(9) The experience we have had with the investigation of educational ideas, and the research we have carried on in connection with the teaching has helped us in many ways over and beyond any concrete results we have reached in research materials. The continuous concern with the progress and growth of individual students has concentrated the attention of the entire College on the learning process and the quality of the teaching. For new members of the faculty, most of whom have not had experience in other than conventional teaching, the prevailing interest in experiment and in the work of students has quickened the process by which their own teaching can develop in quality. It is for this reason that we do not believe that research in teaching or in education should be carried on by separate faculty members who do not teach, since it is only by the close relationship of the results of experiment to the actual teaching and learning process that the institution can benefit by the research itself. Perhaps research is too formal a word for some of the things we do. We investigate the kinds of intelligence and ability which our students possess, we observe their development closely by reports which they receive, we try to assess the value of the various experi-

ences we provide for them, and to adapt our teaching to the weaknesses and strengths which they exhibit. This kind of research is invaluable in any university, large or small, since it makes teachers more conscious of the effect which their own work has in the development of their students. Whether or not such research remains informal, for the use of teachers only within the institution, or becomes more formal by publication, it is a significant part of the evolution of new curricula and the development of greater interest in educational reform.

The list could be extended further, but from the present set of conclusions, it will be obvious that many of the things we are doing at Sarah Lawrence College are being done in other institutions throughout the country. The difference rests only with the fact that we follow these practices consistently as a means of developing maturity in the individual student, and we carry them through the entire scope of the College program rather than in those parts of it where it is convenient or allowable by administrative authority.

Each college makes its own contribution toward the solution of the problem of educating the individual as soon as it begins to think about the students themselves, who they are, what they want, what they need. They need, as does everyone else, a sense of belonging to a special community which accepts them and sustains them and with which they can identify. It is the task of the teachers in each college to create that community within the context of the larger student body, no matter how large it becomes.

Our own experiments at Sarah Lawrence College have proven the value of a philosophy of education which is itself experimental. We do the most we can to educate each person, using everything we know, and have made our own program. In order to carry out its aim, we have built a community with which each person can identify, and within which each person has certain privileges and responsibilities in a total kind of democracy. What we are able to do is, in its turn, limited by the fact that we are small, that we have no source of funds except tuition income and gifts for scholarships. Other institutions have other limitations, many of them coming from the fact of bigness coupled with financial shortages. But the philosophy of education which rests upon contemporary knowledge of human nature, which recognizes the importance of individual differences, and which conceives its aim as that of developing maturity in the emotional and intellectual life of young people, is a philosophy which finds its own way of solving its own problems, no matter what form they may take.

The unity which educators seek in the field of knowledge is to be found in a common core of liberal values to which the students are committed, rather than in a common core of subjects which each has studied. What humanity needs in a world which has become too large, too powerful, too neglectful of individuals, is a restoration of those liberal values which mark the ideals toward which civilizations slowly move and from which we have now receded. This restoration must be the aim of liberal education.

In the essays collected here, we have provided some descriptions of the way a modern philosophy of education is being applied to the problems of teaching and learning in the liberal arts. There are many other teachers who approach the tasks of liberal education in a similar way, and who may recognize in our experience a pattern similar to their own. The aim we share with those others is that of improving the quality of teaching and learning in the American college, and through such improvement, helping to enrich the quality of life in contemporary society.

Index